SECURED TRANSACTIONS AND PAYMENT SYSTEMS

Problems and Answers

D1199566

SECURED TRANSACTIONS AND PAYMENT SYSTEMS

Problems and Answers

Second Edition

LEO L. CLARKE
Associate Professor of Law
Ave Maria School of Law

JOHN F. DOLAN
Distinguished Professor of Law
Wayne State University Law School

LARRY T. GARVIN
Associate Professor of Law
Florida State University College of Law

ALLEN R. KAMP
Professor of Law
John Marshall Law School

KERRY LYNN MACINTOSH
Professor of Law
Santa Clara University School of Law

ASPEN
PUBLISHERS

1185 Avenue of the Americas, New York, NY 10036
www.aspenpublishers.com

Permissions
Aspen Publishers
1185 Avenue of the Americas
New York, NY 10036

Printed in the United States of America

1 2 3 4 5 6 7 8 9 0

ISBN 0-7355-3924-3

Library of Congress Cataloging-in-Publication Data

Secured transactions and payment systems : problems and answers / Leo L. Clarke . . . [et al.]—2nd ed.
   p. cm.
  Rev. ed. of: Secured transactions and payment systems / John F. Dolan. c1995.
  Includes index.
  ISBN 0-7355-3924-3
   1. Security (Law)—United States—Problems, exercises, etc. 2. Negotiable instruments—United States—Problems, exercises, etc. 3. Payment—United States—Problems, exercises, etc. I. Clarke, Leo L., 1950- II. Dolan, John F. Secured transactions and payment systems.

KF1050.Z9 S39 2003
346.7307′4—dc21

2002038335

About Aspen Publishers

Aspen Publishers, headquartered in New York City, is a leading information provider for attorneys, business professionals, and law students. Written by preeminent authorities, our products consist of analytical and practical information covering both U.S. and international topics. We publish in the full range of formats, including updated manuals, books, periodicals, CDs, and online products.

Our proprietary content is complemented by 2,500 legal databases, containing over 11 million documents, available through our Loislaw division. Aspen Publishers also offers a wide range of topical legal and business databases linked to Loislaw's primary material. Our mission is to provide accurate, timely, and authoritative content in easily accessible formats, supported by unmatched customer care.

To order any Aspen Publishers title, go to *www.aspenpublishers.com* or call 1-800-638-8437.

To reinstate your manual update service, call 1-800-638-8437.

For more information on Loislaw products, go to *www.loislaw.com* or call 1-800-364-2512.

For Customer Care issues, e-mail CustomerCare@aspenpublishers.com; call 1-800-234-1660; or fax 1-800-901-9075.

Aspen Publishers
A Wolters Kluwer Company

To Kathleen
LLC

*To Patrick, Allison, Shane, Tristan, John, Meghan, Courtney, Ryan,
and Brendan*
JFD

To my grandmother, Ruth Kepes
LTG

To my teacher, Soia Mentschikoff
ARK

To my sons, Peter and Quinn
KLM

Contents

Using This Book

You can use the book by yourself as a study tool—to prepare for class and to review for exams. The problems work best as a reference tool. We have written and arranged them to explain specific sections that are problematic. When you work in this fashion, it will often be profitable to do a cluster of problems. The problems appear not according to the sequence of the Code sections but according to the way the sections interact in a typical commercial transaction. Code rules tend to be part of a complex of rules, and seeing that complex is helpful in understanding the Code. The table of Uniform Commercial Code citations, the index, and the subject headings will help you find the relevant problems.

You might also find it worthwhile to read the short introductory comments that precede the problems, though those comments will often repeat textual discussion or class lecture. The introductory comments are not essential. Read them if they help.

Problems and Answers

Generally, the problems begin with simple questions, often questions that have obvious answers. That method builds gradually on knowledge that is necessary for the more confusing aspects of a provision.

From time to time as you proceed with the questions, you may want to check your answers against the answer sections in the book. But remember that the purpose of the problems and the answers is not to test but to explain. Don't feel out of it if you don't know an answer. Just look to the book's answer and see whether it makes sense to you. If it does, you're probably doing just fine.

The agencies that sponsor the Code are currently redrafting and have recently redrafted much of it. There are new articles since the publication of the first edition of this book: Article 5, Article 8, and, most importantly, Article 9. These changes, especially the last, prompted this second edition. The sponsoring agencies have adopted a new Article 1 and revisions to Articles 3 and 4, though no states have adopted these new articles. One of the sponsoring agencies is now redrafting the article on documents of title (Article 7). Our problems here usually deal with the official text of the Code; but because we believe many states will adopt the new Article 1 and the revisions to Articles 3 and 4, we have cited to both the official version (in brackets) and the revised versions of Articles 1, 3, and 4.

The problems do not attempt to make you an expert. They do not go into some complex issues and sometimes do not cover all of the exceptions to the rule of a section. Sometimes the problems do not cover sections that your teacher will want to cover. But these problems cover most of the basics, so that you will be in a position after you do them to deal with the more sophisticated questions. We would be claiming too much if we said that commercial law study in law school makes you a complete commercial lawyer. It can, however, make you literate in commercial law. And that's a lot. Your teachers' efforts, your efforts, and these problems and answers are steps toward that end.

Acknowledgments

We prepared these problems as law professors with experience teaching UCC courses in more than ten law schools over a period of years lengthy enough that some of us are not anxious to count them. Foremost thanks, then, go to our students, whose thoughts and questions largely framed this exercise.

LLC

JFD

LTG

ARK

KLM

October 2002

SECURED TRANSACTIONS AND PAYMENT SYSTEMS

Problems and Answers

PART ONE

SECURED TRANSACTIONS

Secured Transactions: Problems

Section 1. *Transferring Property Interests: Security of Property, Good-Faith Purchase, and Fraudulent Conveyance*

It is helpful to think of a secured transaction as a transfer of a property interest, a transfer of one of those sticks in the bundle of sticks that comprise ownership of an asset, in this case, a personal property asset. A lien, a claim, a special property interest, and a security interest are examples of interests in personal property that may be the subject of a transfer or conveyance. The law of secured transactions is law that governs the transfers of those property interests and the respective rights and liabilities that attend them.

You can facilitate your study of Uniform Commercial Code Article 9 by pausing to consider the transfer categories. Generally, transfers fall into one of three categories, under which the taker receives (1) exactly the same interest as that of the transferor, (2) an interest greater than that of the transferor, or (3) an interest less than that of the transferor.

The second kind of transfer is rather famous in commercial law and has its own name: good faith purchase. The third is also common. It is the fraudulent conveyance against which commercial law must take precautions and impose penalties. The first kind of conveyance is the most common of all but it has no name, though it lends itself to poetic license or Latin logic. "No stream can rise higher than its source." "*Nemo dat quod non habet.*" The less erudite among us refer to the first rule as the security-of-property or the no-more rule, the taker receives no more rights than its transferor enjoyed. Professor Harris calls the first rule the *"nemo dat"* rule. Professors Jackson and Baird call it the derivation principle. Sometimes the first rule allows a party to come within the "shelter" or under the "umbrella" of its transferor. All these appellations are descriptive.

3

Note that "title" to property is generally *not* a material concept in conveyancing law under the UCC. *See, e.g.,* §2-401(1) and §9-202. For example, students who remember the importance of title from their real property course sometimes assume that the way the conveyance of a security interest is described has legal significance. Thus, we can say that a seller of equipment conveys the entire bundle of ownership rights in the equipment to the buyer and the buyer then grants a security interest to the seller to secure payment of the purchase price. Or we can say that the seller "reserves" a security interest in the equipment to secure payment of the purchase price and conveys all other ownership sticks to the buyer. Under the UCC, there is no legal difference between these two ways of describing the conveyance. *See* Comment 2 to §9-202, which states: "[T]he characteristics of a security interest that secures the purchase price of goods are the same whether the secured party appears to have retained title or the debtor appears to have obtained title and then conveyed title or a lien to the secured party."

The following problems illustrate the operation of the three types of transfers and hint at the policies that produced them.

Problems

1. Dealer entered into a contract to sell earth moving equipment to Mine Co. on credit. Mine Co. agreed to pay 10 percent of the total price at the time of delivery and the balance in 120 equal monthly installments. Mine Co. took delivery of the equipment at its mine on May 1. It is now December 15, and Mine Co. has made none of the monthly payments. Dealer tells you that the equipment is sitting on a parcel of real estate near the mine, and that Dealer could easily take a flatbed truck and remove the equipment. What do you tell Dealer? Is title to the equipment in Dealer or Mine Co.? Does Dealer have any interest in the equipment?

2. *§2-401(1) (2d sentence).* Woolen Co. delivered wool to Distributor Co. under a contract of conditional sale providing that Distributor would pay only for wool it sold to garment companies and that title to the wool would remain in Woolen Co. until such sales occurred. What interest does Woolen Co. have in the wool on Distributor's premises? What interest does it have in wool Distributor sold to a garment manufacturer? Can Distributor's creditors defeat Woolen Co.'s claim to the wool? Would your answers differ if Woolen Co. names Distributor its agent for purposes of soliciting orders from the garment industry?

3. *§2-401(1) (2d sentence).* Seller Co., a tool and die business, agreed to sell all of its assets to Buyer Co. with payment of the purchase price to be made over a five-year period. Seller and Buyer also agreed that title to the tools and dies would remain in Seller Co. and that in the event Buyer does not pay all of the purchase price, Seller could repossess the goods. What interest does Seller have in the goods?

4. *§2-403(1).* In each of the following cases, on May 1 *A* conveyed all of his rights in a shipment of toluene to *B*. What does *B* get:
   a. If *A* has absolute ownership rights in the cargo?
   b. If, on April 30, *A* had granted a security interest to *C*?
   c. If, on May 2, *A* conveyed his interest in the cargo to *C*? (Why might the law fashion a different answer to this question if *B* had left the cargo in *A*'s possession?)
   d. Identify the policies that your answers to each of the foregoing questions serve.

5. *§2-403(1).* On May 1, Seller granted a security interest in an aircraft to First Bank. On May 2, Seller sold the aircraft to Buyer Co. On May 3, Buyer Co. granted a security interest to Second Bank. Seller Co. and Buyer Co. are now insolvent and have defaulted on their respective obligations to the banks. Both banks claim the equipment. If you assume that both security agreements are fully enforceable, which bank should prevail? Would your answer differ if First Bank's security interest is invalid with respect to Buyer Co.?

6. *§2-403(1).*
   a. On May 1, *A* lost his gold watch, and *B* found it. On May 2, *B* conveyed the watch to *C*. If *A* sues *C* to obtain possession of the watch, what result? How would you describe *C*'s interest in the watch if *A* could not find *C*? (Assume that *C* is unaware of *A*'s interest in the watch.)
   b. Answer the preceding questions assuming that *B* did not find the watch but stole it. Are there considerations of public policy that dictate one result in the case of loss and another in the case of theft?

7. *§2-403(2).* Owner delivered a Ming Dynasty vase to Cash & Carry Gallery, telling the Gallery manager, "Display this vase as my agent for 30 days with a price tag of $500,000, but don't sell it. I merely want to know what kind of interest it will generate at that price." Gallery duly displayed the vase next to a card that read, "Owner proudly authorizes Gallery to offer this one-of-a-kind Ming Dynasty vase for $500,000." Collector took the vase off the display shelf, brought it to the counter and tendered $500,000 in cash. Gallery manager refused to accept the cash or complete the sale. Collector left the cash on the counter and ran out of the store with the vase. Who owns the vase? Is title in Collector or Owner? §2-403(2). Does it matter? §2-403, preamble and §1-103(b) [§1-103].

8. *§2-403(2), (3).* Smith took her Stradivarius to Dealer, who sold new and used violins. She asked Dealer to solicit bids but did not authorize Dealer to sell the violin. Dealer entered into a sales contract with Jones, who paid for the violin and took delivery. In a dispute between Smith and Jones, who will prevail? Why does the law deprive Smith of her title? Was Smith at fault? Was Jones? Who can more efficiently avoid this loss? Would your answer differ if Smith took the Stradivarius to Dealer solely for purposes of having the fiddle stored in Dealer's climate-controlled vault? That Smith delivered the instrument to Dealer with instructions to rent it to symphony performers, with Smith receiving 60 percent of the receipts and Dealer receiving the balance? (Bear in mind that neither Smith nor Jones wants a cause of action against Dealer, though the loser in the dispute would surely have such a cause of action. In the real world, dealers that behave this way are usually insolvent when their misconduct comes to light.)

9. *§2-403(1)(b).*   Manufacturer sold a carload of greige goods to Middle, who took delivery and paid for the goods with a check that later bounced. ("Greige" goods are the stuff of commercial-law lore, akin to grayish-beige widgets.) Before Manufacturer could do anything about it, however, Middle sold the goods to Dealer. In a dispute between Manufacturer and Dealer, who prevails? Would your answer be different if you knew that Manufacturer had never delivered the goods to Middle? That Dealer had never paid Middle? (See the definition of "value" in §1-204 [§1-201(44)].) Why does the statute protect Dealer's expectation interest?

10. *§2-403(1)(a).*   Owner shipped 100 cartons of short-sleeved women's blouses to Jones, a poor credit risk. Owner, misled by Jones' misstatements, believed that Jones was Reed, a wholesaler of impeccable credit reputation. Jones then sold the blouses to several retailers. In a dispute between Owner and the retailers, who prevails? Did Owner intend that Jones take title to the garments? If Owner had sued Jones before he entered into a contract with the retailers, could Owner have maintained successfully that he had title to the blouses?

11. *UFTA §4.*   Ace Electric Co. owed First Bank $400,000. When Ace defaulted under the terms of the loan agreement and note, the bank sued and obtained a judgment against Ace. During the course of that lawsuit, Ace, whose sole stockholder is Joe Ace, sold all of its assets (most of them consisting of trucks, tools, and other equipment) to Joe for "one dollar and other good and valuable consideration." First is now seeking to levy against the assets. Will it succeed?

12. *§2-402(2).*   On May 1, Edison Co. purchased a truck from Dealer, paying $50,000, but left the truck on Dealer's lot with plans to pick it up a week later. On May 2, First Bank, a creditor of Dealer, made a claim on the truck. In a dispute between First and Edison, who prevails? Would it matter that Edison had left the truck with Dealer to have a hydraulic hoist mounted on it? Would it matter that Edison had left the truck with Dealer for a month? What result if Dealer sold the truck to Dealer's sole shareholder?

   a. *UFTA §4.*   Doc's med school loans are overdue, and the guarantor is threatening to sue to collect the $120,000 now owing. Doc transfers ownership of the equipment in his office (but not the right to use the equipment) to a newly formed corporation owned by his father and mother in exchange for their promise to let him live and eat for free in their home until they die. Doc also assigns to the corporation all his existing and future accounts receivable in exchange for a promise to pay him in 8 years an amount equal to 60 percent of the amount the corporation collects on those receivables. Are the transfers valid against the guarantor?

b. *UFTA §5.* Dot is an insolvent former executive of iPhantom.com. Since the company folded, she has been unemployed and living off cash advances against her credit card. Over the last year, she has been paying PBS $2000 a month on a pledge she made, when she was still a high-flyer. Can the credit card issuer recover the payments from PBS?

c. *UFTA §4.* Parent Inc. is a holding company whose only assets are the stock of two wholly-owned subsidiaries. Sub *A*'s sole asset is a very valuable patent. Sub *B* is developing a new product that it hopes to patent, but it needs a cash infusion to continue doing business. Bank refuses to lend to Sub *B* because Sub *B* does not have sufficient assets or income to support a loan to it without a guarantee. Parent offers to have Sub *A* guarantee the loan. Bank's credit officer is willing to lend on that basis. Should Bank accept Sub *A*'s guarantee? Is there a better way to structure the transaction from Bank's viewpoint?

Section 2. Scope

The original version of Article 9 of the Uniform Commercial Code was a signal achievement. Its architects, Gilmore, Kripke, and Llewellyn, among others, rationalized a system of law governing personal property security that had up until then defied rationalization in the United States and that still defies it elsewhere. It is a tribute to the Code drafters that Article 9 achieved ubiquitous adoption in the United States and ubiquitous regard, and even some emulation, abroad.

The drafters of Revised Article 9 did not enjoy the luxury of writing on a clean slate. By the time they began the project, Article 9 had a long history; borrowers and lenders, especially banks, knew the weak spots and the ambiguities. Most commentators agree that the courts have handled those spots and ambiguities quite well. However, many lawyers for commercial parties, especially for banks, insisted that revisions to the Code itself were necessary so that they could provide the types of legal opinions required by their clients. Unfortunately, the lawyers got their wish, and the drafters were given the impossible task of drafting a secured property code that contained no ambiguity.

The result is a rather long statute with significantly more detail than Gilmore, Kripke, and Llewellyn fashioned. We can only predict that the revised article will ultimately raise as many questions as the old one. In fact, given the degree of detail, we would not be surprised if there aren't even more ambiguities lurking in the revision than the bankers found in the pre-revised version. But we don't have to rely on predictions concerning the learning challenge revised Article 9 poses for you. Revised Article 9 is not an easy statute to learn.

Parties often disguise secured transactions, describing them as sales, consignments, leases, or retention of title arrangements. A remarkable achievement of the Article is its scope provision, which looks through the disguises and lets the realities govern the application of the statute. The scope provision is not without its problems, but by and large it has been an outstanding success.

The following problems illustrate the key scope provision, §9-109, and the difficulties that attend it. Some problems in this section deal with the transactions that the drafters felt should be excluded from the operation of the Article.

Problems

13. *§9-109(a)(3).* May, a garment manufacturer, sells all of its accounts receivable ("accounts" in Article 9 parlance) to Finance Co. with the understanding that Finance Co. will collect them and charge May back for any account that is bad. Should Finance Co. comply with Article 9? Would your answer differ if May sold the accounts to the finance company without recourse (with the understanding that the finance company would take the loss on bad accounts)? What is the difference between the sale of accounts and the creation of a security interest in accounts?

14. *§9-109(a)(3) and §9-109(d)(4).* Dealer sells battery-powered forklift trucks. He has found a new line of customers—independent supermarket operators. The operators need credit, however, and Dealer has agreed to 120-day terms. Dealer insists that the purchasers sign installment sales contracts (which are chattel paper in Article 9 parlance) obligating the purchasers to make monthly payments for the trucks and granting Dealer a security interest in the trucks to secure those payments. Dealer finds that the volume of his paper has risen to the point that he can no longer afford to carry it. Dealer, therefore, approaches Bank and asks Bank to take the paper as collateral for a loan. Must Bank comply with Article 9? Would your answer differ if Dealer sold the paper to Bank? What if Dealer sold its paper to New Dealer along with all of the other assets of Dealer's business?

15. *§9-102(a)(65), §9-109(a)(3).* Mortgage Co. generates second mortgages by lending money to customers of home improvement contractors. The contractors steer the customer to Mortgage Co., which lends the money directly to the customer to pay for the home improvement. Mortgage Co. takes a second mortgage on the customer's home from the customer as security for the note it also takes. It then quickly turns the note and mortgage over to National Bank, which usually pays Mortgage Co. 95 percent of the face amount of the note. Must the bank comply with Article 9? Is the bank's interest in the note a security interest? Is its interest in the mortgage? Does it matter whether Mortgage Co. sells the note and the mortgage to the bank or whether it grants the bank a security interest in the note and the mortgage?

16. *§9-109(a), §9-109(c)(1) & cmt. 8.* First National Bank loaned $1 million to rock star Andy Swinger for a Lear jet that Swinger is buying. First National took a security agreement under Article 9 that properly creates a security interest in the aircraft. Thus, in Article 9 parlance the security interest "attached." The bank also filed a financing statement in the office designated by Article 9 as the place to file for security interests in Swinger's personal property. Is it accurate to say that having complied with Article 9, the bank can now safely conclude that it is adequately protected? Would the answer be any different if the collateral were a yacht registered under the Federal Ship Mortgage Act? A patent? A copyright?

17. When Swinger went to the bank to borrow for the aircraft, he also wanted to borrow additional sums for an investment he planned to make in a Las Vegas casino. In which of the following assets might he grant the bank a security interest under Article 9?
    a. Sums due from a recording company under a recording contract. §9-102(a)(2).
    b. A claim against Andy Zinger for pirating Swinger's songs. §9-102(a)(13)(B), §9-109(d)(12).
    c. Sums due from American Casualty Co. for losses Swinger sustained when thieves stole his Grammy. §9-109(d)(8).
    d. One thousand pounds Swinger has on deposit with the O'Connell Street Branch of the Bank of Ireland. §9-109(d)(13).

Section 3. The Concept of Security

If a security interest is a property interest, as most agree it is, there must be rules for its creation. The Code rule is that it is created by the voluntary act or sufferance of the debtor, the party that is conveying the security interest to the secured party or is allowing the secured party to retain a security interest. A security interest arises when the debtor grants it to the secured party or when a seller of goods retains a security interest in them with the buyer's acquiescence.

Problems

18. Seller entered into a contract to sell a drill press on credit to Buyer. More than ten days after delivery, Buyer had not paid. What might Seller do to obtain payment from Buyer? May Seller sneak into Buyer's premises and retrieve the press?

19. *Bankruptcy Code §362.* Assume the same facts as in the preceding problem with the additional fact that Seller retained a perfected security interest in the press. How would this additional fact alter your answers to the preceding question? Would Buyer's bankruptcy have any effect on Seller's actions? What effect would Buyer's bankruptcy have on Seller's position in Problem 18?

20. *§9-315, §9-320(a).* In the preceding problem assume Buyer sold the press to Sub-Buyer. Can Seller recover the press from Sub-Buyer? Would it matter whether Sub-Buyer is a buyer in ordinary course, that is, a buyer without knowledge of Seller's claim who buys in the ordinary course of business from a merchant who sells goods of the kind? Should the law prefer ordinary course Sub-Buyer to Seller?

Section 4. Creating the Security Interest: The Security Agreement

A security interest is not a lien or claim that arises by operation of law. It is a form of purchase, that is, it arises by virtue of voluntary transfer. *See §1-201(b)(29) & (30) [§1-201(32) & (33)]* (defining "purchase" and "purchaser"). The Code forges this feature of the security interest through the concept of "attachment." Attachment occurs only when the parties satisfy certain Code requirements that protect the debtor by insisting that the transaction reveal that the debtor created the security interest voluntarily. Those requirements also relate to the scope of the interest transferred. *See §9-203.*

Problems

21. *§9-201(a).* On May 1, Debtor granted Secured Party a security interest in Debtor's plastic molding machine. Which of the following parties are bound by the conveyance?
   a. Debtor.
   b. Secured Party.
   c. Debtor's unsecured creditors.
   d. X, to whom Debtor sells the machine on May 2.
   e. Y, to whom Debtor grants a security interest in the machine on May 2.
   f. Z, who causes the sheriff to levy on the machine on May 3.
   g. Debtor's trustee in bankruptcy when Debtor files a petition in bankruptcy on May 4.

22. Would any of your answers to the foregoing question differ if
   a. Debtor retained possession of the machine and granted the security interest to Secured Party orally? §9-203.
   b. Secured Party failed to perfect its security interest? §9-301.
   c. Debtor holds title to the machine? §9-202.
   d. Secured Party holds title to the machine? §9-202.

23. *§9-203(b)(2).* On May 1, Debtor, a hardware wholesaler that purchases from manufacturers and sells to hardware retailers, entered into a security agreement granting First Bank a security interest in all of Debtor's "inventory, equipment, and accounts, now owned or hereafter acquired or arising." The secured party, First Bank, made a loan to Debtor of $100,000. In which of the following items of property does Bank have an enforceable security interest on May 1? On August 1?

    a. A truckload of snow shovels Debtor acquired on May 10.

    b. Sums due from retailers for sales Debtor made to the retailers during June.

    c. Two electrically operated forklift trucks Debtor purchased on May 30 for use in its warehouse.

    d. Sums due Debtor under a software copyright license it entered into with a national chain of food wholesalers, the software being something Debtor developed to keep track of inventory.

    e. Thirteen checks Debtor received from retailers as proceeds from June sales of hinges, door knobs, kickplates, and other brass items.

24. *§9-203(b)(3)(A).* Assume in the foregoing problem that Debtor's president, Joe, went to Bank to borrow the funds he needed as working capital. While he was at the bank, the loan officer asked him to sign a number of documents, including a loan agreement, a promissory note, a financing statement, and the security agreement. Joe went about signing the documents but inadvertently failed to sign the security agreement, a fact that did not become evident until six months later when Debtor Co. filed a petition in bankruptcy. Do these altered facts change any of your answers to the preceding question? Would it matter that the bank discovered the missing signature on August 1 and required Joe to execute the security agreement at that time?

25. *§§1-201(b)(35), 1-203 [§1-201(37)].* At the time of Debtor Co.'s default, it maintained 15 work stations located throughout the warehouse where warehouse employees fed data into a central processing unit that kept track of the inventory. The computer hardware that comprised this inventory control system was leased to Debtor by Computer Leasing Co. The system consisted of 15 terminals, a central processing unit, printers, and various peripherals. Under the terms of the lease, which had an original term of 2 years and had 18 months to run, Debtor paid rent monthly and had the right to terminate the lease at any time. What rights, if any, does First Bank have in the computer hardware?

26. On May 1, three farm producers delivered cattle to the slaughterhouse of Samuels & Co. under a contract of sale. Samuels could not pay the producers immediately because the purchase price depended on the weight of the slaughtered animals and the grade that government inspectors gave them. Traditionally, it took a day for the cattle to be slaughtered, dressed, weighed, and graded; shortly thereafter, Samuels would write a check to the producers. On May 2, before Samuels could write the checks to the three farmers, its creditors forced Samuels into bankruptcy. One of the creditors, Commercial Finance, Ltd., had taken a properly signed security agreement from Samuels on April 10, some three weeks before the producers delivered the cattle in question. The security agreement described Commercial's collateral as "all inventory of cattle, now owned or hereafter acquired." The farmers can show that on May 1, Samuels' liabilities greatly exceeded its assets, that is, on May 1, Samuels was insolvent. Under the common law, then, Samuels is guilty of fraud at law, taking delivery of goods on credit while insolvent. Under both the common law and §2-702(2) of the Code, the farm producers have the right to reclaim the cattle they delivered on May 1. Samuels' interest in the cattle on that date was title voidable by the producers. Assume that there is no state or federal statute that preempts application of the Code to this problem.

    a. Is Commercial a purchaser? §1-201(b)(29) & (30) [§1-201(32) & (33)].

    b. Has it given value? §1-204 [§1-201(44)(b)].

    c. Has it acted in good faith? Even if it knew that Samuels had inventory for which Samuels had not paid? §9-102(a)(43).

    d. If the farm producers retained title to the cattle, how does the Code characterize their interest? §2-401(1)(second sentence).

    e. If your or the law's answers to questions a through c are in the affirmative, does Commercial defeat the producers? §2-403(1).

    f. Does the fact that under §9-324(b) the producers had a method to defeat Samuels support the Article 2 analysis implicit in the answers to the above questions?

27. *§9-204(a) & (c).*   On May 1, CNC, Ltd. sold two pieces of robotic equipment to ABC Manufacturing Co. To pay for the equipment, ABC borrowed most of the purchase price from First Bank and granted First Bank a security interest in the two pieces of equipment to secure the loan. On July 1, First Bank extended credit to ABC to cover ABC's payroll. On October 1, ABC defaulted on both loans. First Bank repossessed the equipment and sold it at a foreclosure sale for $2 million. The balance on the equipment purchase is $1.75 million. May First Bank use the $250,000 excess to satisfy the payroll advance? Would your answer differ if the security agreement recited that the security interest secured

    a. all debts due from ABC to First Bank for equipment?

    b. all debts of any kind whatsoever whenever incurred?

28. *§2-401(1), §1-201(b)(35) [§1-201(37)].*   Assume in the foregoing question that ABC did not seek a loan from First Bank but purchased the machines for 10 percent down with the balance payable in monthly installments over a period of 60 months. Assume that in the written sales contract, the parties agreed that title to the equipment would remain in CNC until all of the payments were made. If ABC defaults in its installment obligation, may CNC repossess the machines?

29. *§9-203(b)(3)(A), §9-204(e).*   On May 1, XYZ Manufacturing granted First Bank a security interest in all of its equipment. On May 5, XYZ obtained a metal stamping machine. On May 10, XYZ defaulted on its loan to Bank. Does First Bank have the right to repossess the stamping machine?

30. *§9-204(a).*   On May 1, Beer Distributors, Inc. entered into a working capital loan agreement with First Bank. Under the terms of the agreement, First Bank extended a $1 million line of credit in Beer's favor. In the agreement Beer granted to Bank a security interest in all of its inventory, then owned or thereafter acquired. Beer turns its inventory over (sells its stock and buys new stock) once every 45 days. Under the terms of the security agreement, First Bank allowed Beer to sell its inventory in the ordinary course of its business, so that by the middle of June, Beer held none of the inventory that it held on May 1. Every week, however, Beer received shipments of beer from its brewery suppliers. Beer defaulted on its bank loan on September 1.

    a. Does First Bank have any interest in the after-acquired inventory? §9-204(a).

    b. Does it matter that First Bank left the inventory in the possession of Beer with power to sell it? §9-205(a).

31. *§9-203(a) & (b).* In each of the following illustrations, indicate the date when the security interest of Bank in Debtor's collateral first attached.

    a. Bank made a loan on May 1 and, on May 2, took possession from Debtor of promissory notes for collection through the bank collection system.

    b. Bank made a loan on May 1 and, on May 2, took a written security agreement signed by Debtor covering after-acquired inventory. On May 3, Debtor acquired its first shipment of inventory.

    c. Bank made a loan on May 1. On May 2, Debtor signed a security agreement covering equipment then owned or thereafter acquired. On May 3, Debtor identified a machine that it planned to use in its business and agreed to purchase from Seller. Seller delivered the machine to Debtor on May 4.

    d. On May 1, Debtor signed a security agreement, and Bank made a binding commitment to make a loan. The security agreement covered after-acquired property. On May 2, Debtor acquired property of the kind described in the security agreement. On May 3, Bank disbursed the loan proceeds.

    e. The facts are the same as in d, but the loan commitment is not binding.

    f. Bank made a loan on May 1. On May 2, Debtor signed a security agreement covering inventory. On May 3, Debtor acquired new inventory.

    g. On May 1, Bank made a loan. On May 2, Debtor signed a security agreement covering all inventory. Debtor, on May 3, sold some inventory and received a promissory note from the purchaser.

Section 5. Definitions

By now it should be apparent that Article 9 differentiates collateral by type. The distinctions are functional and accommodate different rules that reflect merchant and banking practices. Much of Article 9 study is the study of the rules that rest on these distinctions, rules relating to priorities and to the manner of perfection being chief among them. Later, you will see that Code provisions defining parties also play a key role in application of Code rules. For now it is enough to be concerned with definitions that relate to collateral.

Problems

32. *§9-102(a)(2).* On May 1, Debtor, a clothing retailer, granted First Bank a security interest in all of its accounts. In which of the following items of Debtor's property does the bank enjoy a security interest?
    a. Office furniture. §9-102(a)(33).
    b. Word processors. §9-102(a)(33).
    c. Stationery, fuel for vehicles, and unsold merchandise. §9-102(a)(33) & (48).

33. *§9-102(a)(48).*
    On May 1, Debtor, an aluminum fabricator, granted First Bank a security interest in all of its inventory. In which of the following items of Debtor's personal property does the bank enjoy a security interest?
    a. Aluminum ingots Debtor plans to melt and mold into parts it will sell to its customers.
    b. Partially manufactured aluminum parts.
    c. Finished goods.
    d. Cartons Debtor uses to ship finished goods.
    e. Stationery and fuel for vehicles.
    f. An aluminum stamping machine Debtor no longer needs and has advertised for sale.

34. *§9-102(a)(2).* Joe Buyer owes Carl Creditor $5,000. In which of the following cases is the debt an account?
    a. When Creditor loaned the money to Buyer.
    b. When the sum is due for goods sold to Buyer on credit.
    c. When the sum is due for services performed by Creditor for Buyer on credit.
    d. In either b or c, if Creditor holds
       i.   a promissory note signed by Buyer. §9-102(a)(47).
       ii. a written lease under which Buyer grants Creditor an interest in goods and agrees to pay the $5,000 in monthly installments. §9-102(a)(11).
       iii. a non-negotiable promissory note or some other written contract evidencing Buyer's obligation to pay Creditor.

35. *§9-404.* Seller's customers buy goods periodically from Seller on open account. On May 1, Seller decided to sell these customer obligations to First Factor Co., which undertook to collect the sums due from the customers. First Factor paid Seller 95 percent of the total amount of the obligations and agreed that the sale was without recourse, that is, Seller does not have to buy back from First any obligation that goes bad by virtue of a customer's default.
    a. *§9-109(a)(1) or (3).* Does Article 9 apply to the transaction? If so, what steps must First take in connection with the sale of the accounts?
    b. What are the Article 9 terms in this transaction for
       i. a customer's obligation to Seller?
       ii. Seller?

        iii. First Factor?

        iv. the customers?

  c. *§9-406.* If First Factor notifies the customers of the sale of the obligations and that the customers are to pay First Factor, may the customers pay Seller? Would your answer to this question differ if the terms of the obligation between Seller and the customers forbade Seller to sell the obligation to anyone?

  d. *§9-406.* If a customer receives notice of the sale of his obligation to First Factor and that the customer is to pay First Factor, but if the customer pays Seller, is the customer's obligation discharged?

  e. If a customer does not receive any notice of the sale of his obligation to First, will the customer's payment to Seller discharge the obligation?

  f. If a customer receives notice of the sale but not that the customer must pay First Factor, will the customer's payment to Seller discharge the obligation?

36. *§9-109.* Dealer sells pipe and pipe fittings to plumbing contractors on 60-day terms. Dealer's accounts from these customers aggregate $2.5 million. In addition, Dealer has inventory, a warehouse, and equipment, all of which are valued at about $650,000. Dealer is retiring and plans to sell his assets to *X* for cash. Must *X* comply with the attachment and perfection rules of Article 9? Must *X* worry about the rule of §9-406?

Section 6. *Defining Proceeds*

In a simpler age, commerce was rather static; debtors' collateral did not move. In the modern day, however, collateral moves with alarming celerity. Furthermore, some collateral—inventory in particular—is *supposed* to move; its sale, presumably at a profit, makes it possible for the debtor to repay the creditor. The creditor's main interest is thus in the proceeds of sale. Sometimes, however, collateral is supposed to stay put. A creditor wants the debtor to use equipment, for example, in order to repay the loan, and would be greatly distressed were the debtor to sell the equipment without the creditor's approval. Indeed, creditors often place covenants in the loan agreement to make sale of the equipment without approval an instant default. In either case, secured parties protect themselves by policing the activity of their borrowers. They can police only so far and so often, though. The Code provides further help for the secured party by fashioning a proceeds rule that is rather generous. To accommodate commercial practices, the proceeds section's rules often differentiate among the kinds of collateral involved.

Problems

37. §§9-102(a)(64), 9-203(f), 9-315(a).   On May 1, Dealer granted First Bank a security interest in all of Dealer's new cars, then owned or thereafter acquired, including all accessories and additions thereto. To which of the following items received by Dealer during the week of May 1, will the bank's security interest attach?

    a. Three used cars and a used truck that customers traded to Dealer as down payments on new vehicles.
    b. Ten retail installment sales contracts signed by customers who purchased new vehicles and that contained a security interest granted by the purchaser to Dealer.
    c. Nine checks that customers used as down payments on new cars.
    d. A check that was a down payment on a used car. (Would it matter that the used car was not a trade-in for the sale of a new car?)
    e. Two hundred dollars in the cash drawer that includes some cash down payments and some payments for work done by the service department. (Would it matter that some of the cash, no one knowing how much, had been used during the week to buy lunches for employees of Dealer?)
    f. Insurance proceeds from damage done to a new car when a customer test-drove it.
    g. A customer's obligation to pay for parts and service.
    h. A deposit account that contains $500 from a check received that day from the sale of a new car. (Would it matter that non-proceeds had been deposited in the account that week? Would it matter that the proceeds were deposited on Monday and the non-proceeds later in the week?)
    i. A deposit account segregated for proceeds from the sale of new vehicles.
    j. A check received from the lease of one of the cars.

38. In the preceding question, who bears the burden of showing that the items are proceeds?

39. On May 1, F granted First Bank a security interest in F's sorghum crop. On May 2, F, who is a member of a local farm cooperative, sold the sorghum to the cooperative in return for the right to draw up to $40,000 in feed, fertilizer, seed, and other products the cooperative sells to its members. Does First Bank have any interest in the drawing rights?

40. In May, F granted First Bank a security interest in all of his grain or legume crops then growing or thereafter to be grown on his 1,000 acre farm in Princeville, Illinois. The following winter, F entered into a government program under which he agreed not to plant any cash or feed crop on his farm, but only clover or prairie grasses. Under the program, at the end of the growing season, F will be entitled to the market price on the day he cashes his entitlement of 40,000 bushels of corn and 30,000 bushels of soybeans. Does the bank have any interest in the entitlements?

41. In the preceding problem, *F* also granted the bank a security interest in all of his livestock, then owned or thereafter acquired. *F* owned 100 head of dairy cattle, 15 of which calved the following spring. Does the bank have any interest in the calves?

Section 7. Commingling and Accessions

Sometimes goods are combined with other goods in ways that change both. If creditors with rights in the uncombined goods claim against the whole, what rights do they have? The answer depends in part on the nature of the combination and the presence or absence of other claimants, as the problems below show.

Problems

42. *§9-336.*   Copper Co. sells copper ingots to Brass Co. for $60,000. Zinc Co. sells zinc to Brass for $60,000. Both sellers sell on credit and retain a security interest in the metal they sell. Brass has made brass (60 percent copper and 40 percent zinc) parts out of the shipments from Copper and Zinc and sold the parts to customers on open account for $75,000. Brass is now insolvent. Copper and Zinc both claim the accounts. What part of the accounts will go to Copper and what part to Zinc?

43. *§§9-102(a)(1), 9-335, 9-336.* Suppose Brass simply bolted the ingots together to make furniture, using sixty percent copper and forty percent zinc. The furniture was sold on open account for $75,000. Brass is now insolvent. Copper and Zinc both claim the accounts. What part of the accounts will go to Copper and what part to Zinc?

44. After granting each of the sellers a security interest in the product they sell, Bakery Co. purchased on credit flour from *F*, butter from *B*, and leaven from *L*. Bakery has turned all of the ingredients into bread. Under *§9-336*, what must each of the sellers show to claim a security interest in the bread?

Section 8. Tracing

Tracing rules are customarily the concern of accountants, but in proceeds cases tracing becomes a problem for the lawyer. The lowest intermediate balance method of tracing funds commingled in an account comes to secured transactions law from trust law. *See* Restatement (Second) of Trusts §202. It is not the only possible tracing rule, but it is the one most commonly used in this field. *See* §9-315, cmt. 3. Note that the courts—for this is judge-made commercial law, not Code law—eschewed some tracing rules (e.g., LIFO or FIFO) that they might have used.

The lowest intermediate balance rule can be thought of as treating proceeds as heavy water that sinks to the bottom of the bucket. The debtor takes water from the top of the bucket and may not dip into the proceeds that have sunk to the bottom until he has taken all the non-proceeds water from the top. If he does dip into the proceeds, however, the proceeds are lost to the secured party. Non-proceeds water poured into the bucket thereafter will replenish the bucket but not the proceeds that remain depleted at the lowest intermediate balance level. So under the lowest intermediate balance rule, proceeds are spared but are never replenished.

Problem

45. The following chart shows proceeds deposits and end-of-day balances of a checking account of Dealer, which has granted a security interest in all of its inventory to First Bank. Each listed deposit consists of checks received from customers as down payments for the purchase of new cars out of Dealer's inventory. What is the amount of proceeds in the account on each day? (Bear in mind that the chart does not show debits, only credits from proceeds deposits and the balance on each day. Not shown are amounts of non-proceeds deposits, even though they affect the balance figures.)

Date	Deposit (of proceeds)	Balance
May 1	$10,000	$20,000
May 2	—0—	5,000
May 3	—0—	1,000
May 4	5,000	6,000
May 5	—0—	1,000
May 6	—0—	100,000

Section 9. More on Classifying Collateral

Definitions are the subject of the next 17 problems. One purpose of these problems is to make the definitions second nature. You cannot understand class discussion without a working understanding of the definitions. It simply will not do for you to refer back to the definition section or your notes as the instructor and fellow students talk about purchase money security interests, accounts, chattel paper, equipment, etc. To be literate in commercial law (the primary object of your commercial law study in law school), you must move these definitions from your passive to your active vocabulary. The problems help.

Problems

46. *§9-108.* If Debtor grants First Bank a security interest in "all of debtor's property no matter where situated, now owned or hereafter acquired," will the bank have a security interest in any of Debtor's property?

47. *§9-102(a)(11), (30), & (47).* Debtor, a commodities broker, granted First Bank a security interest in all of Debtor's "instruments and chattel paper." Debtor has in its safe a negotiable bill of lading covering 200,000 barrels of West Texas crude oil. Debtor and the bank orally agreed that the bank would have an interest in the bill. Thereafter Debtor delivered the bill to the bank. Does First Bank have any interest in the bill? In the oil?

48. *§9-102(a)(48).* Rockford, Inc. manufactures steel door locks, hinges, fasteners, and other hardware for the construction industry. Rockford owns rolled steel sheets, steel wire, and steel rods, all of which it uses in the manufacture of its products. For purposes of Article 9, what kind of collateral would the steel sheets, wire, and rods be? What kind of collateral would partially manufactured products be? Finished goods?

49. *§9-102(a)(33) & (48).* Wausau Co., a modular home builder, owns hinges and door hardware it acquired from Rockford. Wausau also owns electric saws and drills, trucks, and heating oil for the plant it uses to manufacture its products. For purposes of Article 9, how would you classify the hinges and door hardware, the electric saws and drills, the trucks, and the heating oil?

50. Contractor, a sole proprietorship, does small home improvement jobs, driveway repaving, and snow removal work. Over the years customers have paid him by
   a. cash;
   b. promissory note, §9-102(a)(47) & (65);
   c. agreeing in writing to pay him 30 days after he completes the work, §9-102(a)(2); and
   d. trading an oriental rug that he took home and put in his living room, §9-102(a)(23).

How would you classify the various assets for Article 9 purposes?

51. *§§9-102(a)(48), 9-102(a)(30).* Dealer sells personal computers. He has 20 PCs on his showroom floor and a negotiable bill of lading covering 10 more that are en route to his establishment from a manufacturer. How would you classify Dealer's assets?

52. *§9-102.* Cincinnatus sells new and used grand pianos. On May 1, he sold a Steinway to *A* for use in the music studio where she teaches her students. On May 2, he sold a Mason & Hamlin to *B* who took the piano home for her children to use. On May 3, he sold a Baldwin to *C* to use in her piano bar. How do you classify the three pianos?

53. In the preceding problem, Cincinnatus sold the Mason & Hamlin under a written contract that obligated *B* to pay Cincinnatus in 60 equal monthly installments and granted Cincinnatus a security interest in the piano to secure the payments.

    a.   What special character does Article 9 give to this security interest? §9-103.

    b.   In what kind of property does Cincinnatus have a security interest? §9-102(a)(23).

    c.   If First Bank takes a security interest in the retail installment contract, in what kinds of collateral will the bank have a security interest? §§9-102(a)(23), 9-102(a)(11), 9-109(a)(3).

    d.   Does Cincinnatus have to file a financing statement to perfect its security interest in the piano? Would it have to file if it had taken similar retail installment sales contracts from *A* and *C*? §9-309(1).

    e.   Does the bank have to file a financing statement to perfect its security interest in the chattel paper? §§9-312(a), 9-313(a).

    f.   Does the bank have to file a financing statement to perfect its security interest in the piano? §9-310(c).

    g.   Would any of your analysis in this question change if Cincinnatus had sold the retail installment sales contract to the bank? §9-109(a)(3).

54.   *§§9-102(a)(49) & cmt. 6, 9-313(a) & cmt. 1.*   On May 1, Investor subscribed and paid for 4,000 shares of preferred stock in ABC Co. The company could not issue the stock certificate to Investor until the Securities and Exchange Commission issued a letter to the company validating the company's opinion that the stock was not covered by regulations requiring registration of the offering. On May 2, Investor granted First Bank a security interest in her rights to the stock. How do you classify Investor's interest? How would you perfect the bank's security interest?

55.   *§§9-102(a)(29), 9-109(d)(13).*

    a.   *D*, the owner of a child care center, has asked First Bank, her banker, for a loan so she can expand. In the security agreement, First Bank has listed her savings and checking accounts, both business and personal, with them as collateral for the loan. Which of these would be subject to an Article 9 security interest? What if *D* uses one account for both business and personal transactions?

    b.   Suppose *D* banks with First Bank but wishes to borrow from Second Bank. Second Bank wants to take a security interest in *D*'s bank accounts with First Bank. How may Second Bank do so? §§9-104(a), 9-342.

56.   *§§9-102(a)(47) & (65), 9-312(a), 9-313(a).*   Syndicator sells limited partnership interests in aircraft that the partnership leases to airlines. Under the syndication, the limited partners invest $500,000, of which $50,000 is to be in cash, with the balance to be evidenced by a negotiable promissory note. Syndicator intends to borrow money from a bank to complete the acquisition of the aircraft. What will he have to offer the bank as security? How will the bank perfect its security interest? May it file a financing statement?

57.   Jones, a lawyer, enjoyed watching motion pictures filmed in the 1930s. Jones bought a DVD player from Chicago, a retailer, that sold the equipment to Jones under a retail installment sales contract. Under the terms of the contract, Jones granted Chicago a security interest in the player to secure payment of the purchase price, which Jones agreed to pay over 24 months.

   a. Must Chicago file a financing statement to perfect its security interest? §9-309(1).
   b. Would your answer differ if Jones had acquired the DVD player to show clients films on estate planning?
   c. What should Chicago do if Jones plans to use the DVD player 25 percent of the time to watch the films and 75 percent for his clients? §9-102 and comment 4a.
   d. What should Chicago do if Jones buys the DVD player for use in the home and a month later takes it to the office? §9-507(b) and comment 4.

58. *§9-102(a)(23), (34), (48).*   Hennery has 100 gross of eggs. It sells them to Farm Distributor Co, which sells them to Ace Food Markets, Inc., which sells one dozen of them to Smith, who takes them home and puts them in the kitchen refrigerator. For Article 9 purposes, how do you classify the eggs in the hands of each of the parties?

59. *§9-102(a)(34).*   Dillon operates a feedlot on which he fattens 10,000 head of cattle. Dillon owns 50 percent of the cattle. The other 5,000 head are owned by a consortium of schoolteachers, ophthalmologists, and attorneys. How would you classify the cattle for Article 9 purposes? Are the cattle in the possession of one engaged in farming operations?

60. *§9-102(a)(42) & (44).*   How would you classify for Article 9 purposes the following assets?

   a. Capital investment of a partner available to the partner upon withdrawal from the firm.
   b. Royalties due from a publisher to an author.
   c. Right to return of membership fees due country club member upon death.
   d. Alimony payments.
   e. Bequests due from an estate under active administration.
   f. A word processing program.

61. *§9-103.*   Which of the following secured parties has a purchase money security interest?

   a. Chicago, which sells a snowmobile to Jones on credit for use on weekends (late September through early May) in Michigan's upper peninsula and takes a security interest from Jones.
   b. First Credit Union, which takes a security interest from Jones and lends her the money to pay Chicago cash at the time she acquires the snowmobile from Chicago. Would your answer to this question differ if Jones used the money from the credit union to pay tuition and borrowed the purchase price from her mother to pay Chicago?
   c. If the credit union is a purchase money secured party, does it need to file a financing statement to perfect its security interest? §9-

309(1). How might the credit union protect its assumption that it is a purchase money secured party?

62. Dealer sells personal computers to farmers and other small businesses on credit. Under the arrangement, the purchasers execute installment contracts granting Dealer a security interest in the computers and reflecting the purchasers' obligation to pay Dealer the purchase price over a fixed period of time, usually 24 months. Dealer also takes a financing statement from the purchaser and files the statement in the proper office.

   a.   What is the nature of Dealer's collateral? §9-l02(a)(33).
   b.   If Dealer assigns its paper to First Bank for cash ("discounts" its paper), what is the nature of First Bank's collateral? Does First Bank have two kinds of collateral? §9-102(a)(11) & (33).
   c.   What must First Bank do to become a perfected secured creditor with respect to the personal computers? §9-310(a).
   d.   With respect to the paper? §9-310(a), -313(a).

Section 10.   The Financing Statement

Part 5 of Article 9 deals with the financing statement. Section 9-502 sets out the requirements for the statement, and section 9-501 indicates the office or offices where the secured party must file the statement in order to be perfected.

You will note that the filing rules are choice-of-law sensitive. Initially, we will assume that there is only one state involved in the transaction. Later, we deal with multiple state transactions. In general, the applicable law is that of the debtor's location, though that rule gives way in some instances to the law of the jurisdiction where the goods are located. *See* §9-301. Note also that there are two offices for filings, one local for collateral associated with real estate, one central for all other collateral. We assume that jurisdictions have selected the office of the Secretary of State for central filings.

It eases study of the filing sections to learn now four simple rules:

(1) For filing purposes, there are individuals, organizations (§1-201(b)(25) [§1-201(28)]), and registered organizations (§9-102(a)(70)).

(2) Individuals are located at their residence.

(3) Organizations are located at their place of business or chief executive office if they have more than one place of business.

(4) Registered organizations (e.g., corporations) are located where they are incorporated.

In this book, we deal with individuals (who conduct consumer affairs or business affairs without the corporate form) and registered organizations, the Code's name for business corporations. If you learn the rules for those entities, you'll have no problem when you deal with partnerships, estates, trusts, municipalities, and the like.

It should not surprise you to learn that the predecessors of these two sections, §9-501 and §9-502 and, we predict these sections as well, prompt a considerable amount of trouble for the careless lender. When a trustee in bankruptcy succeeds to the assets of a debtor's estate, the trustee takes free of unperfected security interests. Filing in the incorrect office or filing an inadequate financing statement are two common mistakes that leave a secured party unperfected. Trustees are aware of that fact and comb through the financing statements carefully to see whether they can upset a secured creditor's claim of perfection. The following problems deal with technical rules, the observance of which is often critical to the secured lender.

Problems

63. *§9-501(a), §9-301(1), §9-307.* Where should First Bank file to perfect a security interest in the following items of collateral?
   a. Farming equipment owned by a farmer residing in Lake County, Michigan, and farming in Mason County, Michigan. Would your answer differ if the owner were a feed store operator who combined for farmers (operated harvesting equipment, for you urbanites) on a contract basis?
   b. A sum due from a dairy incorporated in Indiana for grain sold by First Bank's debtor, a farmer residing in Mason County, Michigan.
   c. A Cleveland, Ohio, doctor's cattle located on a Mason County, Michigan, feedlot.
   d. A boiler in a Detroit apartment building.
   e. Inventory of a Detroit firm that manufactures hydraulic lifts.
   f. Accounts owned by a tool and die manufacturer in Chicago.
   g. Equipment leases under which a national bank is the lessor.
   h. Cash.
   i. A negotiable bill of lading covering
      (1) cattle;
      (2) plastic pellets.
   j. Cattle at a slaughterhouse.
   k. Trotters at Northville Downs race track in Northville, Michigan.

64. *§9-502, §9-503, §9-506.* Which of the following errors in a financing statement would render the filing defective?
   a. "A.B. Jones Mfg. Co." is listed as the debtor, instead of the actual name "A.B. Jones Manufacturing Co., Inc."
   b. *§9-108, §9-504.* A description of collateral as "farm products" for
      i. a dairy herd;
      ii. a race horse.
   c. The secured party is listed as "Joe" Smith instead of "Joseph" Smith. Would your answer differ if Smith were the debtor?
   d. The debtor is listed as Benjamin Smith, when the debtor's correct name is
      i. J. Benjamin Smith;
      ii. JBS, Ltd., a corporation of which Benjamin Smith is sole shareholder.
   e. Does it matter in either of the cases in (d) that no creditor is misled?

f.   That "everyone knows" that Benjamin Smith is J. Benjamin Smith?

65. *§9-516, §9-520(c), §9-502, comment 4.*
a.   Is it necessary for a financing statement to include:
i.   The address of the debtor?
ii.   The address of the secured party?
iii.   The tax identification number of a corporate debtor in a state whose version of Article 9 requires it?
b.   If, by mistake, the filing officer accepts for filing financing statements omitting or incorrectly stating the items mentioned above, what effect would the filing have on the perfection or non-perfection of the security interest?

66. *§9-507(b) & (c).* On May 1, Ace Heating & Supply Co. sold all of its assets to ABC Co., which granted a security interest in the assets to Ace to secure payment of the purchase price. Ace immediately filed a financing statement designating ABC as the debtor and Ace as the secured party. On May 2, Ace changed its name to XYZ Co., and ABC changed its name to Ace Heating & Supply Co. [This is a not uncommon way for a new corporation (ABC) to acquire the assets, including the goodwill of an existing company (Ace).] What are the risks here? Has XYZ (the original Ace and the secured party) behaved in bad faith? Is its filing misleading? Does Article 9 require it to make a new filing? If the sale included substantial inventory and if the security agreement covered that inventory and after-acquired inventory, does XYZ have a problem? When a bank takes a loan application from a customer, do you suppose the application asks the customer whether it has changed its name within the last five years?

67. *§9-503(1).* If First Bank is about to make a secured loan to Hartford Inns, a division of Old Colony Hotel Corp., under what name should it search for previous filings? Under what name should First Bank designate the debtor on its financing statement?

68. *§9-517.* On May 1, First Bank perfected its security interest in Dealer's inventory by filing a proper financing statement in the office of the Secretary of State. The filing officer, however, indexed the filing improperly. On May 2, Second Bank searched for filings against Dealer and, finding none, took a security interest in Dealer's inventory and extended credit. Dealer has now defaulted on both loans. Which bank should have priority?

69. *§9-508.* On May 1, Wholesaler, Inc. granted First Bank a security interest in all of Wholesaler's inventory, including after-acquired inventory. On the same day, First filed a financing statement listing the debtor as "Wholesaler, Inc." On May 2, ABC Co. acquired all of the stock of Wholesaler and merged the two companies under the name "ABC Wholesalers, Inc." On July 2, the merged company received a shipment of inventory. On October 1, the company acquired another shipment of inventory
a.   Is the bank's security interest perfected in the original inventory?
b.   Does the bank have a perfected security interest in the inventory acquired within four months of the merger?

c. Does the bank have a perfected security interest in the inventory acquired after the four months passed?

Section 11. *Introduction to Fixtures*

Fixtures are a problem for two reasons. First, they fall into two categories, real estate and personal property, with different legal regimes. Second, there are times when no one can be sure whether a piece of equipment, say, or a consumer appliance is a fixture. Whether a good stays personalty or becomes part of the realty and therefore a fixture is a matter of non-Code law, which is not a well rationalized body of jurisprudence. The Code responds to these confusing features of fixture law with an array of rules that ultimately make quite good sense but can be a little confusing.

We begin the study of fixtures with problems concerning the definition and the proper place to file. Note that there are two possible filings: a regular financing statement or a fixture filing, which is a financing statement with some additional information. The Code requires a fixture filing to be filed with real property records. We deal with priority rules for fixtures in Problems 157 through 166.

Problems

70. *§9-102(a)(41), §9-501(1)(b).*   Where should a secured party file a financing statement to cover the following collateral? Must the filing be a fixture filing? What are the consequences in each case if it isn't?
    a. Pella windows incorporated into a new house. §9-334(a).
    b. A photocopy machine. §9-334(e)(2), §9-501, cmt. 4.
    c. A four-color, high-speed printing press bolted to the floor of a manufacturing facility that was installed by tearing down a wall that the debtor later rebuilt.
    d. A boiler used as part of a central heating system in an apartment house.
    e. A radio tower bolted to a concrete platform and held in place by guy wires fastened by hooks imbedded in the concrete.
    f. A bolted-down, two-ton sign that can be removed in one hour by one person with a crescent wrench and a hydraulic hoist mounted on the bed of a truck.
    g. Would your answers to any of the foregoing problems differ if the owner of the real estate and the secured party agreed that the equipment would not become part of the real estate?

71. *§9-334(e)(d).*   In the foregoing question, if the equipment mentioned is owned by a business corporation and if the secured lender filed in the office of the Secretary of State,

    a. Would the lender defeat the debtor's trustee in bankruptcy? §9-334(e)(3), Bankruptcy Code §544(a)(3).

    b. Would your answer differ if the secured lender filed a regular financing statement (as opposed to a fixture filing) in the office of the register of deeds?

    c. Would your answer to problem (a) differ if the secured lender were contesting with a purchaser of the real estate?

72. On May 1, Debtor granted First Bank a mortgage on a lot in the city. Thereafter Debtor built a house on the lot, installed a boiler in the house, added a sound system, and moved office equipment into a room of the house that Debtor uses as an office. In which of the foregoing items does the bank have an interest?

73. On May 1, Debtor granted a security interest in a wire-strapping machine to Minneapolis Machines, Inc. The machine was installed in a building. The secured party filed centrally.

    a. If the machine is a fixture under the law of the jurisdiction, will the company defeat Debtor's trustee in bankruptcy?

    b. Assume that the company made a fixture filing locally but did not file centrally. If the court finds the machine to be a fixture, will the trustee defeat the company? Will the trustee defeat the company if the court finds the machine not to be a fixture?

    c. Would your answers to the foregoing questions differ if the company were competing with a lien creditor instead of the trustee in bankruptcy?

    d. A mortgagee of the premises that obtained its mortgage after the machine was installed?

74. *§9-502(b)(3) & (4).* What information must be included in a fixture filing that need not be included in a regular filing? To which of the following sources would you look for that information?

    a. A copy of the deed that the person your client tells you is the owner has in his records.

    b. A real estate tax bill.

    c. Your client.

    d. The county real estate records.

75. If you as counsel for a tenant who is granting a security interest to a secured party are called on by the secured lender to give an opinion that the secured party's security interest in equipment installed in a building is superior to all other security interests, which of the following steps would be sufficient?

    a. File centrally.

    b. File a fixture filing locally.

    c. Obtain the legal description and the identity of the owner of record by getting a title search from a title company.

    d. Obtain a disclaimer (estoppel certificate) from the mortgagee.

    e. Rely on the readily removable equipment exception or the not-used-in-the-operation-of-the-building exception.

76. An equipment lessor suspects that some of its leases are going to be construed by the courts as security agreements. If it files centrally, will it
a. always defeat the trustee under Bankruptcy Code §544(a)(3)?
b. defeat a subsequent purchaser of the real estate?

[You may draw the conclusion from these problems that fixture financing is hopeless. Note, however, that by virtue of §9-334(e)(2) & (3), the risks are small for equipment financing, the major collateral that might become a fixture. Note similar protection for replacements of some less frequently financed consumer goods in §9-334(e)(2)(C). True, for boilers, Tiffany chandeliers, Pella windows, large signs, and a host of other peculiar types of collateral, the fixture rules are problematic. Fortunately, with the exceptions for equipment and some domestic appliances, fixture financing is not commercially common.]

Section 12. More on the Place to File

Filing the financing statement can be a nuisance, but it is the statutory means for effecting the stated purpose of Article 9: to give notice to the world that the secured party is claiming an interest in the collateral.

In the best of all possible worlds, there would be one office for all UCC filings. But because we do not live in that world, we must analyze a secured transaction to determine which office is the appropriate office for filing.

These problems are exercises in that analysis. The answers are relatively easy under Revised Article 9. They were far more complex under the old version. We leave them here as testimony to the fact that the drafters of Revised Article 9 were trying to make things easier. When filing rules are complex and there are millions of filings, it is axiomatic that there will be errors. The Revised version's simplified rules will save lots of people lots of money.

Assume that each state has designated the Secretary of State's office as the place for central filing. Section 9-501 is the section designating the place to file, but you can't use that provision without consulting §9-301. That section tells you what law governs perfection. You cannot use that section, however, without consulting §9-307, the provision that tells you the location of the debtor. These three sections, then, are a complex that works to give you the answers. Note that in every case, the location of the debtor governs.

Problems

77. Indicate the proper office and state for filing a financing statement to perfect a security interest in the following collateral:
a. A plastic extrusion machine used by a tool and die company incorporated in Maryland to make plastic parts for the toy industry.

   b.   Plastic pellets used by a competitor tool and die company to make
        the parts. The competitor is a sole proprietorship. The owner lives in
        Pennsylvania.
   c.   A riding mower that Joe Smith, a resident of Adams County,
        Mississippi, uses to mow lawns for a living. If Smith bought the
        mower for personal use while living in Washington County,
        Mississippi, where should the secured lender file? Must it refile if
        Smith thereafter moves to Tennessee?
   d.   Payments due Weaver, a Vermont dairy farmer, from Hood Milk
        Co. for milk Weaver delivered to Hood last month.
   e.   Weaver's herd of cows.
   f.   Sums due Weaver under an oral lease of his prize breeding bull.
   g.   Sums due from a chain of Illinois supermarkets owned by a New
        York corporation for bread that International Baking Co., a
        Delaware corporation, delivered last week.
   h.   Equipment leases that cover earth moving equipment that Leasing
        Co., a California corporation, leases to construction companies in
        California and Nevada.
   i.   An income tax refund due Weaver, a resident of Michigan.
   j.   An income tax refund due Ace Motor Co., a Michigan corporation.

78. On May 1, Weaver, a resident of Michigan, purchased a tractor from Ace
   Tractor Co., granted Ace a security interest in the tractor to secure payment
   of the purchase price, and took delivery of the tractor. At the time Weaver
   was living in Michigan, but he planned to use the tractor in Indiana, where
   he had recently rented a farm. On May 1, Ace filed in Indiana. On May 2,
   Weaver moved to Indiana. Was Ace perfected on May 1? Was Ace perfected
   on May 2?

Section 13. *Perfection Without Filing (Pledges and the Like)*

There are four ways to perfect: (1) file; (2) take possession, (3) effect control,
and (4) do nothing. The following problems deal with the second category
(the pledge), the third (control), and the fourth (the case of automatic
perfection).
   Historians think that the oldest secured transaction was a pledge.
Pledges figured prominently in societies without juridical institutions to
enforce promises. In those days, the pledge looked much like a hostage
arrangement. It still does, but we do not pledge our youngsters anymore, we
only pledge our property.
   There is some property that cannot be pledged: intangible property.
There is other property that is so negotiable, so readily passed from one hand
to another, that it *must be* pledged if it is going to be the subject of a security
interest. Finally, there is property that falls between the two categories. In
those cases, the Code allows a secured party to perfect by filing but makes so
many exceptions to protect third parties who deal with the collateral that the

secured party facing any risk will hold the collateral, that is, will insist on a pledge.

Control is a concept new to Revised Article 9. It covers intangible collateral that cannot be the subject of a pledge (deposit accounts, letter-of-credit rights, and electronic chattel paper) and investment property that includes some collateral that is intangible and some that isn't. *See* §9-102(a)(49). In all of these cases, however, filing is not efficient; and the need may arise for the secured party to use third parties to protect the security interest. The methods of control differ for each of the four categories and are governed by §§9-104 through 9-107.

The Code allows automatic perfection when the costs of filing or control outweigh the benefits of requiring the secured party to file.

Problems

Pledges (§9-313)

79. If Debtor grants Bank a security interest in Debtor's jewelry, may Bank perfect its security interest by appointing Debtor its agent to hold the jewelry?

80. If Debtor has securities in a safety deposit box, can Debtor pledge the securities to a finance company by giving the finance company the key to the box?

81. How do you take possession of an account? Of a general intangible? Of letter-of-credit rights in a letter of credit issued by SWIFT in electronic data interchange (EDI) format? Of electronic chattel paper?

82. *§§8-301, 9-312(a).* On May 1, Debtor granted Broker a security interest in 100 shares of ABC Co. common stock to secure a loan of $50,000. The stock is worth $200,000, and Debtor would like to grant a second security interest in the stock to Uncle to secure a loan that Uncle is now making to Debtor.
    a. How should Broker perfect its security interest?
    b. How should Uncle perfect his?

83. *§9-207.* On May 1, Debtor pledged shares of XYZ Co. common stock and ABC Co. convertible debentures with First Bank as security for a loan. On May 2, ABC Co. called the debentures, but the bank failed to act and missed the deadline for converting the shares. Had the bank converted the debentures into common stock, the shares of ABC common would be worth $100,000. Today, the debentures are worth $15,000. Over the period that First Bank held the XYZ stock, its value has diminished by 50 percent.
    a. Is First Bank liable to Debtor for any of these losses?
    b. Would First Bank be liable to Debtor if it pledged the securities with Second Bank as security for a loan from Second to First? Would the amount of the loan or the ability of Debtor to redeem the stock from Second matter? (Would your answer differ if Second sold the

debenture after First defaulted on its loan? *See* §9-207(c)(3) and cmts. 5 and 6.)

84. *§§3-503(a) & (c), 9-207(c).* Debtor pledged a promissory note in the amount of $100,000 to First Bank. The note was drawn by *M* and indorsed by *E*. The note came due on May 1, 1993. The bank did nothing about the note until May 1, 1994, when it presented it and learned that *M* had become insolvent. *M* duly dishonored but *E* was not given timely notice of dishonor. Is the bank liable to Debtor?

85. *§8-313(1)(a).* *D* owns a certificate covering 1,000 shares of ABC Co., which *B*, a broker, is holding for *D* in a securities account. How does *D* grant a security interest in the certificate to First Bank? Would it be sufficient for *D* to cause the broker to deliver a certificate for the shares to the bank or its broker?

86. *§9-107.* For the account of Buyer, First Bank issued a commercial letter of credit in favor of Seller. Seller wants to use that letter of credit to secure a loan Second Bank is going to make to Seller. Seller needs the loan to pay Supplier, which is providing Seller with the goods to fill Buyer's order. What does the UCC call the collateral, and how should the bank proceed to perfect its security interest?

87. *§9-104.* On May 1, Debtor borrowed $100,000 from First Bank. On May 2, Debtor's checking account at First Bank has a balance of $75,000. What must First Bank do to perfect a security interest in the checking account?

88. *§9-309(1).* On May 1, *C* purchased for cash a refrigerator from *S*, a retailer. On May 2, *C* purchased from *S* a DVD player on credit and granted *S* a security interest in the refrigerator and the recorder. *S* did not file a financing statement.
    a.   Does *S* have a perfected security interest in the refrigerator?
    b.   Does *S* have a perfected security interest in the DVD player?

89. *§9-320(b).* If *C* sells the refrigerator to neighbor *X* on June 1, is *S*'s security interest good against *X*? Would the security interest be good against *X* if *X* were a merchant who took the refrigerator in trade?

90. On May 1, *S* sold *C* on credit $50,000 worth of antiques for *C*'s home and retained a security interest in the goods. How does *S* perfect its security interest? If the security agreement stipulates that any articles *C* acquires thereafter for his home will serve as security for *S*'s debt, will *S* have a security interest in antiques *C* subsequently acquires?

91. *§9-312(e).* On May 1, Broker granted First Bank a security interest in all of Broker's instruments and documents. On the morning of May 2, Broker acquired a batch of documents (negotiable warehouse receipts) and instruments (negotiable promissory notes). That afternoon, the bank covered Broker's overdraft. Bank did not file any financing statement and has not taken possession of the receipts or the notes. On May 3, Broker acquired a second batch of instruments and documents, but the bank made no further advances. On May 31, Broker was still in possession of the paper.

a. Was the bank perfected on May 3?
b. Was the bank perfected on May 31?

92. *§9-312(f).* First Bank issued a letter of credit for the account of Importer, naming the seller as beneficiary. On May 1, First honored its credit by paying the seller and took a negotiable bill of lading covering the goods sold by the seller to Importer. On May 5, the goods arrived in a U.S. port; and First released the bill to Importer, so that Importer could take delivery of the goods from the carrier and store them in a warehouse. On May 8, Importer stored the goods with a warehouse that issued a negotiable warehouse receipt to Importer. Importer delivered the warehouse receipt to First that same day. Was the bank perfected during the various stages of this transaction?

Section 14. *Multistate Transactions*

Just as you start to get a grip on the filing and perfection rules of Article 9, the real world intrudes and reminds you that in commercial transactions often the parties and the collateral are not in the same state. In that case, the perfection rules become sensitive to the reasonable expectations of third parties.

The rules of §9-316 reflect concern that a third party dealing with collateral or with a debtor not be required to look for filings in unexpected places. To some extent, the Code cannot protect everyone. Generally, as you know, §§9-301 through 9-306 specify the law that governs the perfection of a security interest. That complex of provisions not only tells the actual secured party where to file. It also tells the prospective secured party where to search.

These rules are complicated by the fact that sometimes debtors move goods from one jurisdiction to another or move themselves from one jurisdiction to another and by the fact that parties having control of collateral may move from one jurisdiction to another. The Code must take account of these perfectly normal but troublesome facts of commercial life.

To a considerable extent Revised Article 9 simplifies filing and searching rules by making the location of the debtor the place to file. (Section 9-307 tells you how to determine the location of a debtor.) Since filings are generally good for five years, prospective lenders will ask a debtor about any moves during the five years prior to the prospective loan. Note, however, that §9-316 introduces a four-month rule into the equation.

Problems

93. *§9-316.* In each of the following questions, assume that on May 1, Debtor and the secured party (Bank) are located in State *A* and that on that date Debtor signed a proper security agreement covering Debtor's equipment then owned or thereafter acquired. Is the filing by Bank effective to perfect Bank's security interest in the following cases?

    a.   On May 2, while the goods are in State *A*, Bank made an advance to Debtor. On May 3, Debtor moved the equipment to State *B*, and Bank filed in State *A*.

    b.   On April 10, Bank filed in State *A*. On May 2, Bank made an advance just after the goods were moved to State *B*.

    c.   Same facts as in b. On May 3, Debtor moved the goods back into State *A*.

    d.   Bank filed in State *A* on May 10. Bank made an advance on May 15. On May 20, Debtor acquired an interest in goods by taking delivery of them in and keeping them in State *B*.

94.   On May 1, Debtor Inc. entered into a contract with Barney, a specialty manufacturer in State *B*, for the manufacture of four rotary dryers for use in preparing corn by Debtor in its distillery operation in State *A*. Debtor granted Barney a security interest in the dryers, and Barney filed a financing statement in the office of the Secretary of State in State *A*—the state where Debtor was incorporated and where Debtor intended to use the dryers. The purchase price of the dryers was $1 million. On February 1 of the following year, Barney notified Debtor that the dryers were complete and that Debtor, pursuant to the sales contract, should send its flatbed trucks to Barney's plant in State *B* to pick up the dryers. Debtor paid Barney half of the purchase price, and Debtor's workers loaded the dryers onto the trucks on February 2. At that point, a transport union strike resulted in the establishment of pickets at Barney's loading dock. As a consequence, Debtor's drivers left the trucks, waiting for the strike to settle.

    a.   Is Barney perfected during the times it was manufacturing the dryers? Is it perfected on February 2?

    b.   If the strike prevents removal of the trucks for a period of five weeks, will Barney be perfected at the end of that period? What should Barney do to avoid becoming unperfected if the goods remain in State *B* that long?

    c.   Would your answer to any of these questions differ if Debtor originally intended to keep the dryers at a facility in State *B* but changed its mind on February 3 and decided to move them to State *A*?

    d.   If Debtor intended from the start to move the goods to State *A*, would Barney be perfected on March 15 if Debtor moved the dryers into that state on that day?

95.   On May 1, First Bank took a security interest in Ace Printing Co.'s printing presses and filed a financing statement in the office of the Secretary of State in State *A* where Ace Printing is incorporated. On May 2, Ace reincorporated in State *B*. On October 1, First Bank refiled in State *B*. In a contest between First Bank and the following parties, who prevails?

    a.   A buyer of one of the presses who took delivery of the press on June 1 for value and without knowledge of First Bank's security interest.

Would your answer change if the buyer failed to take delivery of the press until after the Bank filed in State *B*?

b. A creditor of Ace that obtained a judgment against Ace and levied on one of the presses on June 5

c. Second Bank that took a security interest from Ace in the presses on June 10 and filed a financing statement in the office of the Secretary of State of State *B* on the same day.

d. Would your answer to this question differ if Second Bank failed to file or filed in the wrong office in State *B*?

e. The trustee in bankruptcy of debtor if debtor files his bankruptcy petition on June 1.

f. Would your answer to this question differ if First Bank did not file in State *B* at all and if the bankruptcy filing occurred on September 25?

Goods Subject to Certificate of Title Laws

Certain goods that are extremely mobile, such as motor vehicles, are subject to certificate of title laws to make ownership more certain and to assist law enforcement agencies in their regulatory efforts. Once again, we find that a complex of provisions governs the rules for perfecting a security interest in such goods. In this case, we begin with §9-311(b), which stipulates that perfection of a security interest in goods subject to a state's certificate of title law must follow the rules of that law. Next, §9-303(c) provides that the law of the jurisdiction issuing the certificate of title governs perfection while the goods are subject to the certificate. Section 9-316 (d) & (e) governs situations when the goods become subject to a second certificate of title in a state other than the one that issued the first certificate. Finally, §9-337 governs the priority of conflicting claims to good subject to a certificate of title.

96. **§9-316(e)(2).** First Bank obtained a perfected security interest in Debtor's automobile on May 1 by noting its interest on the automobile's certificate of title pursuant to the law of State *A*, the state in which Bank was located and in which Debtor lived. Bank, pursuant to sound lending practices, retained possession of the certificate. On June 1, Debtor moved to State *B*.

a. If nothing else happened with respect to the automobile, is the bank perfected on July 1? December 1?

b. If Debtor obtains a new certificate of title in State *B* on June 15 and if the new certificate fails to show the bank's security interest, is the bank perfected on that date?

c. If Debtor obtains a new, clean certificate in State *B* on June 1 and sells the vehicle on June 2 to a used car dealer who gives value and takes delivery of the vehicle without knowledge of First Bank's interest on June 2, does the dealer defeat the bank? What if the dealer purchased the vehicle on October 2?

d. Would it matter that the buyer in sub-part (c) above is not a dealer? *See* §9-337(1).

e. If Second Bank obtains a security interest in the vehicle after issuance of a new certificate that does not disclose First Bank's interest, will Second Bank prime First Bank? Does it matter when Second takes its security interest or whether Second Bank perfects?

97. §9-301(1). Debtor, a corporation organized under the law of California, is a freight forwarder in Oakland, California. Debtor owns 40-foot containers that it delivers via rail and truck to customers throughout that state. The customers "stuff" the containers and notify Debtor when they are ready to be picked up, returned to Oakland, and transshipped by ocean-going vessel to other parts of the world or by rail to other parts of the United States. Debtor has granted First Bank a security interest in the containers.
   a. Where should First Bank file?
   b. Would your answer differ if Debtor maintained two classes of containers: (i) 20-foot containers that it used only to transport produce from farms in central California to California's coastal cities, and (ii) 40-foot containers that it used in the fashion described earlier in this problem? Would your answer differ if Debtor's chief executive office were located in New York?

98. Tridelt Co., a New York Corporation, which manufactures computers, maintains its chief executive office in Texas. Tridelt borrowed from First Bank and granted First Bank a security interest in all of its accounts. First Bank filed with the office of the Secretary of State in New York.
   a. Does the bank have a perfected security interest in accounts arising from the sale of computers by Tridelt's warehouse and sales office in Florida?
   b. Tridelt leases hardware to customers throughout the country under leases that are not true leases but security agreements disguised as leases. Tridelt files a financing statement against the "lessees" in the states where the lessees are located. If First Bank takes an assignment of those security interests, will it have a perfected security interest
      i.   in the hardware?
      ii. in the leases?
   c. How should First Bank perfect its security interest in the leases described in the preceding question?
   d. How should First Bank perfect a security interest in Tridelt's inventory? Are there any acts the bank should take in this financing in the event Tridelt moves its chief executive office from Texas to Florida? If it reincorporates in Oregon?

99. §§9-109(3), 9-203(g), 9-309(4).
   a. On May 1, Developer, an Illinois corporation, sold a parcel of real estate and a dwelling located on it to Buyer. Buyer gave Developer a down payment, a twenty-year promissory note in the amount of $250,000, and a mortgage of the property to secure the note. On May 2, Developer sold the note to First National Bank for $250,000 discounted. Is the Developer/bank transaction subject to Article 9? What steps should the bank take?
   b. §9-102(a)(77), §9-203(f), §9-308(d). Would your answer differ if instead of being secured by a mortgage, the buyer secured the

promissory note with a standby letter of credit issued by Second Bank?

100. *§§9-309(l), 9-316(a).*   On May 1, while she lived in Georgia, *C* purchased a grand piano for use in her home and granted First Bank a security interest in the piano to secure the purchase price that the bank loaned to *C* to enable her to acquire it. On May 2, *C* moved to Alabama. Is the bank perfected on September 10?

101. *§9-316.*   On May 1, Sam sold a printing press to Bob, a printer doing business as "Bob's Printing." The sale was on credit, and Sam retained a security interest in the printer and filed a financing statement in Missouri, where Bob conducted his printing operations. On June 1, Bob moved his home and enterprise across the river to Kentucky. On November 1, Sam filed in Kentucky.
   a.   If Bob becomes bankrupt on November 2, and assuming no preference problem, will the trustee defeat Sam?
   b.   If Lee obtained a lien on the press in Kentucky on June 10, would Lee's lien have priority over Sam's security interest? Would your answer differ if Sam refiled in Kentucky on August 1? What if Lee were a secured party rather than a lien creditor and perfected on those dates?

Section 15. *Perfecting the Security Interest in Proceeds*

Often, secured parties are unconcerned about proceeds. Some proceeds (cash proceeds) have a tendency to disappear rapidly; others (accounts and chattel paper) may be the subject of another lender's security interest. The working capital lender is well advised, however, to position itself in such a way that if the debtor defaults, the lender can effectively claim the proceeds of the collateral. Because the working capital lender is more willing to lend in that circumstance, even the borrower is well-advised to prefer rules that permit the secured party to have quick and, often automatic, access to proceeds. The lender, then, must be concerned about the perfection rules of §9-315. They are moderately tricky; and while the tricky parts have little operational scope, you need to know how they work in order to understand the section.

Problems

102.   First Bank has a security interest in all of the inventory, now owned or after-acquired, of Bell Furniture, an Iowa retailer. First filed in the Iowa office of the Secretary of State a financing statement describing the collateral as "all inventory." On May 1, Bell sold some furniture on open account, some in return for chattel paper, and some for cash.

    a.   Does the bank have a perfected security interest in the accounts, the chattel paper, and the cash on May 1?

    b.   Does the perfection continue after May 20 for the accounts and chattel paper?

    c.   Does the security interest in the cash remain perfected if Bell commingles the cash?

    d.   Would your answers to any of the foregoing questions differ if Bell were the local branch of a national enterprise incorporated in New York?

103. On May 2, Bell Furniture (referred to in the preceding problem) purchased a word processor that it used in the office with cash it received from customers who bought furniture. Does the bank have a perfected security interest in the word processor on May 23? Would your answer differ if the filing described the collateral as "inventory and equipment"?

104. Assume that the bank's filing referred to in the two preceding problems covers only inventory manufactured by "Maple Wood Products, Inc." Does the bank have a perfected security interest in chattel paper Bell receives upon the sale of Grand Rapids Furniture Co. furniture? If Bell receives cash from the sale of inventory manufactured by Grand Rapids and deposits that cash in an account designated "Maple Wood Products Proceeds Account," does the bank have any interest in that cash?

105. On May 1, Bell received the following cash proceeds, $100,000 in cash and $75,000 in checks. Later that day Bell used the cash to purchase a certificate of deposit from Second National Bank. Does First Bank have any interest in the certificate and the checks on May 1? On May 22? Would your answer differ if Bell had deposited the cash into a checking account?

Section 16. *Introduction to Priorities*

Claims to collateral drive secured transactions disputes. Article 9 fashions a regime for dealing with most of them. That regime distinguishes claimants on the basis of policy concerns that may not be readily apparent to you. These are best dealt with in class discussion and thus will be treated here only interstitially.

For the purposes of these problems, it is enough to know that the Article 9 priority rules rest on three schemes. The first is a hierarchy that distinguishes among the following creditors: the unsecured creditor, the secured creditor (that is, the creditor whose security interest has attached), the perfected secured creditor (that is, the creditor whose security interest has attached and is perfected), and the lien creditor.

The second scheme involves buyers, lessees, and licensees. That category includes, among others, a distinction between those who take in ordinary course of business, and those who don't. Recall the *nemo dat* principle from Section 1.

The third scheme is a timing rule that essentially favors the first perfected secured party to file or perfect.

In the following eight problems, assume that the security interests are created in equipment. In each problem, indicate the priorities of the various creditors.

Problems

106. *§§9-201, 9-317.*

      a. May 1.   Bank took a security interest in after-acquired equipment.
           May 2.   *S* sold equipment to Debtor on credit.
           May 3.   Bank filed.
           May 4.   *S* obtained a judgment lien against Debtor's equipment.

      b. *§9-317(b) & (c).* Alter the facts by assuming that the actor that intervened on May 2 was *B*, a buyer not in ordinary course, and that *B* took possession on that date. What result? If *B* does not take possession until May 4, what result? Why treat the buyer differently depending on the day it takes delivery? Is a buyer that prepays different from a buyer that does not?

      c. *§9-317(c).* What result if *B* is not a buyer but a lessee that takes delivery on the dates indicated?

      d. Would your answer to the original problem differ if the bank filed on May 1 and took its security interest on May 5? Would your answer differ if *B* bought not in the ordinary course from Debtor on May 2 and took delivery on that date? Took delivery on May 5? If the bank filed on May 1 and took a security interest on May 5? (Do you see why *B* loses if he takes delivery on May 5 but wins if he takes delivery on May 2?)

      e. *§9-317(d).* Does a "buyer" of accounts need to take delivery in order to defeat an unperfected secured party? How does one take delivery of an account?

107. *§§9-204(a), 9-317(a), 9-322.*

    May 1.   First Bank takes perfected security interest in all equipment, including after-acquired equipment.
    May 2.   *S* sells equipment to Debtor on open account and obtains judicial lien.
    May 3.   Debtor acquires more equipment.

108. *§§9-103, 9-317(e).*

    May 1.   *S* sells on credit and retains a security interest.
    May 2.   *L*, who sold services on credit, obtains a judgment lien.
    May 3.   *S* files.

Would your answer to this question differ if the party intervening on May 2 were a buyer not in ordinary course that took delivery without knowledge of the security interest? A bulk buyer?

109. *§9-317(a)(2)(A).*

May 1.   First Bank lends $50,000 to Debtor and takes a security interest.
May 2.   Utility Co. obtains a judgment and levies.
May 3.   First Bank files.

110. *§9-317(e).*

May 1.   First Bank takes a purchase money security interest.
May 2.   Utility Co. obtains a judgment and levies.
May 3.   First Bank files.

111. *§9-322(a).*

May 1.   First Bank takes a security interest and possession under an agreement with Debtor.
May 2.   Second Bank takes a security interest and files.
May 3.   First Bank lends $50,000.

112. *§9-322(a).*

May 1.   First Bank files.
May 2.   Second Bank takes a security agreement, lends, and files.
May 3.   First Bank takes a security agreement and lends.

113. *§9-322(a)(1), (b)(1).*

May 1.   First Bank lends $25 and takes possession under a security agreement.
May 2.   Second Bank takes a security agreement, lends $50, and files.
May 3.   First Bank lends an additional $10.
May 4.   Collateral sells for $35.

114. *§9-322(a)(1).*

May 1.   First Bank lends $25.
May 2.   Second Bank lends $25.
May 3.   Second Bank takes security interest and files.
May 4.   First Bank takes security interest and files.

115. *§9-324(a).*

May 1.   Bank takes a security interest.
May 2.   S sells to Debtor on credit and retains a security interest.
May 3.   Bank files.
May 4.   S files.

Would S prevail if it filed on May 23?

116. *§9-324(g).*

May 1.   Bank lends 10 percent down payment for the purchase of a press.
May 2.   S sells the press to debtor on 90 percent credit.
May 3.   S files.
May 4.   Bank files.

Assume that the collateral sold for 50 percent of the purchase price and that neither creditor had been paid. Would your answer differ if the bank filed first?

117. *§9-324(a).*

May 1.   First Bank takes a perfected security interest in all equipment then owned or thereafter acquired.
May 2.   S sells Debtor a drill press on credit, retaining a security interest.
May 3.   S files.
May 4.   Debtor sells the press and holds a check from Sub-buyer after Sub-buyer takes delivery of the press.

118. *§9-324(b).*

April 29.   S files a financing statement and gives notice of a security interest to First Bank.
May 1.   First Bank takes a perfected security interest in all inventory now owned or thereafter acquired by Debtor.
May 2.   S sells beer to D, a beer wholesaler, retaining a security interest in the beer.
May 4.   D sells some of the beer and holds a check from its buyer after its buyer takes possession of the beer.

Who prevails? Would S get the check if D had received it as a down payment from a retailer to whom it had resold the beer S had delivered on May 2? Would S get any accounts due from retail sub-buyers of S's beer if the wholesaler sold S's beer to them on open account? Would S have priority over the bank as to the beer S delivered to the wholesaler?

119. *§§9-103, 9-322, 9-324.*
    a.   Debtor, an auto parts manufacturer, with $20,000 of its own money and a $50,000 loan from First Bank, purchased an industrial furnace for $70,000. First Bank took a security interest in the furnace and filed a financing statement covering "industrial equipment." Earlier, Second Bank had lent $30,000 to Debtor, taking a security interest in equipment, then owned or thereafter acquired, and filing appropriately. A year after its first transaction with Debtor, First Bank lent it an additional $10,000, again taking a security interest in the furnace. If Debtor defaults and the furnace is the only piece of equipment, who prevails and to what extent?
    b.   Suppose First Bank decided not to make a new loan, but rather chose to refinance the whole loan as one package. Would the result

change? If not, would payments on the new loan first pay down the part relating to the first loan, the second loan, or each pro rata?

   c. Suppose Debtor was an individual buying a furnace for her home. Would the answers change?

120. *§§9-102(a)(34) & (35); 9-324(d).* Assume that the collateral in Problem 118 was 1,000 steers held by *S*, a cattle feed lot operator, and that *S* sold the steers on credit to the debtor, another feed lot operator, on May 2 under a security agreement granting *S* a security interest in the steers. Would *S* defeat First Bank if *S* filed on May 3? Is it necessary for *S* to notify the bank before it delivers steers to the debtor? During what time frame must *S* give the notice?

121. *§§9-516(a), 9-517.* On May 1, First Bank took a security interest in all of Debtor's equipment. First Bank filed the same day in the office of the secretary of state and loaned Debtor $100,000, but a clerk in the secretary's office inadvertently failed to note the filing in the records.

On May 2, Debtor went to Second Bank and borrowed another $100,000. Second Bank ran a check of filings in the secretary's office and found no filings. Second filed its financing statement in the office of secretary on May 2. On May 3, Debtor defaulted on both loans. First and Second claim the equipment. Which has priority?

122. *§9-322.* *D* is a beer wholesaler who sells on credit to retailers. Because the retailers had been taking longer and longer to pay, *D* found itself short of cash. On May 1, *D* borrowed from First Bank, giving as collateral all present and future accounts. First Bank filed a financing statement to that effect. On May 5, *D* borrowed from Second Bank, giving as collateral all present and future inventory. Second Bank filed a financing statement to that effect. Who has priority in (a) accounts from the sale of inventory, (b) inventory, and (c) a bank account containing proceeds from the sale of inventory on credit? Would the results change if First Bank had filed on May 5 and Second Bank on May 1?

123. *§9-327.* *D*, a toy store, borrowed $50,000 from First Bank on May 1, giving a security interest in accounts and deposit accounts as collateral. *D* defaulted on its loan from First Bank, at a time when *D* had $10,000 on deposit with First Bank. The security agreement gave First Bank the right to set off any defaulted payments against deposit accounts with First Bank.

   a. *§9-314(a).* May First Bank take the $10,000 as partial payment of the defaulted loan?

   b. Suppose Second Bank had taken a security interest in accounts, present and future, on April 1 and had filed a financing statement to that effect the same day. If the $10,000 in the deposit account is wholly proceeds of accounts, which bank has priority in it?

   c. *§§9-104, 9-339.* On these facts, suppose First Bank's security interest was only in accounts. Then which bank would have priority?

   d. *§9-332(d).* Suppose *D* paid its utility bill with a check drawn on its deposit account with First Bank shortly before it defaulted on the First Bank loan. When does First Bank lose its security interest to the utility? Suppose the check was written to the daughter of *D's* owner?

    e.   Return to the scenario in part b. Second Bank now has persuaded *D* to make Second Bank the customer on *D's* bank account in order to provide more security. *D*, saying that it uses the account for routine expenses, in turn persuaded Second Bank to let it draw checks on the account. May *D* write checks that would drain the account? What if Second Bank learns of this and protests to First Bank?

Section 17. Future Advances

In the old days, as they say, bank loans were made against discrete items of collateral and were self-liquidating. The residential real estate mortgage is a classic case of lending against a discrete asset. The bank that lends to a commodities broker that borrows to purchase a given shipment and repays the loan when he sells that shipment has made a classic self-liquidating loan.

Commercial lending sometimes works that way, but most of the time asset-based borrowers, the middle market enterprises that borrow against assets and that engage in Article 9 transactions, are interested in a working capital loan. Under that kind of loan, the borrower typically grants the lender a security interest in all of its assets, or nearly all of them, and receives in return a commitment from the lender giving the borrower a line of credit. The borrower draws on that line when he needs cash and makes payments against the outstanding balance when he has a positive cash flow. At any given time, the loan balance can be anything from zero to the maximum amount of the line.

The working capital loan makes the floating lien and the future advance essential components of Article 9. You have already confronted the floating lien in the after-acquired property illustrations that appear frequently in these problems. The following problems deal with the future (sometimes called "after") advance.

Note that the future advance sections deal with four parties with whom the secured party is competing for the collateral: (1) lien creditors, (2) buyers, (3) lessees, and (4) other secured parties.

Problems

124.   *§§9-322(a)(1), 9-323(a).*

    May 1.   First Bank takes a security interest in Debtor's equipment, lends $25, and files.

    May 2.   Second Bank takes a security interest in Debtor's equipment, lends $25, and files.

    May 3.   First Bank lends an additional $10.

a. If the equipment is sold on May 3 for $35, how should the court allocate the sales price?

b. Would your answer to the preceding question differ if First knew of Second's May 2 filing when, on May 3, First Bank made the second advance? Would First Bank enjoy priority over Second Bank if First had made no loan until May 3? If Debtor had paid the balance on the loan with First down to zero on the morning of May 2? Would your answer to this question differ if First Bank perfected its security interest on May 1 by taking possession of the equipment? If First Bank's security interest was perfected not by filing and not by possession but temporarily under §9-312(e), (f), or (g)?

c. Would your answers to any of the questions in b differ if the security agreement between First and Debtor granted First a security interest to cover only the May 1 loan? If the security agreement is so limited, would the security interest secure the renewal of the loan on May 1 of the next calendar year?

d. If the security agreement Debtor executed on May 1 covered only the May 1 advance, is there anything First Bank can do on May 3 to make a loan to Debtor that is prior to Second Bank's security interest?

e. If, on May 1, Debtor and First Bank were thinking only of equipment loans but drafted the documents to cover all loans, would First's priority over Second be affected by the fact that the May 3 advance was made to permit Debtor to acquire inventory?

125.   *§9-323(b).*

May 1.   First Bank obtains a perfected security interest in Debtor's equipment and lends $25.

May 2.   L obtains a judicial lien for $25.

May 3.   Bank lends an additional $25.

How should the court divide the proceeds of the sale of the equipment if it yields $50? Would your answer be the same if the bank advanced the second $25 on May 15 without knowledge of the lien? On June 20 without knowledge of the lien? What should L do to prevent the bank and the debtor from squeezing L out? Should he notify the bank on May 9? On June 17? Is there anything L can do to prevent the squeeze-out if the bank enters into a commitment to make future advances on May 1? On May 20 without knowledge of the lien?

126.   *§9-323(d).*

May 1.   Bank obtains a perfected security interest in Debtor's equipment and lends $10.

May 2.   B, a buyer in bulk, buys the equipment.

May 3.   Bank makes an additional advance of $5. Will the bank defeat B if the equipment is worth only $15? Would your answer differ if the bank had made its advance on May 20 without knowledge of B's interest? On June 17 with or without knowledge of B's interest? Would your answer to the last question differ if the bank had on May 1 made a commitment to lend the $5? If it had made the commitment to lend on May 1? On May 20 with (or without) knowledge of the sale? Will the bank defeat *B* if *B* is a buyer of "receivables," i.e., a buyer of accounts? *See* §9-323(c).

Section 18. *Purchaser Priorities*

The following questions deal with sections that protect purchasers that are usually buyers. A secured party, of course, is a purchaser. *See* §1-201(b)(29) and (30) [§1-201(32) and (33)]. But a secured party is not a buyer (*cf.* §1-201(b)(9) [§1-201(9)]), and a secured party must guard against prior filings made by other secured parties. There are exceptions to that rule when the collateral is of a type that moves without inquiry, but usually that is the rule for secured lenders even though they are purchasers. Buyers, on the other hand, usually cannot pause to determine the state of the seller's interest in goods. Here, then, we see the tension between the standard conveyancing rule of *nemo dat* and the need to protect the free flow of goods in commerce. Buyers in bulk, the buyer of a company's assets, for example, usually are concerned with the seller's interest in goods. The following problems illustrate the way Article 9 deals with reasonable commercial expectations in these transactions.

Problems

127. *§§1-201(b)(9) [§1-201(9)], 9-320(a).*   On May 1, *D* granted First Bank a security interest in all of *D*'s inventory of earth-moving equipment. In the security agreement First forbade *D* to sell any earth-movers without obtaining the bank's prior written authorization. Which of the following parties will defeat the bank?
    a.   *A*, an ordinary course buyer of an earth mover who knows of the bank's security interest. Would your answer differ if *A* had agreed to buy the equipment but had not paid for it? Had agreed to buy it but had not taken delivery?
    b.   *B*, a buyer of an earth mover that knows of the security agreement provision forbidding *D* to sell without the bank's prior written approval. Would your answer to this question differ if the bank had not enforced the prohibition of sale over a period of two years during which period *D* made many sales?
    c.   *C*, a pawnbroker that takes an earth mover in the course of his trade as a pawn broker.
    d.   *D-2*, a dealer in earth moving equipment that competes with *D* and that often buys from *D* when *D-2*'s own inventory is inadequate to

satisfy its customers, and that sells to *D* when *D*'s inventory is not adequate to satisfy *D*'s customers.

e. *E*, who is buying *D*'s business and all of *D*'s inventory.

f. *F*, a finance company that wanted to lend to *D* but declined to do so after finding First Bank's filing; *F* instead bought two earth movers from *D*.

g. *G*, a buyer that prepaid the purchase price for one earth mover that is identified but has yet to be shipped. (How might a prepaying buyer protect itself from *D*'s creditors?)

h. *H*, *D*'s cousin, who paid 30 percent of standard retail price.

128. *§1-201(b)(9) [§1-201(9)].* On May 1, *D*, an appliance dealer, granted First Bank a security interest in all of *D*'s inventory of white goods. First duly perfected its security interest by filing on the same day. On May 2, *D* sold three washers and three dryers to *B*, who bought them for his apartment building. *B* purchased the goods on credit and executed a retail installment sales agreement that granted *D* a security interest in the goods and included a promise to pay for them over a period of 36 months. *D* made a proper filing in the proper office.

a. Does *B* take free of First Bank's security interest? If *B* sells the washers and dryers to *C*, does *C* take free of First Bank's security interest?

b. Does *B* take the goods free of all security interests?

c. If *D* assigns the retail installment sales agreement to First Bank, does *B* defeat First Bank?

129. *§§9-315, 9-320.* On May 1, *D*, a hardware store, granted a perfected security interest to First Bank in all of *D*'s inventory. Assume that the security agreement contains a clause allowing *D* to sell inventory in the ordinary course. Which of the following purchasers will defeat the bank's security interest:

a. *B*, a buyer in ordinary course;

b. *C*, a lender that takes a perfected security interest in the same inventory. *§9-322(a)(1)*;

c. *E*, *D*'s son to whom *D* makes a gift of a lawn mower; or

d. *F*, an investor that buys the hardware store and all of the inventory?

130. *§9-315(a).* Debtor granted Bank a perfected security interest in all of Debtor's equipment. The security agreement forbade Debtor to dispose of the equipment without Bank's prior written consent. Subsequently, Debtor sold a piece of the equipment to *B*.

a. Does Bank's security interest follow the goods into *B*'s hands?

b. How does Bank enforce its security interest against *B*?

c. Would your answers to the prior questions differ if *B* were a donee?

d. If *B* gives value to Debtor, does Bank have any claim to the value?

131. On May 1, *R*, a mobile home dealer, granted a perfected security interest in all of its inventory to First Bank. On May 2, *R* sold a mobile home to *B* on credit and took back a retail installment sales contract in which *B* granted *R* a security interest in the mobile home and agreed to pay for the home over a

60-month period. Assume that under governing law mobile homes are not subject to any certificate of title law.

    a. Does *B* take free of the bank's security interest?

    b. Does *B* take free of all security interests?

    c. If *B* sells the mobile home to his neighbor *C*, will *C* take free of the bank's security interest? Of *R*'s security interest? §9-320(b).

    d. Would your answer to the last question differ if *R* had filed a financing statement? §9-320(b)(4).

132. *§9-320(a) ("the buyer's seller").* Assume in the foregoing problem that *B* decided to sell the home and sold it to *X*, a used mobile home dealer, and that *Y* purchased the home from *X* in the ordinary course.

    a. Does *Y* defeat *R*'s security interest?

    b. If *R* assigns its security interest to the bank, would *Y* defeat the bank's security interest?

133. *Food Security Act of 1985, 7 U.S.C. §1631.* On May 1, *F*, a farm producer, granted First Production Credit Association (the PCA) a perfected security interest in all of *F*'s corn growing on *F*'s farm. The security agreement stipulated that *F* could not sell the corn without the PCA's prior approval. On May 2, *F* sold his corn to *B*, broker. On May 3, *B* sold the corn to *K*, a cereal manufacturer. On May 4, *K* sold cereal made out of the corn to *S*, a retail chain store; and on May 5, *S* sold a box of cereal to *T*, a consumer. (In answering the following questions, assume that the state whose law governs the sale from *F* to *B* did not enact any change in its statutes after passage of the Food Security Act.)

    a. Does *B* defeat the PCA's security interest?

    b. Does *K* defeat it?

    c. Does *T*?

    d. Absent protective legislation such as the Food Security Act, which parties are liable to the PCA in conversion?

134. *§9-320(e).* On May 1, *M*, a carpet mill, sold 100,000 yards of greige goods (unfinished fabric) to *B* on a bill-and-hold basis. Under the bill-and-hold contract familiar to all parties, *M* retained possession of the goods until *B* desired to take delivery. The sale was on credit, and *B* granted *M* a security interest in the goods to secure payment of the purchase price. On May 2, *B* sold the goods to *C*, who bought in the ordinary course. *B* has never paid for the goods. *C*, something of a commercial knucklehead, has paid *B*, who is now insolvent. Does *C* cut off *M*'s security interest?

135. On May 1, *D* granted a perfected security interest to First Bank in all of *D*'s inventory of computer parts. On May 2, *D* defaulted on the loan by the bank, and the bank repossessed the inventory. On May 3, *B* bought a carload of computer parts from *D* in the ordinary course. Does *B* cut off the bank's security interest?

136. *§9-320(e).* On May 1, *M*, a lumber mill, sold lumber to *R*, a lumberyard, on credit. *R* granted *M* a security interest in the lumber. *M* perfected its security interest by designating an agent, a field warehouse, to take possession of the lumber by placing it in an area of the yard that was secure and to which they did not have access. On May 2, *B*, a contractor, purchased 20,000 feet of lumber for a construction job in the ordinary course of business and paid *R*. Does *B* cut off *M*'s security interest? Should the law be that no one is a buyer in ordinary course when the seller is not in possession of the goods?

Section 19. *Chattel Paper and Accounts*

Chattel paper and accounts are similar types of collateral in that they often arise on the sale of collateral, that is, they are often proceeds of inventory. Since many middle-market enterprises finance their inventory and since some lenders specialize in inventory lending while other enterprises specialize in chattel paper and accounts, often two secured lenders will claim chattel paper or accounts, either as original collateral or as proceeds of original collateral. The inventory lender claims the chattel paper or accounts as proceeds. The chattel paper or account lender claims the chattel paper or the accounts as original collateral.

Chattel paper and accounts are also mildly problematic because they involve three parties instead of two and, therefore, create some conceptual complications.

Problems

137. On May 1, Smith purchased a snowblower from Retailer on credit and executed a retail installment sales contract granting Retailer a security interest in the equipment. Retailer did not file a financing statement. On May 2, Retailer "sold" the contract along with other such contracts to First Bank, which took possession of them.
    a. Did Retailer have a security interest in the equipment on May 1? Did First Bank have a security interest in the equipment on May 2?
    b. Did First Bank have a perfected security interest in the contract on May 2? §§9-102(a)(11), 9-310(c), 9-313(a).
    c. If First Bank had chosen not to take possession of the contract, would it have a perfected security interest in the equipment? Would it have a perfected security interest in the contract? Where should First Bank file its financing statement covering the contract? Who should sign that financing statement as debtor? §§9-309(a), 9-310(c).

138. Computers, Inc. manufactures computer hardware, which it leases to its customers nationwide. Most of the leases are disguised security agreements, but some are true leases. Computers assigned "all of its leases" to First Bank as security for loans that First made to Computers. First Bank filed a financing statement signed by Computers covering "chattel paper" in the

office of the secretary of state in the state where Computers is located. Computers is now bankrupt.

    a. Describe First Bank's interest, if any, in the computers subject to true leases.

    b. Describe First Bank's interest, if any, in the lease payments under the true leases. §§9-102(a)(11), 9-312(a).

    c. Describe First Bank's interest, if any, in the leases that are credit sales disguised as lease arrangements. Is First Bank protected against the possibility of the bankruptcy of a purchaser-lessee under one of these arrangements? §2-401(1) (2d sentence).

139. *§1-203 [§1-201(37)].* On May 1, Leasing Co., a New York company, entered into a lease of 10 earth movers with Construction Co., which is located in New Jersey. The lease provided that Construction Co. could use the earth movers, which had a projected life of 8 years, for 48 months at a monthly rental of $10,000. At the end of the 48 months, the contractor was to return the equipment in good condition, normal wear and tear excepted. On May 2, Leasing Co. assigned the lease to First Bank as security for a loan. The security agreement between the bank and the leasing company provided that the bank would also have a security interest in the equipment.

    a. If Construction Co. executes a security agreement granting Second Bank a security interest in the equipment, what interest will Second Bank have? How does Second Bank's interest relate to the interests of Leasing Co. and First Bank in the equipment? How would Second Bank perfect its security interest? If it takes a financing statement, who should sign it as debtor, and where should Second file? §9-301(1).

    b. How should First Bank perfect its security interest in the lease? §§9-312(a), 9-313(a). If it takes a financing statement, who should sign as debtor, and where should First file? How should First describe its collateral in that filing? How should it perfect its security interest in the equipment? Who should sign the financing statement covering the equipment as debtor? Where should First file? How should the filing describe the collateral?

    c. On May 1, First properly perfected its security interest in the lease and in Leasing Co.'s reversionary interest in the equipment. On May 2, Construction Co. filed in bankruptcy. What rights does the bankruptcy trustee have against First? Bankruptcy Code §365.

    d. On May 3, Leasing Co. filed in bankruptcy. May Leasing Co.'s trustee defeat First's rights to the equipment? What would Leasing's trustee's rights be if First took possession of the lease and filed as to the equipment in New Jersey? Bankruptcy Code §544(a)(1).

140. *§9-406.* On May 1, Debtor "sold" all of its accounts, then owned or thereafter arising, to First Bank. First duly perfected its security interest. On May 2, Debtor performed services for Buyer under a contract that required Buyer to pay Debtor $10,000 per month for ten months. Over the next ten months Buyer paid Debtor under the contract, and Debtor remitted none of the proceeds to the bank.

a. May First Bank make a claim against Buyer for those payments?

b. Would your answer differ if First Bank had notified Buyer on May 2 that it was assignee of this account?

c. If First Bank had notified Buyer of the assignment on May 1 and directed Buyer to make its payments directly to the bank, could Buyer assert against the bank

   i. a defense it has against Debtor under the contract? §9-404.

   ii. a setoff Buyer has against Debtor by virtue of Debtor's breach of another contract it had with Buyer? §§2-717, cmt. 1 & 9-404.

d. Would your answer to the preceding question differ if the contract between Buyer and Debtor provided that Buyer would not assert against assignees of the contract any defenses it had against the Debtor? §9-403(b) & (d).

141. *§9-404.* On May 1, Construction Co. granted First Bank a security interest in all of its accounts to secure its indebtedness to the bank. On May 2, Construction Co. entered into a contract with Owner to construct a building on Owner's real estate. Under the contract, Construction Co. was to receive payments twice each month for work done and materials delivered to the job. Over a period of months, Construction Co. falsely verified that it had done work and paid for materials. On the basis of these false applications, Owner made payments directly to First Bank, and the bank reduced the construction company's loan balance. Owner has now discovered the construction company's fraud and seeks recovery of the payments from the bank. Did First Bank take those payments subject to the Owner's "claim"?

Section 20. *More on Purchasers, This Time of Paper*

Previously we have considered the Article 9 rules that apply when purchasers take goods from a debtor who has already granted a security interest in them to a lender. Here we consider the rules that apply when the purchaser is taking paper: chattel paper, negotiable documents, and negotiable instruments.

In these and the prior problems, the Code is fashioning rules that protect buyers from having to inquire into the state of the seller's or transferor's title to the subject of the transfer. Security of property may be the first rule of transfer law, but in commercial law it admits of many exceptions.

A transaction in goods is the unlikeliest candidate for the second rule of conveyancing law, good faith purchase; and yet we find that there are instances in which goods enjoy some measure of "negotiability," if we can murder that term for a moment. Goods held in inventory travel without baggage when the merchant sells them to a buyer in ordinary course. Paper is a much likelier candidate for such treatment. Even with paper, however, we find that there are degrees of protection, with the highest degree accorded the favored purchasers of the three kinds of negotiable paper: negotiable instruments, negotiable documents, and negotiable securities. Chattel paper falls in between.

As you do these problems, remember that a lender can be a purchaser and that the priority rule of §9-322(a)(1) may fall before the purchaser protections these problems invoke.[1]

Problems

142. *§9-330.* On May 1, Dealer granted First Bank a perfected security interest in all of Dealer's inventory of golf carts. On May 2, Dealer leased a cart to *B* for the summer. On May 3, Dealer took the lease to Finance Co., which took possession of it and gave Dealer new value.

    a. If it did not know of First Bank's interest, does Finance Co. defeat the bank?

    b. If it did know of First Bank's interest, does Finance Co. defeat the bank?

    c. If it did not know of First Bank's security interest, does Finance Co. defeat the bank if Finance Co. loaned money to Dealer on April 1 and is taking the lease as further security for its loan?

    d. Would your answers to any of these questions differ if First Bank's security agreement covered "all inventory, accounts, and chattel paper?" If the evidence showed that the bank relied in fact on the proceeds from the sale of inventory?

    e. Would any of your answers differ if *R* purchased the cart and gave Dealer a promissory note rather than a lease? §§9-102(a)(47) & (65), 9-331(a).

    f. What might First Bank have done to prevent losing to Finance Co.?

143. *§9-330(c).* On May 1, Dealer granted First Bank a perfected security interest in all of Dealer's inventory of sailboats. On May 2, Dealer sold a sailboat to *B* under an agreement in which *B* agreed to pay for the boat in equal monthly installments over a period of 30 months and to grant Dealer a security interest in the boat. On May 3, Dealer sold the contract to Ace Finance Co. in a nonrecourse transaction. Ace took possession of the contract and gave Dealer value in the ordinary course. On May 4, *B* defaulted on the contract, and Dealer repossessed the boat. Dealer and *B* are now bankrupt.

    a. Does First Bank have a security interest in the boat on May 2?

    b. Does First Bank have a security interest in the boat on May 4?

    c. Does Ace have a security interest in the boat on May 3? §9-109(a)(3).

    d. Between Ace and First Bank, who has the prior claim to the boat?

    e. Suppose that on May 4 *B*, dissatisfied with the boat, returned it to Dealer. Between Ace and First Bank, who has priority over the returned boat? Does it matter whether *B* returned the boat for repairs or through rejection or revocation? §§9-315(d), 9-403, 9-404.

---

1. Some of you may be unfamiliar with the way commercial parties use documents to transport and store goods. You might find it useful to consult chapters 31 through 36 in John F. Dolan, Commercial Law—Essential Terms and Transactions (2d ed. 1997).

144. On May 1, Broker granted Bank a security interest for new value in a stock certificate covering 10,000 shares of Microsoft. Bank perfected under the temporary perfection rule of §9-312(e). On May 2, Broker entered into a repurchase agreement with R. Under the repurchase agreement, or "repo," R bought the stock from Broker, and Broker agreed to repurchase it 30 days later for an amount equal to the purchase price and 30 days' interest. (Not surprisingly, courts treat repurchase agreements as secured transactions.) R protected itself by taking possession of the certificate. On May 3, Broker became insolvent.
    a. Does Bank have a perfected security interest? §9-312(e).
    b. Does R have a perfected security interest? §§8-301(a), 9-313(a).
    c. What type of collateral is this? §§8-102(a)(15), 9-102(a)(49).
    d. If it applies, who would prevail under §9-322(a)(1)? Under §9-331(a)?
    e. Does §9-331(a) interdict the application of §9-322(a)(1)?
    f. If under §8-303 R is a bona fide purchaser that cuts off the claims of prior parties, can the bank use §9-322(a)(1) to defeat R? §9-331(a).

145. On May 1, Bank loaned money to Broker to cover Broker's overdrafts and took a security interest in all of Broker's negotiable instruments and negotiable documents. Bank perfected by doing nothing under the terms of §9-312(e). On May 2, Broker took a negotiable promissory note in the face amount of $100,000 and a negotiable warehouse receipt covering 10,000 bushels of soybeans to Ace Finance Co. and asked Ace to make it a loan. Ace took the note and the receipt, both properly endorsed, and made the loan. On May 3, Broker became insolvent.
    a. Does the bank on May 1 have a perfected security interest in the note and the receipt? §9-312(e).
    b. Does Ace Finance Co. have a perfected security interest in the note and the receipt on May 2? Does it have title to the receipt as well? See §7-502.
    c. If it applies, which of the secured lenders would prevail under §9-322(a)(1)?
    d. Does §9-331(a) interdict application of §9-322?
    e. If Ace is a holder in due course under Article 3 and if §3-306 gives a holder in due course superior rights to a prior claimant, will Ace defeat the bank as to the note?
    f. If Ace is a holder by due negotiation of the warehouse receipt and if §7-502 gives such a holder rights superior to those of a prior claimant, will Ace defeat the bank as to the receipt?

146. On May 1, First Bank paid S, a foreign seller, by honoring S's draft drawn under the letter of credit issued by the bank to S. B, the bank's customer, is the buyer in the international sale, and B has yet to reimburse the bank for the payment the bank made under the letter of credit. The goods which were the subject of the sale are on a container ship in the South Pacific. The ship's captain issued a negotiable bill of lading for them. First Bank took the bill from S when it paid S and is holding the bill as collateral for B's

reimbursement obligation. On May 2, *B* sold the goods in question to *C*, who claims to have bought the goods in the ordinary course of business.

    a.   Is First Bank a perfected secured party, or is it the owner of the goods? §7-502(1)(a). If the goods are worth more than the advance First Bank made in *B*'s behalf, do you think the court would let the bank keep the difference between the advance and the value? (We don't.)

    b.   Is First Bank's security interest created by *B*? Does it arise by statute? §5-118.

    c.   If the bank is a perfected secured party and if the security interest is created by *B*, does §9-320(a) apply to cut off the bank's security interest? Does §9-320(a), a rule in Article 9, operate to limit the rights of a holder of a negotiable document of title by due negotiation? *See also* §9-331(a).

Section 21. *Bailments*

Parties often will want to finance goods while they are in the possession of a bailee, usually a warehouse or a carrier but sometimes a manufacturer or fabricator performing outsourcing functions. In those cases, Article 9 distinguishes, as much of commercial law does, between goods in the possession of a bailee who has issued a negotiable instrument of title covering them and a bailee who has issued a nonnegotiable document or no document at all.

Section 9-312, the potpourri section, details the treatment. Note in that section and in these problems that the negotiable document stands for the goods, and the nonnegotiable document does not.

(Documents of title and the law that governs them are moderately recondite. The following problems illustrate typical document of title transactions. For further problems dealing with Article 7, see Problems 261 through 282 in Part II, Payment Systems.)

Problems

147.   *§9-312(d).* On September 1, Oklahoma Gas Co. (Seller) sold propane to Distributor Co. (Buyer) under a contract that required Seller to deliver the propane to Southwest Pipeline Co. (Carrier). Seller delivered a nonnegotiable delivery order to Carrier, and Carrier accepted it and reaffirmed it to Buyer. Buyer will not need the propane until October but must pay Seller on September 30. Buyer has asked First Bank to lend it money to pay Seller and has offered to grant the bank a security interest in the propane. How will the bank take and perfect its security interest?

148.   *§9-312(c).* On May 1, Farmer bailed cotton with Gin Co. On May 2, Gin

Co. issued Farmer a negotiable warehouse receipt covering the cotton. On May 3, Farmer granted First Bank a security interest in the cotton. First filed a proper financing statement in the proper office on the same day. On May 4, Farmer granted Second Bank a security interest in the warehouse receipt by delivering the receipt to Second Bank as security for a loan. Farmer has defaulted on his loans to both banks.

    a.   Is First Bank perfected?

    b.   Is Second Bank perfected?

    c.   If both banks are perfected, which bank has priority?

149. *§7-501.*   Cotton producer *P* delivered cotton to *G*, a gin. *G* issued a warehouse receipt to *P*, who put the receipt in his desk. *T* stole the receipt and delivered it to *B*, a cotton broker.

    a.   In order for *B* to rise to the level of a holder by due negotiation, which of the following facts must be true?

        i.   The receipt must be negotiable.

        ii.   The receipt must be endorsed by the producer or be in bearer form.

        iii.   *T* must negotiate to *B* in the regular course of business or finance and not in satisfaction of a debt.

        iv.   *B* must take for value in good faith, and without notice of the producer's claim.

    b.   Is *T* a holder by due negotiation?

150. *§7-501.*   In the preceding question, which of the following circumstances would render the transfer to *B* such that *B* would not be a holder by due negotiation?

    a.   The endorsement of *P*, the producer, is forged.

    b.   *T* is a truck driver, a tramp, or a professor.

    c.   The receipt is in order form and is not endorsed to *B*.

    d.   *B* takes the receipt as security for an antecedent debt from *T*.

    e.   The receipt recites that it is nonnegotiable.

    f.   *T* endorses the receipt after *B* takes it and after *B* learns that the receipt was issued fraudulently.

    g.   *T* gives the receipt to *R* as a birthday gift.

    h.   *B* is a bank.

    i.   *T* is a bank.

151. *§7-502(1).*   If, in the foregoing transaction, *B* is a holder by due negotiation, does *B* have greater rights than *T* in the receipt? Than the producer in the cotton? Would your answer to this question differ if *B* were a lender taking the receipt as collateral for a contemporaneous loan, rather than a broker buying the cotton for resale?

152. *§7-504.*   If *B* would defeat the producer in the foregoing problem and if *B* transfers to *C* not by due negotiation, so that *C* is not a holder by due negotiation, what are the rights of *C*?

153. *§7-504.*   In the transaction illustrated in Problem 149, if *B* is not a holder by due negotiation, does *B* have greater rights in the cotton than the producer?

154. *§7-503(1) & cmt. 1 (second sentence).* T, a cotton farmer, steals cotton from a producer and bails the cotton with a gin, which issues T a negotiable receipt. T then negotiates the receipt to B, as security for a loan. B takes for value, in good faith, and without notice of the theft.

    a.   Does B defeat the producer?

    b.   Does B defeat First Bank, to whom the producer granted a perfected security interest in the cotton before T stole it?

    c.   Would your answer differ if T were a truck driver? If he were, what section would govern, and what would the result be? §7-504.

155. *§7-503(1)(a).* Would your answer to the preceding question differ if the producer had entrusted the cotton to T with directions to deliver it to the gin?

156. *§7-502(1)(c).* W, a trader in metals, anticipated a delivery of copper ore on May 1 that W planned to deliver to S, a carrier, for shipment to a foreign customer. The delivery of the ore was late, and W desperately needed a negotiable bill of lading to present to the foreign buyer's bank under a letter of credit that was about to expire. In order to accommodate its customer, S fraudulently issued a negotiable receipt to W, which W duly negotiated to Bank on May 1. Two days later, the ore arrived, and W delivered it to S. W is now insolvent, and his trustee in bankruptcy claims that the bill of lading stood for nothing on May 1, the day the bank took it. What argument should the bank make? Could the bank make that argument if the bill had been a straight bill, that is, if it had been nonnegotiable?

Section 22. Fixture Priority Rules

The following problems deal with conflicts between a lender secured by a real estate encumbrance and a lender holding a security interest in a fixture. For our purposes, real estate encumbrancers fall into two categories: owners and mortgagees. We worry about owners when the borrower granting the security interest is a tenant. Often, of course, the debtor granting the security interest will be the owner, and the potential conflict will be with the mortgagee.

The general rule for priorities between a security interest in fixtures and a mortgage of the real estate is in §9-334(c), which provides that the mortgage interest will prevail over the security interest in the fixture. That general rule is subject to exception, however, as these problems illustrate.

In all of these problems, assume that the real estate encumbrancer's interest is perfected under real estate law.

Problems

157.

May 1.   *O* granted a mortgage in its factory to S&L.

May 2.   *O* granted a non-purchase-money security interest in a furnace to Heating Co., which perfected by a fixture filing.

May 3.   Heating Co. installed the furnace.

   a. Who has priority? §9-334(c).

   b. Would your answer to this question differ if on May 4 S&L transferred its mortgage to Mortgage Investment Co.? §9-334(e).

   c. Would your answer to either question differ if Heating Co.'s security interest were a purchase money security interest? §9-334(d).

158. *§9-334(d).*

May 1.   *O* granted Heating Co. a purchase-money security interest in a furnace to Heating Co. Heating Co. perfected by an ordinary filing and installed the furnace.

May 2.   *O* granted a mortgage to S&L.

   a. Does Heating Co. defeat S&L?

   b. Would your answer differ if Heating Co. made a fixture filing after May 2 but before May 21?

159. *§9-313(d).*

May 1.   *O* granted mortgage to S&L.

May 2.   *O* granted a purchase-money security interest in a furnace to Heating Co.

May 3.   Heating Co. installed the furnace.

May 4.   Heating Co. made a fixture filing.

   a. Does Heating Co. defeat S&L?

   b. Would your answer to this question differ if

     i. the mortgage were a construction mortgage and Heating Co. installed it during construction?

     ii. Heating Co made the fixture filing on May 25?

160. *§9-322(A)(1).* On May 1, First Bank took from Ace Apartments Co. a security interest in a copying machine that Ace installed in its apartment building office on May 3. First filed a non-fixture financing statement on May 1. On May 2, Second Bank took a security interest in the same machine from Ace and also filed a non-fixture filing the same day. Under governing state law, the copying machine is a fixture. Ace defaults on both loans.

   a. Which bank gets the machine?

   b. What provision in Article 9 governs?

   c. Does it matter that neither bank made a fixture filing?

   d. Would either bank defeat a mortgagee that held a mortgage at the time the machine was affixed? §9-334(e)(2).

161. Would your answer to the preceding question differ if the goods were a modular home that the owner of the real estate had affixed on May 3 to a concrete foundation on May 3 and that would be a fixture under applicable state law? Would it differ if First Bank were a purchase-money secured party?

162. *§9-334(e)(3), Bankruptcy Code §544(a)(1) & (3).* Assume in Problem 160 that the machine is worth enough to pay both banks but that the owner, the debtor, is bankrupt. Who gets the machine?

163. *§9-334(e).* On May 1, Dealer sold a Tiffany window to consumer C on credit for installation in C's home. Dealer retained a security interest. The home is subject to a mortgage C granted S&L two years earlier. On August 1, C defaulted on both loans. If you assume that the window is a fixture, who gets it? Would your answer differ if there were no mortgage and C's trustee in bankruptcy were claiming the window? Would your answers to any of these questions differ if the collateral were a new refrigerator replacing the refrigerator that was in the home at the time of the mortgage?

164. *§9-334(d).*

May 1. O granted a mortgage on her apartment building to S&L, which recorded the same day.
June 1. Heating Co. installed a furnace in the building and retained a security interest to secure the purchase price.
June 9. The heating company filed a financing statement centrally.

O is now in default on the mortgage and the sales agreement. Who has the prior claim to the furnace? Would your answer differ if the heating company had filed a fixture filing on June 9? On June 29? Does it matter whether the mortgage is a construction mortgage?

165.

May 1. O granted First Bank a mortgage on its steel plant. The bank recorded the same day.
May 2. O granted Second Bank a security interest in a boiler in the plant, and Second perfected by making a fixture filing on the same day.
   a. If O defaults on the loans to First and Second, which bank will have the prior claim to the boiler? What section governs? §9-334(c).
   b. Would the result differ if First Bank took its mortgage on May 3? §9-334(e)(1).

166. *§9-334(e)(2)(A).* St. Paul Co. manufactures personal computers that it sells on credit throughout the country. St. Paul's buyers typically grant St. Paul a security interest in the computers. St. Paul has followed the policy of taking a financing statement from its customers and making non-fixture filings in the state where its customer is located before it delivers the goods. If a customer becomes bankrupt, will St. Paul defeat the customer's trustee? If the customer's premises are subject to a mortgage and if the customer defaults on the mortgage, will the mortgagee have superior rights in the computers?

Section 23. Further Scope Questions

Earlier problems [see Problems 13 through 17] illustrated the operation of §9-109, the scope and excluded transactions section. That discussion omitted an important area of controversy, however, namely that involving the definition of a "security interest."

The definition becomes problematic in several settings. The first is the lease transaction. For a number of commercial reasons, users may prefer to lease goods rather than buy them. In the simplest case, a traveler will lease an automobile for a few days and return the vehicle at the end of the lease to the leasing company. In other cases, manufacturers lease production equipment for long periods. Sometimes the lease is a disguised sale, but sometimes it is a "true" lease designed to take full advantage of income tax laws, of bank capital adequacy regulations, and of covenants in loan agreements requiring the manufacturer to maintain certain ratios of assets and liabilities. Leasing is a huge industry, but Article 2A, which governs leasing, is traditionally not included in courses on Secured Transactions or Payments Systems, which are the subject of this book. The following problems, then, deal with leases to the extent that they may be disguised security agreements.

The second transaction that has given rise to scope questions is the consignment. At first blush, the consignment looks like an inventory loan under which the consignor holds title to the goods as security for payment by the party in possession of them, the consignee. In some industries, however, parties market products on the assumption that the consignee will probably not sell some of the merchandise. Jewelry and book stores and art galleries, for example, often assume that they will return a significant portion of inventory to their suppliers. Many courts are not comfortable applying Article 9 to consignments in those cases and in commercially marginal operations such as used-goods stores.

Finally, a manufacturer's practice of contracting out certain work to fabricators or other manufacturers that can perform manufacturing services more efficiently than the owner of the work in process has given rise to claims that the fabricators or secondary manufacturers are really engaging in inventory borrowing.

The following problems involve mildly complicated conceptual problems. They begin here with an easy problem, however: the case of the mechanic's lien.

Problems

167. *§9-333.*   Dealer sold a new automobile to C on May 1. C executed a retail installment sales contract granting dealer a security interest to secure the installment payments that C agreed to make over a three-year period. Dealer assigned the paper to its floor planner, First Bank. On May 2, C was involved in a collision that left the vehicle with extensive body damage. C took the car to G, who repaired the vehicle. C is now bankrupt, and G, who has yet to be paid, is holding the car and refusing to return it to the bank that is claiming it. Must First Bank pay G before it can claim possession of the car? Would your answer differ if the garage's lien were based on common law holdings that made the lien subordinate to prior perfected security interests? Would it differ if the garage's lien were statutory and the statute rendered the lien subordinate to prior perfected security interests?

168. *§1-203 [§1-201(37)]*. Lessor, Inc. purchases heavy equipment for the oil industry and leases it to oil exploration companies. On May 1, it leased 20 diesel engines to Oil-Ex Co. for a period of four years. In which of the following cases would you as counsel for Lessor recommend to your client that it file a financing statement?

    a.   The lessee has an option at the end of the four-year term to purchase the equipment for $1.

    b.   At the end of the first four-year term, the lessee has an option to lease the equipment, at a fair rental price, for an additional four years, with the option to purchase the equipment at the end of the second term for $1. Would your answer to this question differ if the rental for the second four-year term were "nominal"? How do you determine whether the rent for the second term is nominal?

    c.   The equipment has an estimated useful life of ten years, the lease is for four years, and the lessee must return the goods at the end of the lease term in its original condition, normal wear and tear excepted.

    d.   The equipment has a life of ten years, the lease term is for four years, and the lease provides that the lessee must purchase the equipment at the end of the four-year term at a price equal to the then market value of the equipment.

    e.   The lease is for four years, and the goods have an estimated useful life of three years. (For the purposes of this problem, as of what date does the statute direct the estimate of useful life to be made?)

    f.   The lease is for ten years, the estimated useful life of the equipment is twenty years, and the lessee has the option to continue the lease for an additional ten years for

        i. $1; or for

       ii. $100; or for

      iii.   a sum of money equal to 50 percent of the estimated value of the equipment at the end of the ten-year term.

    g.   Would your answer to any of the questions in this problem differ if the lessee had the right to terminate the lease?

169. *§§9-102(a)(20), 9-109(a)(4)*. M, a bicycle manufacturer, consigned bicycles to R, a retailer, for resale at R's bicycle shop. Under the terms of the consignment, any goods that R did not resell would be returned to M. The consignment agreement stipulated that title to the goods remained in M and that R was only an agent with power to transfer title to customers of R. R is now bankrupt, and its trustee in bankruptcy is claiming the goods. In

determining whether the trustee or M should recover the goods, which of the following facts would be relevant?

   a. That R's bicycle shop had a sign at the entrance reading "M Bicycle Shop."
   b. That there is a small sign over the door of the shop reading "R, authorized dealer."
   c. That R posted a notice in the shop window reading "M bicycles in this store are on consignment."
   d. That M filed a financing statement centrally designating M as consignor and R as consignee. §9-505.

170. *§§9-109, 9-324(b).* W, a wholesaler, has granted First Bank a security interest in all of its inventory of beer and wine. B, a brewer that is trying to enter the market, offers to sell 20,000 cases of wine to W "on consignment." You are counsel to B, who has asked for your opinion on the action it should take to protect itself from First Bank. What do you advise?

171. P, a farm producer, delivered cotton to C, a gin, for ginning and baling. Traditionally, C, has manufactured cotton for its customers by distributing samples of the cotton and taking orders. When G sells cotton, it subtracts its ginning and baling costs, its storage charges, and its commission, and remits the balance to the customer.

   a. G is now bankrupt, and its trustee claims the cotton that P delivered to G. Does the trustee defeat P? Would your answer differ if P could show that the trustee knew of the bailment?
   b. Prior to its bankruptcy, G granted First Bank a security interest in all of its inventory, then owned or thereafter acquired Does First defeat P? Would your answer differ if P could show that First knew of the bailment?

172. On May 1, Wool Co, which manufactured woolen textiles at its plant, entered into a sale of fabric with Mill Co. Mill did not want to take delivery of the goods and, after paying for them, asked Wool Co. to hold them pending delivery instructions. In the meantime, Wool was having difficulty with Aussie Co., its wool supplier to whom it owed $1 million. On May 2, Wool conveyed to Aussie, in satisfaction of the debt, all of Wool's textile inventory, including Mill's fabric. Wool delivered the goods to Aussie, which was unaware that it was taking property to which Mill would later make a claim. Wool is now bankrupt. Mill claims that Aussie has converted its property.

   a. Is Aussie a buyer in ordinary course?
   b. Is Aussie a secured party that has repossessed its collateral?
   c. Is Aussie liable in conversion to Mill? §2-402(2).

173. *§2A-307.* A&B Co. sells metal strapping to manufacturers that use the strapping to seal containers in which they ship product. A&B also "leases" wire-strapping machines to its customers for use in applying the wire to the containers. The machines are costly, but A&B does not profit from the leases. It profits from the sale of the strapping. If a customer becomes insolvent, will A&B lose the machines to the trustee? Do the customer's bank holding a perfected security interest in the customer's equipment? Does your answer to this question depend on the amount of rent that A&B charges the customer? What result if the rent is $1 per year? What result if the rent is a reasonable rental?

Section 24. The Seller's Right to Reclaim

In the discussion of the doctrine of voidable title in Problems 9 and 10, we noted that a seller loses something when a fraudster with violable title conveys goods to a good-faith purchaser for value. We never identified, however, what it is that the seller loses. He loses the right to reclaim, and the following problems deal with the attempt of the seller to assert that right against third parties. As we already know, he will not be successful when he asserts the right against the good-faith purchaser for value; but we will also see that not every important commercial personage fits the definition of such a good-faith purchaser and that the seller can assert the right against parties that frequently appear in the real commercial world, most notably the trustee in bankruptcy.

This set of problems is an introduction to the bankruptcy issues that are the subject of the problems under the next section.

Problems

174. S contracts to sell diesel engine components to B, an engine manufacturer, for $75,000. B submits a purchase order to S calling for payment within ten days of shipment. S accepts the purchase order. Under the purchase order, S must manufacture the parts to B's specifications and must ship in two installments. S has shipped one installment, but B failed to pay within the ten-day period. S has completed the second shipment and prepared it for delivery in cartons marked with B's name and address.
   a.   What is B's interest in the second shipment? §2-501(1).
   b.   May S cut off that interest? §2-703(a).
   c.   Would B's inventory lender have an interest in the shipment? §9-203(b)(2). If so, would S be able to cut off that interest?

175. §§2-707(1), 2-705(1).   If S had shipped the second installment, under what circumstances could S stop delivery?

176. If S had delivered the parts included in the second installment and if B did not pay for them, does S have any interest in the parts after the delivery? Would B's inventory lender? B's trustee in bankruptcy? What must S do to obtain an interest in goods that it delivers on credit to B when B is guilty of no fraud but does not pay?

177. §2-702.   If B practiced fraud on S, does S have any interest in the goods after delivery? What must S do to "perfect" this interest? Are there circumstances that relieve *S* from its perfection duties? What might *S* do to avoid having to make the demand referred to in §2-702? If *B* gives *S* a check drawn on insufficient funds, is that check a written representation of solvency? What proof of fraud must *S* marshal in these cases? Is common law fraud good enough? Anything else? At common law did *S* have to "perfect" its interest? Is it fraudulent for *B* to receive goods on credit while it is insolvent? Does it matter whether *B* knows it is insolvent? For the definition of "insolvent," see §1-201(b)(23) [§1-201(23)].

178. *§2-507(2).*   *S* entered into a sale of lumber with *B*. Under the terms of the contract, *S* was to deliver the lumber to *B*'s shed. When *S* arrived at *B*'s yard, *B* told *S* to unload the lumber into the shed and return to the office for payment. After *S* unloaded the lumber, he drove his truck to the office, which he found locked. When he returned to the shed, it was locked also. *B* has refused to return the lumber.
   a.   Does *S* have any rights in the lumber?
   b.   Is it necessary for *S* to show that *B* planned all along to defraud *S*?
   c.   Must *S* "perfect" his rights?
   d.   Would your answers to this question differ if, when *S* went to the office, *B* gave *S* a check drawn on insufficient funds? §2-511, comment 6. Does it matter whether the check was postdated. Does it matter whether *B* knew that the check was an overdraft?

179. *§2-507(2).*   Which of the following parties does a cash seller with the right to reclaim defeat?
   a.   A buyer in ordinary course to which *B* resells the goods.
   b.   A purchaser for value in good faith, such as a lender with a security interest in all of *B*'s after acquired inventory. Does it matter whether the secured party is perfected?

180. *§2-507, cmt. 3.*   Must a cash seller that is asserting its right to reclaim under §2-507(2) give a notice of demand for return of the goods?

181. *§2-403(1).*   Customarily, the seller's right to the goods §§2-507(2) and 2-702(2) is characterized as the seller's right to reclaim. The rule of §2-703(a) is probably a codification of what the common law called the seller's lien. What other name might we give the seller's lien?

182. *§2-403(1) (second sentence).*   There are at least four kinds of fraud: (1) common law fraud in which *B* defrauds *S* with scienter and in a manner that satisfies the traditional tort definition of "fraud'; (2) taking delivery of goods on credit under a contract of sale while insolvent; (3) taking delivery under cash sale in return for a check drawn on insufficient funds; and (4) grabbing the goods in a cash sale and refusing to pay for them. In these four instances, what do we call the interest of *B*, the fraudster, in the goods?

183. *§2-403(1) (second sentence).*   If *B* holds voidable title to goods it purchased from *S* under a contract of sale, what interest relative to *S* passes to the following parties:
   a.   A lender that holds a perfected security interest in *B*'s after acquired inventory.

    b.   *C*, a customer of *B* to whom *B* resells the goods in the ordinary course of business.

    c.   *D*, a buyer in bulk to whom *B* resells the goods.

184.   *§2-702(3).* In voidable title cases, will a lien creditor of *B* defeat *S*'s right to reclaim? What does §2-403(1) suggest? In some jurisdictions, the Code includes a "lien creditor" in the list of persons in §2-702(3) to whose rights the seller's right to reclaim are "subject." What does that version of §2-702(3) suggest? How should we read the words "subject to" in §2-702(3)?

185.   *Bankruptcy Code §546(c).* Assume that *B*'s lien creditor in the foregoing problems is the trustee in bankruptcy.

    a.   Does the Bankruptcy Code fashion rules for *S*'s right to reclaim to the extent it is not codified in UCC §2-702? What about UCC §2-507? Is there a negative implication in Bankruptcy Code §546(c)(1) to the effect that it is the sole source of relief for *S*, that is, that *S* may not rely on common law fraud or on UCC §2-507(2) in bankruptcy?

    b.   Must *S* "perfect" to defeat the trustee? How do the perfection requirements of the Bankruptcy Code differ from those in UCC §2-702?

    c.   Does "subject to" in Bankruptcy Code §546(c) mean what those words mean in UCC §2-702(3)? Where do we look to find the meaning? Does the Bankruptcy Code use the term "subject to" to mean "subordinate to"? If the common law of the jurisdiction gives the lien creditor rights superior to those of the reclaiming seller, does the trustee defeat the reclaiming seller? If Bankruptcy Code §546(c) changes the law in those states, does it change it with respect to the seller's right to reclaim under common law fraud? Under UCC §2-507(2)?

    d.   Will *B*'s periodic statements of solvency obviate *S*'s need to demand return of the goods under Bankruptcy Code §546(c)(1)?

186.   *§§1-201(b)(35) [§1-201(37)], 9-109(a)(1).* Does Article 9 apply to *S*'s right to reclaim? If *B* resells the goods delivered by *S*, does *S* have a right to the proceeds? If so, does that right defeat third parties (that is, lien creditors, *B*'s trustee in bankruptcy, *B*'s inventory lender, *B*'s account lender)?

187.   *§§1-201(b)(35) [§1-201(37)], 2-505(1)(a), 2-711(3).* Is the seller's right to reclaim a security interest? Can it be a security interest under Article 9? Are there security interests in Article 2? How does the seller's right to reclaim differ from the Article 2 security interest defined in those provisions? If the seller's right to reclaim is not a security interest, what is it?

Section 25. *Article 9 and the Powers of the Trustee in Bankruptcy*

Article 9 is state law, and it is subject to the provisions of the Bankruptcy Code and of the powers granted under that federal law to the trustee in bankruptcy.

Secured lenders often face the perils of bankruptcy. There are a number of sections in the Bankruptcy Code that traditionally fall within Article 9 study. Chief among them are (1) the trustee's power to assert the rights of a lien creditor that obtains a lien on all of the debtor's property on the filing of the bankruptcy petition, and (2) the trustee's power to set aside transactions that are preferences. In addition, §362 of the Bankruptcy Code, the automatic stay provision, impacts the rights of the secured creditor. The rules of Bankruptcy Code §552 also are particularly relevant.

The following problems examine the effect of these Bankruptcy Code sections on the security interest. Notably absent from these problems is discussion of the effects of Chapter 11 on the rights of the secured party. Study of that complex of bankruptcy rules is better left to courses on creditors' rights.

Assume in the following problems that the debtor filed a Chapter 7, straight liquidation, petition on December 1, which makes September 2 the 90th day before bankruptcy. Assume further that at all times, unless the problem otherwise states, the secured party is undersecured.

Problems

188. *Bankruptcy Code §§544(a)(1), 552(a); UCC §9-301(1)(b).* On October 1, Debtor executed a security agreement that purported to grant First Bank a security interest in all of Debtor's equipment, then owned or thereafter acquired. The bank filed a proper financing statement in the proper office on October 5. On December 2, Debtor obtained rights in a press that it had paid for in November. Does the trustee as a lien creditor defeat First Bank's interest in the press?

189. *Bankruptcy Code §552(b).* On May 1, Debtor granted First Bank a perfected security interest in all of Debtor's inventory, then owned or thereafter acquired. On December 2, Debtor in possession, who has the rights of a trustee, sold on open account inventory that it had owned on May 1 and immediately before the filing. Does Debtor in possession defeat First Bank's claim to the account?

190. *Bankruptcy Code §§362(b)(3), 546(b); UCC §9-317(e).* On November 15, debtor granted Manufacturing Co. a security interest in kitchen equipment Manufacturing Co. was selling on credit. Manufacturing Co. delivered the equipment on November 27 and filed a proper financing statement in the proper office on December 5. Does the trustee as a lien creditor defeat Manufacturing Co.?

191. *Bankruptcy Code §362(b)(3).* On November 28, Supply Co. delivered a truckload of inventory to Debtor on credit when Debtor was insolvent. May Supply Co. on December 5 successfully demand in writing that the inventory be returned?

192. *Bankruptcy Code §362(a)(5).* On May 1, Debtor granted First Bank a perfected security interest in all of Debtor's equipment. If Debtor is in default on the note secured by the equipment, may First repossess the equipment under UCC §9-609(a) on December 2? If First repossessed the equipment on November 30, may First sell it under UCC §9-610 on December 2? If First Bank's security interest were unperfected on December 1, could it file a financing statement on December 2?

193. On August 30, Debtor granted First Bank a security interest in all of Debtor's equipment to secure a debt of $10,000. On September 3, Electric Co. obtained a judgment in the amount of $100 against Debtor and levied on Debtor's equipment. On September 4, First filed.

    a. May the trustee defeat First under the preference section, or is the transfer deemed to have occurred on August 30? Bankruptcy Code §547(e)(2)(A).

    b. May Electric Co. defeat First Bank? UCC §9-317(a)(2)(A). (Bear in mind that this is not a purchase money security interest.)

    c. May the trustee defeat Electric Co. under the preference section? *See* Bankruptcy Code §101(54) (defining "transfer").

    d. If it defeats Electric Co., will the trustee step into Electric Co.'s shoes as a lien creditor as of September 3; and will the trustee, therefore, defeat First? Bankruptcy Code §551.

    e. If the trustee defeats First under Bankruptcy Code §551, is the trustee's victory limited to Electric Co.'s $100, or may trustee upset First's security interest in its entirety?

Section 26. *Preferences*

The following four problems deal with preferences as defined in §547(b) of the Bankruptcy Code, with the exceptions to that definition in subsection (c) of §547 and with the timing rule of subsection (e). The emphasis is not so much on the preference rules as it is on the intersection of those rules with secured lending practices.

Problems

194. *Bankruptcy Code §101(54) (defining "transfer" for Bankruptcy Code purposes) and §547(b) (listing elements of voidable preference).* On September 5, Manufacturing Co. became anxious about the security of its claim against Debtor for equipment Manufacturing Co. delivered to Debtor on credit. Manufacturing demanded a payment on that open account. On the next day, Debtor paid $10,000 to Manufacturing Co.

    a. May the trustee recover the payment?

    b. Would your answer to the preceding question differ if instead of paying cash to Manufacturing Co. on September 6, Debtor had granted Manufacturing Co. a perfected security interest in Debtor's equipment on that date? Could the trustee set the creation of that security interest aside?

   c.   Would your answer differ if instead of obtaining a cash payment or a security interest, Manufacturing Co. obtained a lien by judicial proceedings against Debtor on September 6? Could the trustee set the lien aside?

195. *Bankruptcy Code §547(b), (c)(3), (c)(4), (e)(2).*   Which of the following transactions is a preference that the trustee in bankruptcy may recover under §547?

   a.   On November 1, Debtor paid $1,000 to First Bank on First Bank's demand note. §547(b).

   b.   Would your answer differ if the note were completely secured by a perfected security interest in Debtor's property? §547(b)(5).

   c.   On May 2, Debtor gave $100 to its president in satisfaction of a loan the president had made to the company. §547(b).

   d.   On October and November 1, Debtor paid $1,000 to First Bank on an installment note that called for payments of that amount on the first day of each month. §547(c)(2).

   e.   On November 3, Debtor granted First Bank a security interest in all of its equipment as security for a $100,000 loan made on that date. §547(e)(2). Does it matter whether First files its financing statement before or after November 13?

   f.   On August 1, Second Bank made an unsecured loan to Debtor of $50,000. On August 31, Second deemed itself insecure and asked Debtor for a security interest in Debtor's inventory. Debtor granted the security interest on that date. Does it matter whether Second files its financing statement before or after September 10? Id.

   g.   On November 29, Seller Co sold and delivered inventory to debtor on credit, and debtor granted Seller Co. a security interest in the inventory. Does it matter whether Seller files before or after December 19? §547(c)(3) and (e)(2)(A). Would your answer differ if the security interest were not a purchase money security interest? Is the date of delivery critical?

   h.   On August 15, Debtor executed a security agreement purporting to grant Fourth Bank a security interest in all of Debtor's general intangibles. Fourth made a loan to Debtor for the first time on September 10. Fourth filed on September 17. §547(e)(2)(A). Would your answer differ if Fourth had made a commitment to lend on August 15?

   i.   On August 15, Fifth Bank loaned Debtor $50,000. On September 15, Debtor granted Fifth a perfected security interest in a piece of Debtor's equipment that was worth, and is still worth, $50,000. On October 15, Fifth made a second unsecured loan to Debtor of $20,000. §547(c)(4).

   j.   On August 20, Supply Co. delivered a month's supply of fuel to Debtor on 20 days' open account. On September 9, Debtor paid for the August delivery. On September 20, Supply Co. delivered another month's supply of fuel, for which Debtor made payment on October 10. Supply Co. made a third delivery on November 20. §547(c)(2).

196. On August 15, Debtor granted First Bank a perfected security interest in all of Debtor's accounts, then due or thereafter arising. On the same day, First loaned Debtor $100,000.

    a. Under the UCC, when does the bank first obtain an interest in an account that arises out of the sale by Debtor of inventory on September 15?

    b. If the bank first obtains an interest in the account on September 15, is there a transfer by Debtor of that account on that date, and is that transfer not on account of the antecedent debt of August 15? Bankruptcy Code §547(e)(3). Can the UCC alter this result by saying, for example, that the transfer "shall be deemed to be taken for new value?" Given this analysis, is it correct to say that under the UCC and the Bankruptcy Code revolving account financing would be seriously problematic for lenders if there were no accommodation for it?

    c. Does the Bankruptcy Code interdict this analysis for revolving account (and revolving inventory) loans? Bankruptcy Code §547(c)(5).

    d. Would your answers to any of the foregoing questions differ if the collateral were equipment rather than inventory or accounts?

197. *Bankruptcy Code §547(c)(5).* On May 1, Debtor granted Lender a security interest in inventory then owned or thereafter acquired. In which of the following examples would the revolving inventory lender have received a preference?

    a. On September 2, the value of the inventory was $10,000, and the balance due on the inventory loan was $8,000. On December 1, the value of the inventory was $20,000, and the balance due on the loan was $19,000.

    b. Would your answer differ if the value of the inventory on September 2 was $5,000 and the debt $19,000?

    c. On September 2, the value of the inventory was $10,000, and the balance due on the loan was $12,000. On the date of bankruptcy, the respective figures were $10,000 and $10,000. $20,000 and $22,000. $4,000 and $6,000.

198. *Bankruptcy Code §547(c)(1).* On the morning of November 20, First Bank loaned Debtor $20,000. That afternoon, Debtor granted the bank a perfected security interest in Debtor's chattel paper. May the trustee recover the chattel paper?

199. *Bankruptcy Code §547(c)(1).* On the morning of November 20, First Bank loaned Debtor $20,000. That afternoon, Debtor granted the bank a perfected security interest in Debtor's chattel paper. May the trustee recover the chattel paper?

Section 27. The Trustee as Lien Creditor

More powerful, though less intellectually challenging, than the trustee's power to recover preferences is the trustee's power under Bankruptcy Code §544(a)(1) to set aside security interests that fall before the avoidance power of lien creditor. This provision coupled with the rule of UCC §§9-201(a), 9-317(a)(2) permits the trustee to defeat the unperfected secured party and makes the Code's perfection rules critical. Assume, again, that the debtor filed in bankruptcy on December 1.

Problems

200. *Bankruptcy Code §§544(a)(1), 547(e)(2)(C).*   On April 1, Debtor granted First Bank a security interest in return for a loan, and the bank filed a proper financing statement in the proper office on December 5. Does the trustee have the right to set the secured transaction aside as a preference? May the trustee avoid the security interest under its strong-arm power as a lien creditor?

201. *Bankruptcy Code §§544(a)(1), 547(e)(2)(C); UCC §9-317(e).*
    a.   In the preceding question, if the bank had loaned and taken the security interest on November 30, would your answer differ?
    b.   Would it matter whether the bank's security interest was a purchase money security interest?

Section 28. Part 5: Default

In the event the debtor defaults on the underlying obligation that the security agreement supports, the secured party may want to enforce the rights it enjoys under the provisions of the security agreement and under Part 6 of Article 9.

There has been some litigation here, fostered for the most part by disputes over debtor protection provisions that turn on factual determinations. As you will see, some of the rules of Part 6 require reasonable conduct. Often, parties will disagree on the question of reasonableness.

The purpose of these problems is not to deal, however, with those issues but only to provide you with an understanding of the sections themselves.

Problems

202. *§9-609(a)(1).* On May l, Seller sold and delivered goods to Debtor, and

Debtor agreed to pay Seller $10,000 on June 1. On May 2, Bank loaned Debtor $10,000 and took a security interest in the goods that Seller had delivered. Debtor executed and delivered to the bank a promissory note for the $10,000. There was a provision in the security agreement under which Debtor covenanted that she would not allow judgments or allow liens to attach to the collateral. Bank perfected its security interest in the goods on the same day. On June 1, Debtor defaulted on both debts, and Seller obtained a judgment against Debtor. The bank has obtained no judgment.

    a.   Does Bank have the right to take possession of the goods? §§9-601(a)(2), -609(a)(1).

    b.   Would your answer differ if Seller had obtained a lien on the goods by having the sheriff levy on them? §9-317(a)(2).

    c.   Would your answer differ if Debtor was not in default on the promissory note that she signed when she borrowed the money from the bank? §9-601(a).

203. *§9-609(b)(2).* Assume the same facts as in the foregoing problem. Under which of the following circumstances has the bank exercised its rights properly under Part 6 of Article 9?

    a.   Bank called Debtor's employee and told the employee that a truck would be arriving that afternoon to pick up the goods. The employee, without speaking to Debtor, allowed the bank's agents to take the goods.

    b.   Banker arrived at Debtor's place of business, told the employee of Debtor that he was there to pick up the collateral, walked into the premises, and took the goods.

    c.   The goods were inside Debtor's plant, and Banker broke a lock, went into the premises at night, and took the goods. Does it matter whether Bank has offered to repair the lock? Does it matter whether the security agreement gave Bank the right to enter the premises and remove the collateral?

    d.   The goods included a truck that Debtor had parked on the street in front of Debtor's plant. During the night, Banker forced the lock on the truck, hot wired it, and drove it away.

    e.   The goods were sitting on public property when Banker arrived to pick them up. Debtor was present, and when she saw the banker, she told him not to take the goods. Banker took them anyway. Would your answer differ if Debtor had told Banker that if he tried to remove the goods that there would be trouble? Would your answer differ if the banker used vulgar language?

204. *§§9-610, 9-627.* Assume in the following problem, that the bank repossessed the goods properly and took the following actions in connection with them. In which of the following cases has the bank acted improperly? In all cases assume, unless the facts state otherwise, that the bank gave the debtor(s) timely notice of the proposed dispositions. (In answering these questions, ask yourself how the bank would prove the reasonableness of its conduct.)

    a.   The bank sold a drill press to one of its best customers at a price below the market price for a used drill press. §9-610(b).

    b.   The bank sold a second drill press through a used equipment dealer at the fair market price and paid the dealer a commission.

    c.   The bank sold a third drill press six months later at the market price for used drill presses but at a price substantially below the market price on the day it repossessed the press.

    d.   The bank kept for itself a personal computer and credited the debtor with the fair market value of the computer.

205. *§9-617(b).* If the bank sold the defaulting debtor's collateral to an innocent third party and made the sale in violation of the debtor's rights under the security agreement or under Part 6 of Article 9, will the third party take good title to the goods?

206. *§§9-504(2), 9-507.* A secured party sold collateral of its debtor and received $9,000 as proceeds after deducting the costs of the sale. The debt that the collateral secured was for $10,000. In which of the following cases may the secured party obtain a judgment against the debtor for the deficiency?

    a.   The secured party sold the collateral without giving the debtor notice of the sale, but the sale was reasonable, and the evidence indicates that the secured party received a fair price.

    b.   The secured party disposed of the collateral without giving notice to the debtor, but the security agreement contained a provision under which the debtor waived its statutory right of notice. §9-624(a).

207. *§9-506.* A debtor borrowed $10,000 and granted secured party a security interest in goods. The promissory note that the debtor executed stipulated that in the event of a default on a payment of principal or interest, the full amount of the note would come due. The security agreement provided that a default under the note would be a default under the security agreement. After the debtor defaulted on an interest payment, the secured party repossessed the collateral. The debtor now seeks to reclaim the collateral and offers to pay the secured party the full amount of interest due. The secured party proposes to sell the collateral, apply the proceeds of the sale to the note, and seek a deficiency judgment against the debtor for the balance.

    a.   May the secured party pursue that course of action?

    b.   Would your answer differ if the debtor proposed to pay the secured party the interest and the full principal balance due on the note?

Secured Transactions: Answers

Section 1. Transferring Property Interests: Security of Property, Good-Faith Purchase, and Fraudulent Conveyance

1. You tell Dealer not to remove the equipment. Under §2-401(2), "title" to the equipment passed to Mine Co. on delivery. Dealer did not retain any interest in the goods, so Dealer has no interest in the equipment. Although §2-401(1) provides that "title" is generally immaterial, this is a situation where the Code, namely §2-401(2), specifically mentions that title is transferred simply upon completion of Dealer's performance regarding delivery. By failing to reserve any of the ownership rights, such as a security interest, Dealer has lost all interest in the equipment.

   Dealer's repossession of the equipment would therefore be tortious and, perhaps, larcenous. Dealer and Mine Co. could have structured the transaction differently (of course) by reserving a security interest in Dealer, but they didn't. Dealer, moreover, has no common law right to repossess the equipment.

2. *Woolen's Interest.* Woolen Co. has only a security interest in the Wool delivered to Distributor Co. The agreement that title remains in Woolen Co. brings the transaction within the second sentence of §2-401(1). So Distributor Co. obtains title to the wool, and all Woolen Co. has is a security interest in the wool. This security interest is not governed by Article 2, but is a "consensual" security interest that falls within the definition of "security interest" in §1-201(b)(35) [§1-201(37)] and is therefore governed by Article 9. The facts given do not establish that the transaction is a "consignment" as

69

defined in §9-102(a)(20). But even if it were such a "consignment," Article 9 would still apply.

Buyers from Distributor. Under the good faith purchase rules in Article 9, garment manufacturers buying from Distributor are probably buyers in ordinary course from Distributor Co. They will therefore take free and clear of Woolen's security interest §9-320(a). Other buyers will take free and clear unless before delivery (1) Woolen perfected its security interest or (2) the customer had knowledge of the security interest. §9-317(b).

Distributor's Creditors. Under §9-109(a)(4) this is a secured transaction, and Woolen must comply with Article 9. Distributor's perfected creditors will defeat Woolen's claim to the goods. §9-322.

The notion that Distributor Co. can act in these circumstances as an agent for Woolen Co. is a subterfuge that should not fool anyone in this day and age, though American Woolen Co. fooled the U.S. Supreme Court in an earlier day. This arrangement is one of inventory financing, whether the parties dub Distributor Co. "agent" or anything else. This is not to say that a seller cannot sell through a representative. The situation would be different if Woolen did not deliver the goods and if Distributor did not make any undertaking to pay for the goods.

3. The analysis here is the same as that in Problem 2. Article 9 will not work if parties can avoid its scope by characterizing their arrangements in archaic or arcane terms. Both this reservation of title and the earlier "consignment" were truly secured transactions, and Article 9's scope rule, §9-109(a)(1), correctly commands that all such arrangements fall within the purview of that Article. The sellers' interest is a security interest and no more. *See also* §1-201(b)(35) [§1-201(37)].

4. The first sentence of §2-403(1) codifies the *nemo dat* and the umbrella (or "shelter") principles of conveyancing law. This is the first rule of conveyancing, a security-of-property principle, to the effect that the transferee gets what the transferor had and what he conveyed. Under *nemo dat*, the transferor cannot convey greater interests than he has; under the umbrella principle, the transferee gets everything the transferor has, provided the transferor conveys what he has. If he conveys only a one-half interest, the transferee only gets the one-half interest, even though the transferor has a full interest.

Using this first rule of conveyancing, the starting point in any conveyancing analysis, the answers to the questions follow.

   a. *B* gets absolute ownership.
   b. *B* takes subject to the security interest. (Note that the rules of Article 9 may alter this conclusion by invoking either the second or the third conveyancing rules. Under the first rule of conveyancing, however, *B* cannot take more than *A* has; and after the conveyance to *C*, *A* has title subject to a security interest. *B*, therefore, takes subject to the interest.)
   c. *A* has already conveyed all of his interest to *B*, *B* takes all, and *C*

takes nothing. (If *B* had left the toluene with *A*, *B* may have permitted *A* to defraud *C*.)

  d. The first rule of conveyancing serves the free transferability of goods and the security of property principle. To say that *A* owns goods but may not transfer them is to say that ownership does not mean much. In commerce, the ability to transfer ownership, to convey, is essential. The law's recognition of the right to convey title to goods doomed feudalism, for it permitted the lowly merchant to create wealth and make himself and his contemporaries wealthier than the lords and to reduce the lords to the point of having to rent out their estates on the weekend for the merchants' employee picnic. (The merchants' struggle to have the law recognize the right to own goods and convey them was not an easy one; it took centuries for the merchants to prevail. Lords do not surrender privilege easily. They knew what the merchants were about. The lords may have been lazy, but they were not stupid. Modern society has lords. Some of them sit in the Congress or in state legislatures. Most of them, however, teach law.)

5. Under the first sentence of §2-403(1), the first rule of conveyancing (*nemo dat*), Buyer Co. takes subject to the security interest of First Bank. *Nemo dat* also dictates that Second Bank takes subject to the security interest. Buyer Co. cannot give Second Bank what Buyer Co. does not have.

  If for some reason First Bank's security interest is not good against Buyer Co. (under one of the good-faith purchase exceptions to the *nemo dat* principle), Second Bank will come under Buyer Co.'s umbrella, take what Buyer Co. has (title free of First Bank's security interest), and defeat First Bank.

6. In the case of loss, *C* may retain the watch as against the whole world, except for *A*. In the case of theft, *C* has nothing. The different results reflect in the first case the romance of a young chimney sweep named Armory, in the latter, the law's animus toward theft. In both cases, *C* has a legitimate expectation of ownership. The difference in result rests on the policy of preventing thieves from being rewarded by their wrong and to discourage thievery by limiting their markets, i.e., forcing a buyer to be more careful about dealing with a thief.

7. Owner and Gallery may think of themselves as clever chaps, but commercial practice and the law regard them as odious creeps. Buyers such as Collector should be able to rely on Gallery's at-least-apparent authority and should be able to complete what seems to be a normal commercial transaction. There is perhaps more than one way to justify that conclusion.

  First, the display with the card appears to be an offer for sale. Customer accepted that offer by carrying the vase to the counter and tendering the cash. Because the Gallery was "cash and carry," Gallery's/Owner's performance regarding physical delivery was complete at that time. Under §2-401(2), title to the vase passed to Collector at that time.

  Second, even if there was no offer and acceptance so as to create a contract of sale, Gallery had apparent authority or authority by estoppel (at least) to sell the vase. (There may even have been actual authority, because, although Owner did not authorize a sale, he did authorize the display and resulting offer.) Owner's delivery of the vase with the knowledge of display may estop him from asserting title. If the law of the jurisdiction recognizes that estoppel, then Collector has title. This is the beginning of the second conveyancing rule, the notion that a transferee may take something extra, more than he would get under the first, *nemo dat*, rule.

8. In this problem, the two contenders are innocent, but Jones is more innocent (innocenter?) than Smith, who permitted Dealer to mislead Jones. Efficiency analysis helps here. While some goods, such as automobiles, are subject to certificate of title laws, which permit a buyer to check on a seller's title, most goods, including violins, are not subject to such laws. It would be grossly inefficient in sale-of-goods transactions to insist that buyers check on the seller's title. Why? Because defects in title are relatively rare, and checking title without a recording system would be very time-consuming and unreliable. Moreover, if a search is necessary, a seller will have to do it only once whereas each potential buyer would be forced to conduct a search. To put the loss on Jones would force many different potential buyers to make that costly search. Smith can avoid the loss by entrusting his violin to an honest/careful dealer or by taking dealer's bond or other security. It is easier for Smith to protect himself than it is for Jones to protect herself.

   Whether the result should differ if Smith took the violin to Dealer for storage is a matter of some dispute. Those who would protect buyers think it makes no difference. The efficiency analysis holds. At least one court disagrees. Note that there is tension here between the first rule of conveyancing, a security-of-property rule, and the good-faith purchase doctrine, which is a security-of-purchase rule. You will not be surprised to learn that the lords often prefer security of property while merchants usually prefer security of purchase. In this transaction, the merchants seem to have won. *See* §2-403(2) & (3).

9. Taking delivery of goods using a check drawn on insufficient funds is fraud at common law. [The Code drafters expect us to know lots of law not codified in the Code.] Under the voidable title rule, which is only partly codified in §2-403(1) (second sentence), a fraud feasor has power to transfer good title to a good-faith purchaser for value. Dealer is such a purchaser even if she has not paid for the goods. The law protects her expectation interest—an important interest, evidently more important than Manufacturer's security-of-property interest. Note again that efficiency analysis helps explain the rule. Manufacturer could protect itself by checking on Middle's credit rating, by insisting on cash or other security before payment, or by refusing to do business with Middle. In fact, merchant sellers do all of these things, while buyers such as Dealer do exactly what Dealer did. They rely on Middle's "ostensible ownership" of the goods. Dealer has behaved in commercially reasonable fashion. Manufacturer has made a mistake. It is not a bad rule that lets people who make mistakes pay for them.

10. The retailers should prevail under the same economic analysis that we used in the preceding answer. Owner intended Reed, not Jones, to get title. So, if

Owner had sued Jones, Owner could get title "back" (Jones shouldn't benefit by his own fraud), and §2-403(2) so provides. On the other hand, some of the early voidable title cases used the notion of intent to hold that a seller such as Owner should lose. If an owner intended to convey title to the fraud feasor, the fact that the owner was defrauded did not overcome the fact that there was intent. If Owner intended to vest title in Reed, however, Jones took void title, the courts reasoned. The intent rationale fails in the impostor case. Owner did intend to vest the impostor, whatever her name, with title. The Code drafters eschewed the "intent" theories, opting instead for efficiency analysis, which prevails under the Code's version of the voidable title doctrine, as subsection (1)(a) of §2-403 indicates.

11. This problem illustrates the operation of the oldest fraudulent conveyance rule. Fraudulent conveyance law comprises the third conveyancing principle, the second exception to the notion that the transferee receives that which the transferor had. In good-faith purchase, the taker receives more than the transferor had. Under fraudulent conveyance, the taker receives less. Here, Ace and his company have defrauded the bank. The law regards the transfer as not having occurred, and First Bank will be able to levy on the equipment.

12. Under the common-law rule of *Twyne's Case*, it is fraud at law for a buyer to pay for goods and leave them with the seller, unless the buyer can provide a good-faith reason for his conduct. To leave a truck with a seller to have a hydraulic lift installed strikes us as such a reason. Edison would prevail over First Bank. Note that §2-402(2) does not codify *Tywne*. It merely refers to *Twyne*. Section 2-402(2) codifies only the good-faith reason proviso of *Twyne*.

   a. The guarantor could seek to avoid the transfer under UFTA §4(a)(1) as a transfer by Doc with actual intent to hinder, delay, or defraud the guarantor. However, because actual intent is so hard to prove (do you think the Docs of the world will admit their intent?), courts traditionally looked for "badges of fraud" that would allow a jury to infer the intent to hinder, delay, or defraud. UFTA §4(b) includes a non-exhaustive list of badges. Here, Mom & Pop's corporation is not literally an "insider" within the meaning of UFTA §1(7), but the fact that the transfer is to a company beneficially owned by Doc's relative is close enough to fail the smell test intended by §4(b)(1). Other badges arguably present are those of §4(b)(2), (4), (5) and (8). As to (8), note that "value" does not include the parents' unperformed promise to provide support. UFTA §3(a).

   b. UFTA §5(a) permits present creditors such as the credit card issuer to avoid transfers by an insolvent debtor to the extent the debtor does not receive "reasonably equivalent value in exchange" for the transfer. Here Dot is insolvent, the credit card issuer is a present creditor, and Dot did not receive "value" for her payments to PBS because she received no property in return, nor was an antecedent debt satisfied. (If Dot received as a premium a video of the Three Tyrolean Tenors, she did receive value, but not "reasonably equivalent value.")

c. Bank should not take the guarantee from Sub *A*. This is a "cross-guarantee" which is generally considered a no-no because it might be avoided later by Sub *A*'s present or future creditors under UFTA §4(a)(2)(i). Essentially, §4 might be triggered because (i) it applies to "obligations incurred" (i.e., the guarantee) as well as transfers and (ii) Sub *A* gets no direct benefit from the guarantee and hence receives no reasonably equivalent value. Instead of taking the guarantee of Sub *A*, Bank should have Parent guarantee the loan, and if appropriate, pledge its stock in Sub *B* as collateral for the guarantee. Parent's guarantee is not subject to the same fraudulent transfer risk because the value of its stock in Sub *B* is increased by the value of the loan to Sub *B*. (Note that the guarantee with pledge does not put Bank in the same position as if Sub *A* guaranteed the loan, because Bank's status v. Sub *A* upon default by Parent under the guarantee and foreclosure against the Sub *A* stock will not be that of a creditor but that of a shareholder. Bank can improve its position somewhat by including in Parent's guarantee affirmative and negative covenants relating to Sub *A*'s business.)

Section 2. *Scope*

13. Finance Co. must comply with Article 9, whether it takes the accounts with or without recourse. It matters not that the transfer of accounts is by sale or by creation of a security interest. Both characterizations fall within the scope section, §9-109(a)(3) (sale) and §9-109(a)(1) (security interest). For scope purposes, there is no difference between the sale of accounts and the assignment of accounts as security. (Note that there are exceptions for the assignment of accounts for collection purposes or as part of the sale of a business. *See* §9-109(d)(4) & (5). The exceptions are not commercially significant.) For now, it is enough to know that the sale of accounts to a factor, the name we give the buyer of accounts, is an Article 9 transaction that requires the factor to obtain a security agreement and to file a financing statement. (Note also that there is an exception to the filing requirement in the event of the "occasional" transfer of an account. *See* §9-309(2). This exception can be mischievous.)

14. Bank must comply with Article 9. It does not matter whether Dealer and Bank characterize their transaction as a sale §9-109(a)(3) or as a transfer for security §9-109(a)(1). The Code treats both transactions (which are pretty hard to distinguish anyway) as secured transactions that fall within the scope of Article 9. Section 9-109(d)(4) excludes from Article 9 the sale of chattel paper as part of the sale of the business out of which it arose.

15. By itself, the promissory note is subject to Article 9, whether the contractors grant the bank a security interest in it or sell it to the bank. In this type of transaction, the transfer of the note should be and usually is a full negotiation, so that the transferee is the owner of the instrument, and the

transaction is a sale. Sales of promissory notes fall within Article 9. *See* §9-109(a)(3). The fact that the note is secured by a real estate mortgage does not alter that analysis. *See* § 9-109(b). (Generally, Article 9b does not apply to the creation or transfer of an interest in real property, which includes a mortgage or deed of trust. §9-109 (d)(11). *See also* comment 7 to §9-109.) Note, moreover, that in such a transaction, the security interest in the promissory note is automatically perfected. *See* §9-309(4).

The mortgage is a supporting obligation. *See* §9-102(a)(77). If the creditor has a perfected security interest in the note the mortgage secures, the creditor also has a perfected security interest in the supporting obligation. *See* §9-203(g) (attachment of the security interest to the mortgage), §9-308(e) & cmt. 6 (perfection of that security interest).

Satisfying Article 9 does not protect the bank completely, however. As we will see later, possession of an instrument is essential to that protection, for subsequent takers of the note may rise to the level of a holder in due course. In that case, they can use the Article 9 exit ramp (§9-331(a)) to go to the holder in due course rule of Article 3 (§3-306), which gives the holder in due course rights to the instrument free of the bank's security interest. In these transactions, commercially sophisticated parties take possession of the note if they have any question about the financial integrity of their borrower. That possession satisfies negotiable instrument concerns. Trouble arises in the commercially infrequent cases in which the borrower, the mortgage company in this problem, gets into financial trouble or if the transaction is a homemade one, say, between a small construction company and an unsophisticated lender.

16. Section 9-109(c)(1) provides that Article 9 does not apply to any transaction to the extent that federal law preempts Article 9. Federal statutes govern the perfection (but not attachment) of security interests in aircraft and federally registered watercraft. Federal law also governs the creation and perfection of security interests in patents and copyrights.

17. The challenge of this question is the basic challenge in most secured transactions—classifying the collateral. Lenders will often take a security interest in anything of value, and the listed items all have value. Not all of them, however, are subject to Article 9. The sums due from the recording company for services rendered are either accounts or payment intangibles. *See* §9-102(a)(2). The tort claim is a "commercial tort claim" and falls within Article 9. *See* §9-109(d)(13)(B), which provides that Article 9 does not apply to assignments of tort claims other than commercial tort claims. Article 9 does not apply to transfer of the insurance claim. §9-109(d)(8). The deposit account does not arise out of a consumer transaction and, therefore, is covered by Article 9. *See* §§9-109(a)(1) and 9-109(d)(13). (The Code leaves to non-Code law questions concerning the transfer of deposit accounts as security in a consumer transaction. Most of those questions are matters for assignment law. Under assignment law, transfer of a chose in action is not good against third parties unless they have notice of it or, in some cases, unless they acknowledge the assignment. It is not unusual for a bank taking such assets to ask the obligor (the Irish bank) to acknowledge the

assignment by "attorning," that is, by expressly agreeing to pay whatever is due to the lender rather than to Andy Swinger. That attornment is easier to obtain in some cases than it is in others.)

Section 3. The Concept of Security

18. By now you know that Seller may not sneak the press away. Seller's remedies are its common law remedies: suit for the balance due, levying on the property, judicial sale. These remedies are notoriously time-consuming and, therefore, inefficient. In collections, delay is deadly. During the time that Seller is waiting for Debtor to file an answer to Seller's complaint, Debtor is usually doing one of the following: letting the drill press rust in the rain, letting insurance coverage lapse, failing to maintain the drill press, selling the drill press and skipping town with the proceeds, filing in bankruptcy.

19. If Seller has a security interest, it may repossess the press without notice, as long as Seller does not breach the peace. *See* §9-609. Taking the press in the middle of the night from a vacant lot is probably not breaching the peace. Taking it from the lot in broad daylight is probably not breaching the peace, unless Buyer resists the repossession. Repossession involving trespass or any threats of violence (by Seller or Buyer) is probably a breach of the peace. If Buyer will not let Seller repossess the press peaceably, Seller may maintain an action in replevin. In theory, that relief is summary and should not entail the kind of judicial delays that characterize an action for debt.

Once Seller repossesses the press, it may sell it in accordance with Part 6 of Article 9. That sale is quicker and less costly than the judicial sale. *See* Problems 202 to 207.

Buyer's bankruptcy invokes the automatic stay provision of the Bankruptcy Code. Bankruptcy Code §362. It suffices to say now that the stay prevents Seller from acting against Buyer in any way. The Bankruptcy Code protects Seller, however, by requiring Buyer's trustee to take possession of all assets, to conserve them for Buyer's creditors and allowing termination of the automatic stay if the trustee fails to provide "adequate protection" as provided in §361.

Generally under bankruptcy law, Seller will be preferred as a perfected secured creditor.

20. In fact, Article 9 often protects purchasers in good faith. Here, if Buyer was in the business of selling drill presses, §9-320(a), a provision that is the subject of Problems 127 through 136, would protect Sub-Buyer. As we see there, buyers in ordinary course should not have to check the title of their sellers. The policy that protected the buyer in ordinary course of the watch from the watch merchant in Problem 6 applies here. If sub-buyer cannot fit into one of the good-faith purchase rules, she takes the press subject to the seller's security interest. *See* §9-315(a)(1).

Section 4.   *Creating the Security Interest: The Security Agreement*

21. As a general rule, all of them are bound, though there are exceptions. Once Debtor has conveyed an interest in the molding machines to Secured Party, all subsequent transferees take subject to that conveyance. This conclusion follows from the first rule of conveyancing law, which §9-201(a) codifies. Note, however, that §9-201(a) provides that it controls only to the extent that the Code does not otherwise provide. *The exceptions to §9-201 comprise the bulk of Article 9 study.*

22. Parts a and b of this question illustrate two of the many exceptions in the Act to the general rule of §9-201(a) that the security agreement binds the whole world.

   a. Debtor's failure to execute a security agreement could be fatal under §9-203(b).
   b. The failure to perfect the security interest will be fatal when Secured Party comes into conflict with a later secured party that does perfect, *see* §9-322, or with lien reditors and the debtor's trustee in bankruptcy. *See* §9-317(a)(2); Bankr. Code §544(a)(1).
   c. and d.   The location of title is immaterial. *See* §9-202.

23. The security agreement describes the collateral as "inventory, equipment, and accounts, now owned or hereafter acquired or arising." The snow shovels are inventory. *See* §9-102(a)(48)(B). The sums due from the retailers are accounts. *See* §9-102(a)(2). Both, then, are covered by the security agreement. (However, the bank cannot have a security interest in the shovels as of May 1 because Debtor does not have rights in the collateral on that date, §9-203(b)(2). Nor can the bank have an enforceable security interest in the accounts on May 1, because they have yet to come into existence.) The forklift trucks are equipment and therefore also come within the security agreement. *See* §9-102(a)(33). The bank will have an enforceable security interest in them on August 1. The money due under the copyright license is a payment intangible (a particular subset of general intangibles) and, therefore, is not covered by the security agreement. *See* §9-102(a)(42) & (61). The checks are proceeds from the sale of inventory. Unless the security agreement otherwise provides, a secured party automatically has a security interest in the proceeds of its collateral. *See* §9-315(a)(2). Because the hinges, doorknobs, and other items were inventory and because the bank had a security interest in the inventory, it has a security interest in the checks as well.

   (Note that the proceeds definition section, §9-102(a)(64), defines proceeds in the broadest terms. The burden of proof in proceeds cases, however, can limit the secured party's interest. If the secured party cannot prove that the proceeds are from the sale, exchange, or other disposition of its collateral, generally the secured party has no rights in the proceeds. That proof burden is often heavy. Disputes over "cash proceeds" such as the 13 checks in the problem (*see* §9-102(a)(g)) of course, rarely arise. If the debtor is in trouble, it tends to spend those cash proceeds in a flash.)

24. Joe's failure to sign the security agreement may prove fatal, though some courts have been generous with the secured party, regarding as done that which ought to have been done or looking to the intent of the parties.

The secured party can attempt to salvage the situation with one or both of two different approaches. One is to focus on the definition of "security agreement" in §9-102(a)(73). That definition incorporates the broad definition of "agreement" in §1-201(b)(3) [§1-201(3)] as the "bargain of the parties in fact as found in their language or by implication from other circumstances." Thus, the agreement might be construed to include all documents signed, including the financing statement that reflects at least the intent to grant a security interest. Courts that have bought this theory compare the documents to a collage. A second approach is to focus on the definition of "authenticate," which has replaced the requirement of signing the security agreement. "Authenticate" includes the notion of "processing a record" with the present intent . . . to adopt or accept a record." §9-102(a)(7). The bank might argue that Joe's review of the package of documents, his signing of most of them and his failure to reject the security agreement document was an effective "processing" with intent to accept the security agreement. (Tough bankruptcy judges, of which there are plenty, will not provide much comfort for this secured party.)

Late signing of the security agreement is better than no signing, but the late signing may have the effect of rendering the date of the transfer August 1 instead of May 1. That change in the facts will have significance in bankruptcy, as later study of Bankruptcy Code §547 illustrates. (*See* Problems 194-199.)

25. The question here is whether First Bank has an interest in the computer equipment or only in Debtor's leasehold in the equipment. If the lease is a true lease, Debtor's only interest in the equipment is a leasehold, and Debtor cannot transfer more than the leasehold to First Bank. If the lease is not a true lease but a disguised sales agreement wherein the lessor's retention of title operates as retention of a security interest, then First Bank has a security interest in the equipment, and the priority will depend on the rules of §9-317 and subsequent sections, which sort out disputes of this kind.

Often it is not easy to determine whether an equipment lease is a true lease or a disguised sale. Sections 1-201(b)(35) and 1-203 [§1-201(37)] attempt to answer the question. Under that section, the lease in this problem is probably a true lease. First Bank's interest is in the leasehold, that is, the bank has the right to retain the equipment if the bank pays the rent to the lessor. At the end of the lease term, First Bank would have to return the equipment to the lessor.

26. This problem, taken from a rather famous case, illustrates the operation of the after-acquired property clause found so often in security agreements taken by banks or finance companies in connection with working capital loans. In fact, the notion that inventory and accounts "revolve" is indispensable to the classic working capital loan that is so important to small and medium-sized enterprises.

The answers are as follows:

a. Commercial is a purchaser.

b. It has given value.

c. It probably has acted in good faith, though the answer to that question is less clear under the definition of "good faith" as it has been revised since the Fifth Circuit decided the *Samuels* case. (The definition now includes "observance of reasonable commercial standards of fair dealing." The farm producers would argue that claiming a "security interest" in unpaid inventory is not fair.)

d. The farm producers' interest is merely reservation of a security interest.

e. Yes. Commercial will probably defeat the farmers, then, unless a state or federal statute interdicts application of the Code.

f. The purchase-money priority rule of §9-324(b) supports the Article 2 analysis that gives Commercial, as a good faith purchaser for value, good title as against the farmers. Had the farmers complied with that section, they could have obtained priority over Commercial. Federal law and some state statutes alter the result here when the sellers to the debtor are farmers. Farmers, the legislatures apparently believe, are not sophisticated enough to comply with §9-324(b) or, given the exigencies of livestock sales and prices, cannot be expected to act as quickly as the section requires. The non-Code statutes are limited to farm sellers; non-farm sellers must comply with the section to avail themselves of the priority against Commercial. *See* Section 24 for more on reclamation.

27. The language of the security agreement governs the result. If the security agreement recites that the conveyance is to secure the loan for the equipment (alternative a), as many equipment security agreements would, the later advance to cover payroll would not be covered. "Dragnet clauses" in security agreements (alternative b) provide that the collateral will secure all indebtedness of any kind whatsoever. The clause set forth in alternative b would protect the bank in this problem. The comments to §9-204 indicate that it does not matter that the nature of the second loan differs from the nature of the first. *See* §9-204, cmt. 5.

28. In this modified example, CNC is a secured party and may avail itself of the remedies afforded a secured party under Part 6 of Article 9. Repossession is one of those remedies. *See* §9-609(a). The parties do not have to describe the agreement as a security agreement. Article 9 applies to any transaction intended to create a security interest. The CNC-ABC transaction reflects that intent. *See* §2-401(1) (second sentence), §1-201(b)(35) [§1-201(37)] & §9-109(a)(1).

29. The place in the Code to begin answering this problem is § 9-203(b)(3)(A): a security interest becomes enforceable against the debtor with respect to the collateral in this context when the debtor has authenticated a security agreement that provides a description of the collateral. Section 9-108(a) provides that a description is sufficient "if it reasonably identifies what is described." Section 9-108(b) adds a gloss to that helpful definition by providing a list of examples of reasonable descriptions. One type of

permitted description is the "type of collateral" as defined in Article 9; for example, "inventory," "equipment," or "accounts." Where the parties simply use the type of collateral as a description, the issue can arise, as it does in the problem, whether the parties intended to have the security interest attach to (become enforceable against) property of the type described that is acquired by the debtor *after* the security agreement is executed. The general rule is that after-acquired equipment is generally not covered by a security agreement covering "equipment." A security agreement that is supposed to include after-acquired equipment should recite that it includes after-acquired equipment. On the other hand, many courts consider inventory and accounts as such fleeting collateral that they automatically give the secured party a security interest in after-acquired collateral of that nature unless the security agreement indicates the contrary. In other words, the mere use of the terms "inventory" and/or "accounts" to describe collateral may reflect the parties' intent to include after-acquired property. The careful lawyer, however, will include language in the security agreement that grants the secured party an interest in not only the inventory and accounts on hand at the time but all after-acquired inventory and after-arising accounts.

30. This kind of loan is critical to the small enterprise that typically borrows on secured credit. Under §9-204(a), First Bank does have a security interest in the after-acquired inventory, and it does not matter that the bank left the inventory with Beer and let Beer sell it. The Code rejects pre-Code law to the contrary. *See* §9-205(a)(1)(a). Note that the rule in favor of the lender here is not one of favoring banks over other creditors. It is a rule designed to permit certain borrowers to obtain credit.

31. The three elements of attachment are set out in §9-203(b): (1) value; (2) debtor's rights in the collateral; and (3) one of the four events in subsection (3), a signed security agreement describing the collateral or possession pursuant to agreement being the two most common. For a security interest to attach, all three events must occur. Attachment occurs at the instant when the last of the required conditions is satisfied.

    a. Under Article 9, Bank does not have an enforceable security interest in the notes unless Bank proves that Debtor delivered the notes as collateral pursuant to a security agreement, §9-203(b)(3)(A) or (B), and not for safekeeping. If, however, Bank satisfies the requirements of § 4-210(a), it will have an Article 4 security interest, a security interest that arises by operation of law and that is generally not governed by Article 9. *See* §9-109(a)(6).

    b. May 3. The last required event is Debtor's acquisition of rights in the inventory collateral. §9-203(b)(2).

    c. May 3. On that date, Debtor obtained a "special property and an insurable interest" in the machine. *See* §2-501(1). Some authority suggests that Debtor does not have sufficient interest until it has the right to possession of the after-acquired property as against Seller.

    d. May 2. The binding commitment on May 1 constitutes "value." §1-204 [§1-201(44)].

    e. May 3. It is a common practice for the debtor to sign a note, security agreement and financing statement before the secured party makes or commits to make the loan or deliver goods on credit. Absent a promise ("binding commitment"), the secured party does not give value until it actually extends credit or performs the sales contract.

f. May 2, if Debtor has inventory on that date; if not, May 3.

g. The problem obviously assumes that Debtor has inventory at all times. In that case, the security interest in the inventory first arises on May 2. Under §9-315(a)(2), a security interest in favor of Bank attaches to any identifiable proceeds of the inventory. The security interest in the promissory note, which is "proceeds" from the sale of inventory, cannot arise until the debtor has an interest in it. For the note, the security interest attaches on May 3.

Section 5. Definitions

32. None of these items fit the definition of "account." *See* §9-102(a)(2). It is remotely possible, but unlikely, that the bank can show that one or more of these items were purchased with proceeds from the accounts. In that case, the item would be proceeds of proceeds, and the bank would have a security interest in it. *See* §§9-102(a)(64), 9-315(a)(2). *See* Section 15 for more on proceeds.

33. All of these items fit the "inventory" definition except for f. For goods to qualify as inventory, they must be sold in the ordinary course of business. §9-102, cmt. 4a. Assuming that Debtor does not often sell used machinery, this occasional sale would not make the machine inventory. The machine would remain equipment. §9-102(a)(33).

34. Only Problems b, c, and d(iii) describe accounts. Problem a is not an account because it is not related to any of the events listed in §9-102(a)(2). A pure loan like that in Problem a should be represented by a promissory note, which would be an instrument. *See* §9-102(a)(47) & cmt. 5(c). Debts represented by instruments, as (probably) in a and definitely in d(i), are excluded from the definition of account. §9-102(a)(2)(2d i). If not represented by a negotiable note, the property interest (the right to repayment of the loan) is a payment intangible. *See* §9-102(a)(42) & (61). The lease is chattel paper. *See* §9-102(a)(11).

35. Section 9-404 is the section that describes the assignment of an account and the rights of the various parties.

a. Yes, Article 9 applies, and First Factor should obtain a written assignment authenticated by the debtor. That document will be a security agreement. (As we see later, First Factor must also perfect its security interest.)

b. i.   An account. §9-102(a)(2).
    ii. Assignor (debtor). §9-102(a)(28)(B).
    iii. Assignee (secured party). §9-102(a)(72)(D).
    iv. Account debtors. §9-102(a)(3).

c. The customers may pay Seller, but if Seller does not remit the money to First Factor, the customers will have to pay First Factor and will end up paying twice. §9-406(a). The debtor may be suspicious of a letter that purports to direct its payments to a hitherto unknown recipient. If so, it may demand proof of the assignment. Until that proof arrives, the debtor may continue to pay the original creditor (the assignor). §9-406(c). Presumably this demand must be made in good faith. The clause is not enforceable. *See* §9-406(d)(1). (The struggle to convince the common law courts to render choses in action, such as accounts, assignable was arduous. The law merchant had recognized that need for centuries when the King's courts began exercising jurisdiction over merchant matters. The story is a part of the downfall of the feudal notion that property is personal to its owner—a concept the merchants, of course, found wholly unacceptable. The greater concern of the judges at the Guildhall, however, was with multiplicity of lawsuits and uncontrollable increases in litigation. Those fears have only now been realized but largely not in the merchant context, where filing a lawsuit is courting a reputation as (1) a sore loser, or (2) one who cannot plan transactions properly.)

d. No. §9-406(a). Again, the debtor may request reasonable proof that the notice is valid. §9-406(c). (A young lawyer (Dolan) once delivered to a leading member of the bar a notice of assignment of a chose in action. The curmudgeonly lawyer in the well-appointed office gave the youngster a frosty reception. "We'll look into this and see whether we will comply. We agreed to pay [A], and I don't see why we should have to do business with your firm's client who is a stranger to us" (and a competitor of his client, he might have added). The neophyte resisted the temptation to tell the old so-and-so he had no choice and that if he paid the assignor, his client would be the poorer. To his credit, the lawyer called later to say that his client would comply with the assignment. He was, after all, a good lawyer—nasty, but good.)

e. Yes. Any other rule would be grossly unfair.

f. Probably yes. Section 9-406(a) makes clear that notice must include a statement that payment is to be made to the assignee.

36. No and yes. This sale is not an Article 9 secured transaction (§9-109(d)(4)), but the law of assignment codified in §9-406 requires the buyer to notify the account debtors or run the risk that they will pay the seller and thereby be discharged on their account obligations.

Section 6. Defining Proceeds

37. The items in parts a, b, c, f, h, i, and j are proceeds under the definition in §9-102. (You will find that some older cases say that lease payments, as in question j, are not proceeds. These are now dealt with in the statute. In any

event, the older cases were wrong. Leased equipment is used up by the lessee, and the lease payments in part compensate the lessor for this used-up value.) The check for the down payment on the used car in part d would be proceeds only if the used car was taken in trade for a new car. In that case, the $500 is proceeds of proceeds—something received on the sale of a car that was proceeds. Proceeds are collateral under §9-102(a)(12)(A), so proceeds of proceeds are proceeds for purposes of §9-102(a)(12)(A) & (64); *see also* cmt. 13c.

The $200 in part e is not proceeds because we do not know how much is from the sale of new cars and how much is from repair work. If the bank can establish that, say, $150 in the account is from new car deposits, the bank would be entitled to that money as proceeds. In questions e and h, the proceeds have been mixed with cash that is not proceeds. It thus will be necessary to figure out how to determine what part of the cash is proceeds. These tracing rules, such as the lowest intermediate balance rule, are discussed in Section 8. Usually, proceeds are the last funds to leave an account and thus are subject to claims by secured creditors. That rule sounds very pro-creditor, but the fact is that creditors rarely can show where their cash proceeds went. Generally, the creditor loses the cash proceeds not as a matter of law but under the facts. He cannot prove that the account contains proceeds, or he cannot prove how much is proceeds. *See* Problem 45.

38. The only fair rule requires the secured party to establish the fact that property is proceeds of the creditor's collateral. There is one presumption, favorable to creditors, under the lowest intermediate balance rule discussed in Section 8.

39. Yes, we think so. Section 9-102(a)(64)(A) says that "whatever" is received on the sale of collateral is proceeds; and sections 9-203(f) and 9-315(a)(2) say that the secured party gets the proceeds from the disposition of the collateral.

40. The issue here is whether the entitlements are proceeds. There being no crops, the bank had no collateral, and the entitlements were not received on the disposition of the crops. On the other hand, the decision of the farmer not to plant in return for the entitlements was a disposition of his right to plant the crops and an exchange of the potential crop for the entitlements, included under §9-102(a)(64)(A). Yet, that is not a "right arising out [the] collateral," *see* §9-102(a)(64)(C), there not having been any collateral. A modicum of violence to the language will render these entitlements proceeds. Some courts have considered that violence a proper price to pay for what would appear to be the essential purpose of the section. Some view them as general intangibles. There is contrary authority, which turns on the notion that there was no intent here to grant the secured party an interest in the entitlements.

Note that the Code's policy section not only authorizes but commands liberal implementation of the Code. Section 1-103(a) [§1-102] commands the courts to construe Code provisions liberally. "This Act must be liberally construed and applied to promote its underlying purposes and policies." Comment 1 makes it clear that it is consistent with that command for courts to apply a provision even when its language appears to interdict application and to apply a provision beyond its literal terms. This "casecode" approach makes practice of commercial law a lot more challenging than literal application of the Code would do. Judges and lawyers who use the Code must discern the Code's underlying policies; that is, they must characterize facts and transactions in a way that makes sense out of the Code and their intended use of it. To some extent, all modern American law is an exercise in this form of realism and its implicit rejection of formalism. Yet that conclusion is facile. Formalism survives too in the Code. Knowing when to invoke realism and when to invoke formalism is part of the challenge and renders the practice of commercial law more than reading cases and applying statutory language.

41. The calves are not proceeds in the view of the courts that have considered the matter. The entitlements in the preceding section came into being after many banks took their security interests. It was a little unfair to deprive them of the entitlements when they came into being after the date of the security agreement. Bankers know, however, where baby cows come from. (In rural areas, bankers know more about animal husbandry and agronomy than law professors. They usually know more about banking too and often know a lot about Article 9.) If the banker wanted a security interest in the calves, she should have included a reference to them in the security agreement ("now owned or hereafter owned" or "and any natural increase thereof"). Calves are not received on the disposition of the cow.

Section 7. Commingling and Accessions

42. The sellers will divide the proceeds according to the ratio established by §9-336(f)(2). Note that it is the *cost* of the metals, not their proportion, that determines the ratio. If the cost of the brass is $120,000, §9-336(f)(2) gives $37,500 to Copper and $37,500 to Zinc. As you see from the comments, the calculations can become involved when there are multiple creditors, a mix of perfected and unperfected security interests, or a mix of over- and under-secured creditors.

43. Because the ingots retain their identity, we are now in the realm of accessions, governed by §9-335. Section 9-335(a) makes clear that the security interest persists, so both Copper and Zinc remain secured creditors. Unlike §9-336 for commingled goods, though, §9-335 defers to other law on priorities. §9-335(c). You thus do not have the information you need, in particular the dates of filing or perfection, to answer this question.

44. They must show first that they had a security interest in the ingredients they supplied. Then they need to show the respective costs, the costs of each ingredient, and the cost of the bread.

Section 8. *Tracing*

45. This problem introduces the lowest intermediate balance rule of trust law. We could use last-in, first-out or first-in, last-out or some other accounting rule for determining what happens to commingled funds, but the courts have generally used trust law and its lowest intermediate balance rule. The rule is easier to apply than it is to state.

May 1 $10,000.

May 2 $5,000.

May 3 $1,000. Note that the lowest intermediate balance rule assumes that the proceeds sink to the bottom of the account and do not come out until all non-proceeds are exhausted. On May 1, only 50 percent of the account is proceeds, but on May 2 and 3, the account is 100 percent proceeds. The withdrawals were initially of non-proceeds. When the non-proceeds were gone, the withdrawals began to deplete the proceeds to $5,000 on May 2 and $1,000 on May 3.

May 4 $6,000. Because there has been a deposit of proceeds of $5,000, that deposit and the previous lowest intermediate balance of $1,000 yield a total proceeds figure on May 4 of $6,000.

May 5 $1,000.

May 6 $1,000. The deposits that yield the high account balance on this date were not deposits of proceeds. They cannot, therefore, augment the amount of proceeds in the account. The proceeds balance remains $1,000, the lowest intermediate balance from May 5.

Section 9. *More on Classifying Collateral*

46. No. *See* §9-108(c). Careful drafters use Article 9 categories. The rule of §9-108(c) is perhaps an instance of lingering formalism, but most authorities feel comfortable with it. "All property" will not work in a security agreement, though it will for a financing statement. §9-504.

47. Under the security agreement, First Bank does not get the bill or the oil for which it stands. The agreement does not cover documents. The negotiable bill of lading (something that gives its holder rights in goods against someone, much as a check gives its holder rights in money held by someone) is a document. §9-102(a)(30).

The bank might argue that it is perfected as a pledgee of the document. In order to take a security interest in a document by pledge, however, the bank must take pursuant to the debtor's security agreement. *See* §9-203(b)(3)(B). If it is clear that the bank took possession of the bill pursuant to the oral security agreement, the bank has satisfied §9-

203(b)(3)(B) & cmt. 4. In that event, the security interest will attach. Failure to have a security interest in the document will defeat the bank's claim.

48. They all satisfy the "inventory" definition in §9-102(a)(48).

49. The hinges, door hardware, and heating oil are inventory. The rest is equipment.

50.
    a. Cash is money, and Article 9 applies to money but has no separate category for money. We'll see later that the only way to perfect a security interest in money is to take possession of it. *See* §9-312(b)(3).

    b. A promissory note is an instrument. *See* §9-102(a)(65). It is not an account. Though rights to payment for services fall within the definition of accounts, that definition specifically excludes rights to payment evidenced by instruments. §9-102(a)(2)(2d i).

    c. This agreement is an account because the obligation is not evidenced by chattel paper or by an instrument. *See* §9-102(a)(2). [The agreement is not an instrument because it is not negotiable in form and is not the kind of obligation that is transferred by delivery and indorsement. *See* §9-102(a)(47). The agreement is not chattel paper because it does not include an interest in goods. Leases and installment sales agreements with security agreements are the most common types of chattel paper. *See* §9-102(a)(11). An account is an intangible. It differs from a general intangible, §9-102(a)(42), in that it arises from the sale or lease of goods or the sale of services or for the other marginally important (in this course, at least) items of property listed in the definitional section. *See* §9-102(a)(2).]

    d. The oriental rug is consumer goods. *See* §9-102(a)(23).

51. He has inventory, the 20 computers on the floor, and a document of title, the bill of lading. *See* §§9-105(1)(f), 9-109(4).

52. The Steinway and Baldwin are equipment; the Mason & Hamlin is consumer goods. *See* §9-102(a)(23) & (33). Note that the definition of consumer goods turns on the *actual* use of the goods. Elsewhere in consumer law, most notably in federal warranty law, the line is drawn according to the *normal* use of the goods.

53.
    a. This is a purchase money security interest. *See* §9-103.

    b. Cincinnatus has a security interest in consumer goods. *See* §9-102(a)(23).

    c. The bank will have two security interests. First, as assignee of Cincinnatus, it will get what Cincinnatus had, namely, a security interest in consumer goods, the piano. Second, it will have a security interest in the paper that Cincinnatus assigned to the bank. That paper is chattel paper, and the assignment of chattel paper is a secured transaction under Article 9. *See* §9-109(a)(3).

    d. Cincinnatus does not need to file to perfect its security interest in B's piano. Section 9-309(1) creates for purchase money security interests in consumer goods an exception to the general filing requirement. Cincinnatus must file as to the other two pianos, however, because they are not consumer goods; and even though Cincinnatus has a purchase money security interest, it is not in consumer goods. (It is best to think of this rule as an exception for the department store or national retailer that formerly more than now used to sell "big ticket" items (consumer durables such as refrigerators and washing machines) on secured credit. The customer made a 10 percent down payment and paid the balance over time. The customer granted the seller a security interest by executing a retail installment sales agreement at the time of the purchase. Because the transactions were relatively small and because the goods normally left commerce after the consumer took possession of them, the Code drafters agreed with the national retailers and the department stores that it would only clutter the filing system to require a filing in these transactions. Retailers use the retail installment sales agreement far less frequently today than they did in the 1950s when the prior version of Article 9 was drafted.)

e. The bank may either file or take possession of the chattel paper. *See* §§9-312(a), 9-313(a).

f. No. Cincinnatus does not need to file because it holds a purchase money security interest in consumer goods. The bank does not need to file because it is assignee of a perfected security interest. *See* §9-310(c).

g. No. The Code does not distinguish sales of chattel paper from assignments of chattel paper as security for a debt. *See* §9-109(a)(3). However, assignments purely for collection are not covered by Article 9, as they are considered insufficiently commercial. §9-109(d)(5).

54. Investor's interest is not investment property. *See* §9-102(a)(49). We do not see this right as a "security entitlement," which is defined in Article 8 on investment securities. *See* §8-102(a)(17). (You are referred to this by comment 6 to §9-102.) Security entitlements consist of rights in securities held by a stockbroker or other third party. Probably the investor's property interest is a general intangible. Filing is the only proper mode of perfection for a general intangible. *See* §9-310(a). Because the secured party cannot take possession of an intangible, one cannot pledge an intangible. Accounts cannot ordinarily be pledged either. They are intangible too. (You have to arrive at this conclusion by negative implication. Section 9-313(a) lists everything that may be the subject of a pledge. It does not include intangibles for obvious reasons. Ever see an intangible? *See* comment 2 to §9-313 for a more complete list. There is a small exception for occasional assignments of accounts, which perfect on attachment. *See* §9-309(2).)

(Later problems deal with the perfection rules in more detail. Reference to perfection is helpful here to illustrate the need to discern the type of collateral early in the analysis of a secured transaction. The perfection rules are the locus of some of the important differences in the Code's treatment of various kinds of collateral.)

55.   a.   *D's* business deposit accounts are collateral the rights in which are governed by Article 9. §9-109(d)(13) & cmt. 16. The security agreement must, however, identify deposit accounts as collateral. §9-108. Note that filing a financing statement will not perfect a security interest in deposit accounts. The secured party can only perfect by control. §9-312(b)(1). Since First Bank is both lender and banker, it has control automatically. §9-104(a)(1). *D's personal* accounts remain outside of Article 9. An account mixing personal and business funds is a terrible idea for many, many reasons. If, however, *D* has been incautious enough to do this, her account will fall within Article 9. The exclusion in §9-109(d)(13) is for consumer *transactions*, which this loan is not.

     b.   For Second Bank to effect control over a deposit account in First Bank, it must either enter into a control agreement with both *D* and First Bank, or it must become the customer of the account. §9-104(a)(2) & (3). First Bank need not enter into the control agreement, however. §9-342. *D* could simply make Second Bank the customer, as defined in §4-104(a)(5). This is a problematic solution. It might be easier to close the accounts at First and move them to Second.

56.   The bank can take a security interest in the aircraft and in the partners' notes, which are promissory notes and instruments. *See* §9-102(a)(47) & (65). The bank may perfect its security interest in the notes by filing or taking possession. *See* §§9-312(a), 9-313(a). It will probably not be able to take possession of the aircraft itself but might designate the lessee (some airline) as its agent. At least one court has accepted the theory that this constitutes possession for perfection purposes. We wouldn't rely too heavily on that theory. It is probably best to file as to the aircraft under the federal statute that governs such filings.

57.   There is no need to file if Jones uses the player more than 50 percent of the time as consumer goods. *See* §9-309(1). There is no need to file if Jones starts using the player as consumer goods and then uses it in his office. Jones *bought* the player for personal use. That its use changed does not force the creditor to file. *See* §9-102, cmt. 4a. If Jones' initial use of the player is as equipment, the retailer must file because there is no exception in the filing requirements of §9-309 for purchase money security interests in equipment. Many goods can be put to either personal or commercial use. At the time it makes the loan, the prudent financer will ask the borrower what he plans to do with the equipment. For small-ticket items the creditor may choose not to file anyway, given the size of the filing fee and the usually modest risk of default. For large-ticket items, it may wish to file in ambiguous cases for safety's sake.

58.   In the hands of the hennery, the eggs are farm products. *See* §9-102(a)(34)(D). The eggs are inventory in the hands of the wholesaler and the market, *see* §9-102(a)(48)(B), and consumer goods while in Smith's refrigerator, *see* §9-102(a)(23).

59. They are farm products no matter who owns them. All of the livestock is in the hands of the feedlot operator, who is engaged in farming operations. *See* §9-102(a)(34)(B).

60. These are all probably general intangibles. *See* §9-102(a)(42). Note that "payment intangible" is a subset of "general intangible." Except for f, these assets also satisfy the "payment intangibles" definition. §9-102(a)(61). Item f may be goods if the software is embedded in goods other than the medium in which it is transmitted. §9-102(44).

61. Chicago surely has a purchase money security interest. First Credit has one too, if it can trace the funds and show that they went to Chicago. *See* §9-103(a)(2). The credit union does not need to file a financing statement because it holds a purchase money security interest in consumer goods. *See* §9-309(1). The credit union can protect itself by making the loan proceeds check payable to Jones and Chicago jointly. In some large purchase money transactions, the lender will hold the closing at its own offices to ensure that it can satisfy the tracing requirement. The credit union would not satisfy the tracing requirement and would not be a purchase money secured party if Jones used the credit union's loan proceeds to pay tuition. Money may be fungible as a general rule but not for purposes of §9-103(a)(2).

62.
    a. The dealer has a security interest in equipment. *See* §9-102(a)(33).
    b. First Bank has a security interest in two kinds of collateral. It takes Dealer's security interest in the equipment under the law of assignment. By virtue of §9-109(a)(3), it also has a security interest in the chattel paper that the dealer took from its customers.
    c. Note that because the dealer has filed and perfected, the bank is automatically perfected as to the equipment. §9-310(c). The assignment of a perfected security interest does not require the assignee (the bank) to file again.
    d. The bank must file as to the chattel paper or must take possession of it.

(Note that there is no purchase money exception from the filing requirement as to the personal computers. It is true that the dealer had a purchase money security interest in the computers, but the computers are not consumer goods in the hands of the farmers and other small businesses. They are equipment, and there is no exception from the filing requirements for purchase money security interests in equipment.)

Section 10. The Financing Statement

63.
    a. The answers are the same whether the debtor is a farmer or a feed store operator. (What matters is the debtor's location, which in turn depends on the nature of the debtor. *See* §9-307(b). File with the Secretary of State's office in Lansing (MI's capital) for this collateral when, as here, the debtor is an individual. The place where an

individual does business is not relevant. §9-307(b)(1). If the debtor is a corporation, file in the Secretary of State's office in the state of the corporation's incorporation §9-307(e). If the debtor is an unincorporated firm and has more than one place of business in different states, file in the state where its chief executive office is located. §9-307(b)(3).)

b. File in Michigan. The dairy is the account debtor (§9-102(a)(3)), whose location is irrelevant.

c. File in Ohio.

d. The boiler may be a fixture. In that case, §9-501(a)(1)(B) provides that the filing should be local (in the county where the building is situated; Wayne County, Michigan), and the filing must conform to special rules for "fixture filings." *See* §9-502(b).

e. File centrally in the state where the lift manufacturer is incorporated, if it is incorporated, otherwise in the state where it has its chief executive office.

f. File for accounts in the state where the debtor, here the tool and die manufacturer, is located. It may not, of course, be located in Illinois. See the answer to the previous subparts of this question. Do not file where the account debtors are located.

g. So we lied when we told you we wouldn't cover organizations other than individuals and business corporations. The rule for national banks and their branches is found in §9-307(f). First Bank should file in the District of Columbia, unless Federal law provides otherwise.

h. You cannot file as to money but must take possession of it. *See* §9-312(b)(3). Cash, however, will often arise upon the disposition of other collateral, say, the sale of inventory. In that case, the security interest in these "identifiable cash proceeds" is automatically perfected. *See* §9-315(d)(2). *See* §9-315(b) as to how to identify inventory collateral's cash proceeds that are commingled with other cash.

i. The bill is a document, and the rules for documents govern, the nature of the property covered by the document notwithstanding. *See* §9-102(a)(30), §9-312(c). It is permissible but risky to file as to negotiable documents, *see* §9-312(a). The filing must be central in the state where the debtor is located. Filing as to documents is risky because, as we see later, a person who takes the document may take by due negotiation and defeat the perfected secured party. *See* §9-331(a).

j. The cattle is inventory. *See* §9-102(a)(48). File where the debtor is located.

k. The trotters are probably equipment if the debtor/owner is racing them. *See* §9-102(a)(33). File where the debtor is located. If the debtor/owner is leasing them to another person, the horses are inventory. Id. The place of filing is the same. If the debtor/owner is breeding them, of course, the horses would be farm products. The place of filing is still the same.

These last few questions illustrate the efficiency of the new filing rules. Under the old rules, the character of the collateral had much more of an effect on the place to file than under Revised Article 9.

Nonetheless, the filing rules can be complex. You cannot apply them without first identifying the nature of the collateral and consider whether there are multiple state transaction considerations. Lenders must know a good deal about the debtor: its name, whether it is a corporation, where it is located, the nature of its business, the use to which it will put the collateral. Commercial lenders are usually quite sophisticated in this analysis. Loan application forms ask the questions that elicit the information the lender needs to make the filing decision, and commercial credit departments check on critical facts that determine filing location.

Often, you will be able to rely on your client. But beware. There is a widespread practice among banks and commercial finance companies to take an opinion from the debtor's lawyer that the lender is perfected. You may think of yourself as a general practitioner unconcerned with the rules a bank needs to follow when it makes a secured loan. When that bank lends working capital to your hardware store client, however, you find that the bank makes one condition of the loan your opinion that the bank is fully secured with a first priority. The business planner that helps closely held companies structure their corporate and family affairs and helps them avoid unnecessary taxes may find a similar condition in the lease of a million-dollar machine from a bank subsidiary.

64.   a. The result may depend on the practices of the filing office. If it is clear that a computer search of filings against "A.B. Jones Manufacturing Co., Inc." would reveal the filing in the name of "A.B. Jones Mfg. Co.," §9-506(c) provides that the error is not seriously misleading and the filing good. If the filing agency's practices do not reveal the filing, however, the filing is surely bad. No lawyer worth her salt would take the risk of a misleading filing. Check the articles of incorporation on file with the Secretary of State.

Note: This is harsh, but you may as well learn it now as later. One of the most important parts of your practice as a lawyer is not going to be saving orphans from villains but will be getting little facts right, facts like the name of a debtor or the description of collateral. Incredibly, you will find that sometimes a client does not know his legal name. Businesses may use letterheads and the President of the United States may run for office under pseudonyms. The law, of course, could not care less that debtor Charles R. Hansen has been called "Skipper" by his friends for 70 years. As far as the law is concerned, he is Charles R. Hansen. When your administrative assistant types his name on the form as "Charles R. Hanson," or as "Skipper Hansen," moreover, the mistake is yours, not the assistant's. Lawyers are not just people who have a license to practice law. Lawyers are people who know that Hansen can be spelled with an "o" or an "e" and watch for the error every time. They know that Jimmy Carter is not James Carter's name until he changes it by legal proceedings, as he indeed did, unlike many other politicians.

When a merchant changes its name, the credit agencies send out an all-points bulletin. Name changes are big news in the credit industry. Only in the Old Testament do names receive more attention than in commerce. Of course, the law, especially as applied by some judges who never practiced commercial law and who never read the Old Testament, may not always have much respect for names and the clarity they bring to matters, especially matters of responsibility. But you will not rely in advance on such law. You will structure the transaction properly and avoid the potential problem. In some cases, of course, you will receive the file after someone else has messed up the transaction. Then you will have no choice but to rely on such law.

b. The herd surely falls within the farm products category. The race horse, as we suggest above, may be equipment, inventory, or farm products. You need more information. (If that information is unavailable and time is growing short, you might avoid the broad category designation and describe the collateral specifically as "one thoroughbred trotter, registered as 'Champion' with . . . ." Of course, you'd need information to use that description, too. And if information is really unavailable and time is really short, use all three descriptions in the financing statement. After all, the statement is merely a notice filing. Other creditors can determine the true state of affairs through inquiry.

c. Accuracy in the name of the secured party is less critical than is accuracy in the debtor's name. The filing system indexes use the debtor's name. Probably this type of error in the secured party's name will not render the filing seriously misleading. See comment 2 to §9-506.

d. i.   Probably this filing is bad.
    ii. Surely this filing is bad.
    iii & iv.   It does not matter in bankruptcy court and should not matter elsewhere.

65. Questions concerning the contents of a financing statement illustrate what we meant when we said that Revised Article 9 was not an easy statute. Section 9-502(a) provides that a financing statement (other than a real-property-related filing) is "sufficient" if it includes the name of the debtor, the name of the secured party, and indicates the collateral covered. In short, §9-502(a) provides for a true "notice" filing system, putting on searchers a duty to inquire based on the bare minimum of information. But the lawyer who includes only the §9-502(a) information runs a substantial risk that the financing statement will not be accepted for filing; and if the financing statement is not filed, it is worthless. Section 9-520 provides that the filing officer "must" refuse to accept for filing a financing statement that does not comply with §9-516(b). That section includes a laundry list of information included on the "uniform" financing statement form set forth in §9-521.

Note that the information referred to in this problem is all information listed in §9-516(b). Absence of that information could result in the clerk's refusal to file, which is embarrassing enough, and may be a big deal if the funds have already been disbursed or if the debtor needs the loan quickly.

Potential for mistakes in the content of an financing statement is one good reason why the careful secured party has the debtor authorize the filing of the financing statement, files it, and confirms the filing and priority before disbursing any loan proceeds.

Note also that, as a practical matter, the filing officer will have no way of knowing that §9-516(b) information is erroneous, and may therefore accept the financing statement as long the secured party lists information in each box. Under §9-520(c), that filing may be effective to perfect the security interest even if some of the information is incorrect.

Finally, remember that the secured party is not necessarily home free even if the filing is "effective." Section 9-338 provides that a party who gives value in reasonable reliance on erroneous information required by §9-516(b)(5) will take priority over the secured party. This rule makes sense because §9-516(b)(5) requires information that permits the party searching the records to identify and contact the debtor.

66. The secured party (the original Ace and now XYZ) has a problem if it is looking to after-acquired inventory or equipment as collateral for the buyer's debt. Usually in the sale of a business, the seller must be satisfied with a security interest in the inventory and equipment it sells and does not get a security interest in after-acquired property. To the extent the seller is relying on that after-acquired property, it will lose, if the property is acquired more than four months after the name change. *See* §9-507(c).

Subsequent lenders may also be confused here. When Ace Heating & Cooling (the buyer with the new name) seeks credit, its lender will search for filings under that name (Ace) as debtor and will find nothing or only filings against the old Ace. The lender would not find filing in favor of XYZ since that filing is under the debtor's prior name, ABC Co. If the new lender, then, is relying on the inventory and equipment Ace acquired from the seller, the lender might be surprised to learn that there is a pre-existing security interest—XYZ's.

Commercial lenders, of course, are well aware of this risk and ask borrowers whether they have done business under any other name within the last five years. Filings are good for five years. *See* §9-515(a). The unsophisticated lender may suffer from the confusion inherent in this arrangement. At least one court has found that the seller, knowing in advance that there would be a misleading name change, acted in bad faith by not refiling under the new name after the change.

67. Under §9-503(a)(1), the financing statement is effective only if it lists the actual name of the corporation. The name of a division will not be sufficient. So First Bank should list the debtor as Old Colony Hotel Corp. However, as a matter of prudence, the Bank should search under both names, since the cost of a search is small compared to the downside of litigation.

Incidentally, this is from a real case decided by a judge who did not share your authors' respect for certainty and who held a filing under the name "Hartford Inns" good. The name of this debtor is Old Colony Hotel

Corp. We think the drafters of §9-503(a) sought to overturn that kind of ruling.

Corporations have names that are spelled out usually in the first article of the corporate charter. The Secretary of State will not issue a charter to a company under a name that is already taken or a name that would cause confusion because of its similarity to an already chartered enterprise. States maintain registers of corporations chartered in the state or licensed to do business there and usually have telephone or internet services for those checking on the corporate name. Divisions are not corporations; they are profit centers or marketing entities created unilaterally by the corporation and do not constitute a separate person under the law. Subsidiaries, of course, are separate corporations and are incorporated separately. If a subsidiary borrows and grants a security interest, the subsidiary will be listed as the debtor on the financing statement and must authenticate it and the security agreement. Often related companies assist each other's borrowing. A parent's subsidiary may grant a security interest to secure the parent's debt. Lawyers structuring the transaction must be certain that the party that owns the collateral is designated as the debtor. Making the ownership determination can be problematic and may call for certified audits or opinions, or both, from the borrower's attorneys and auditors.

68. Normally, as you will see when you study the priority rules, the first lender to file prevails under the rule of §9-322(a)(1). Section 9-517 provides that this rule applies even when the filing officer mis-indexes the financing statement, First Bank has priority. Second Bank, in effect, pays for the filing officer's error and must seek relief under the state's tort claim act. *See* §9-517 and comment.

69. Corporate changes can create problems for secured lenders. An acquisition might take the form of a statutory merger where a debtor disappears and its assets and liabilities are assumed by the surviving corporation. Or the debtor might sell its assets to a new company and then dissolve. The debtor might acquire shares of the purchaser and dissolve the purchaser, with the "purchaser's" management and shareholders taking control of the debtor. Cautious and watchful secured parties spot these mergers, acquisitions, spin-offs, and other corporate transmogrifications and act promptly. The well-drafted security agreement will forbid such transactions without the lender's prior approval. In that event, the lender can take additional documentation, including new financing statements, to protect itself. Credit agencies will report this kind of activity. Lenders that adequately monitor their borrowers' activity will spot it.

Cases in which the sophisticated lender is unaware of the corporate change are rare. When they arise, courts will usually attempt to resolve the matter by literal application of the Code—an unsatisfactory resolution. Thus a lender may win if the merger takes one form and lose if it takes another, the result being adventitious. Section 9-508(a) provides that the rule of corporate successor liability generally governs the result. The merged company will be liable, of course, if the lender insists that the merged company execute a new security agreement covering all debts and all collateral, as most lenders aware of the situation will do.

We think the answers are:

a. Yes. ABC Wholesalers, Inc., as survivor of the merger, is vested with Wholesaler's assets and liabilities as a matter of law. Section 9-203(d) provides that ABC becomes bound by Wholesaler's security agreement. Whether First Bank's security interest is perfected is governed by 9-508. Because the name change makes the financing statement materially misleading, §9-508(b) applies. The interest is perfected in collateral existing at the time of the merger.

b. Yes. §9-508(b)(1).

c. No. §9-508(b)(2).

Section 11. Introduction to Fixtures

70. You cannot answer this question just from the definition of "fixtures" in §9-102(a)(41) because that definition refers to the "real property law" of the jurisdiction. However, if you have perchance forgotten some of that real property law, you can still avoid researching the finer points of the law of fixtures by being aware that §9-334, the Code provision that most specifically deals with fixtures, states in subsection (a) that "a security interest does not exist under this article in ordinary building materials incorporated into an improvement on land." (Note that this is really a scope provision that might more appropriately have been included in §9-109.) Therefore:

a. It may not be possible to take a security interest in the windows that will survive their incorporation into a building, because windows sound like ordinary building materials today. That result might not obtain in the case of a Tiffany window taken from an old building and incorporated into a new one.

b. In most jurisdictions, a photocopy machine is not a fixture. If the debtor is a business, the machine is equipment; and the filing should be central under §9-501(a)(2). Some lawyers instinctively fear giving opinions on whether something might constitute a fixture. They view the opinion in the first sentence of this answer as folly. To them, courts are unpredictable and might hold that the copier is a fixture, say, under the "institutional" approach or perhaps because the machine takes special wiring or because there was modification of the building to house the copier. To cover these remote possibilities, the ever-cautious lawyer will not assume that the copier is not a fixture.

[Note, however, that if it is a fixture, a central filing covering a copier will give the secured party priority. See §9-334(e)(2)(A) & (B). The central filing would be sufficient to perfect whether the machine is or is not a fixture.

You could run across a transaction in which the secured party financed a number of fixtures and used a fixture filing filed in the real estate records and containing the additional information required by §9-502(b). That filing is good as to the copier only if the court decides that the copier is a fixture. (Note that the readily-removable-office-machine exception and the not-used-in-the-operation-of-the-building exceptions of §9-334(e)(2)(A) & (B) apply only if the court finds that the equipment is a fixture. If it is not a fixture, those subsections do not apply; and only a centrally filed financing statement will suffice.)

In short, when in doubt, the transactional lawyer may be best advised to file centrally for readily removable factory office equipment. If the equipment fits into either §9-334(e)(2)(A) or (B), that filing will be good if the court finds that the equipment is a fixture, and it will be good if the court finds that the equipment is not a fixture.]

c. This is probably a fixture and will require a fixture filing filed locally. If the court finds it is not a fixture, a local fixture filing will not be sufficient. On the other hand, if it is a fixture, a centrally filed financing statement will not be sufficient unless the secured party can squeeze within one of the §9-334(e) exceptions to the general rule that real estate interest wins.

[Of course, there is no prohibition on filing a "regular" financing statement centrally *and* a fixture filing locally. A common practice (for example, when a transaction is intended by the parties to create a true lease rather than a security interest, *see* §9-505) is to make a "precautionary filing" in the event that a court misconstrues the parties' intent. This practice can be employed in the fixture context, although the nuisance and cost of a proper fixture filing (see the answer to problem 74 below), makes it common only in large dollar transactions. For example, where the dollar exposure is sufficient and there is a question whether the equipment falls within §9-334(e)(2), the secured party may choose to file a fixture filing that includes the statement that the parties do not intend the collateral to be a fixture, but that the filing is made as a matter of precaution. Since the cost of preparation and filing of even a fixture filing is generally trivial compared to the value of the sophisticated equipment (the type that has to be installed or secured to the real estate so as to create the risk of a fixture determination), conservative lenders and their counsel frequently resort to dual filing.]

d. This sounds like a fixture. Make a fixture filing.

e. There is at least one reported case holding this to be a fixture.

f. Professors White and Summers once proposed the rule that anything that could be removed by one worker with a crescent wrench in one hour should **not** be a fixture. Under that definition, this sign would be a fixture, since the truck and hoist are necessary to remove it. Make a fixture filing.

g. Absolutely not. Financing statement searches would be unreliable if debtors and secured parties could alter the filing rules. For this reason, courts do not give much weight to such clauses (especially those in boilerplate forms) in determining whether the good is a fixture.

71.   a. Yes, whether or not the court finds the property to be a fixture. Section 9-334(e)(3) protects the secured party against the trustee in bankruptcy. Bankruptcy Code §544(a)(3) reflects Congress' concern that Bankruptcy Courts not use the Bankruptcy Code to override the UCC, state law.

    b. The lender is unperfected. Filing locally is never "permitted" by Article 9 for equipment, and a local, non-fixture filing is not good for a fixture.

    c. Yes. A central filing will work to defeat a good faith purchaser of real estate only if the equipment falls within the §9-334(e)(2)(A) or (B) exceptions. §9-334(e)(3) grants the central-filing-only secured party priority over subsequent claimants with real property liens. However, the secured lender who has not made a fixture filing cannot use §9-334(e)(3) against a good faith *purchaser* of the real estate. That's the reason Congress decrees in the Bankruptcy Code that the trustee in bankruptcy, who normally has the rights of a good faith purchaser of real estate, does not have such rights in fixtures. *See* Bankruptcy Code §544(a)(3).

72. Any of them that the courts decide are fixtures. Fixtures follow the real estate. This is a rule of real property law, not commercial law. The Code's definition of "fixture" recognizes this principle. *See* §9-102(a)(41).

73.   a. Yes. See problem 70(a).

    b. If the machine is a fixture, the trustee will lose, because the secured party filed properly. If the machine is not a fixture, then the trustee will win because the local filing is not effective. See Problem 70(a).

    c. No, because the trustee has the rights of a lien creditor. *See* §9-102(a)(52).

    d. The secured party would win if the machine was not a fixture or if it was a fixture but was a "readily removable" factory machine within §9-334(e)(2)(A) or fell within the "not-in-the-operation" exception of §9-334(e)(2)(B). If the machine is a fixture and is not within those exceptions, the real estate mortgagee wins despite being later in time. §9-334(c).

74. This problem illustrates the nuisance of having to make a fixture filing. While it is easy to designate the filing as a fixture filing, it is not always easy to determine whether the legal description is satisfactory or to determine whether the debtor is a record owner without going into the real estate records. We counsel against any of the proposed short cuts. Deeds can contain a lawyer's or a scrivener's mistake. So can tax bills. You copy another lawyer's documents and you may be copying his mistakes. There is at least one case in which a secured party tried to make a local filing and filed in the wrong county. [The county line bisected a city.] The cautious lawyer may want a title search. Searches take time and cost money, neither of which make the fixture filing an attractive option.

The problem also illustrates the drafters' wisdom in fashioning §9-334(e)(2) & (3), which protect many secured lenders and their borrowers from the inconvenience and expense of having to make fixture filings, and the wisdom of the real estate lending industry to acquiesce in the exceptions to the fixture filing rule of those provisions.

75. All of these steps may be in order.

76. The correct answer is (a). Whether it defeats subsequent real estate purchasers will depend on whether the leased equipment is a fixture and, if so, whether §9-334(e) applies.

Section 12.   More on the Place to File

77.
    a. Secretary of State of Maryland.

    b. Secretary of State of Pennsylvania.

    c. Secretary of State of Mississippi as long as the debtor lives in Mississippi. If the debtor moves to another state, the lender should refile in the new state within four months of the move. *See* §9-316(a)(2). (Why do you suppose loan application forms ask potential borrowers to list their addresses for the last five years?) We study multi-state transactions in Section 14.

    d. Vermont Secretary of State.

    e. Same.

    f. Same.

    g. Delaware Secretary of State. International Baking will use these sums, accounts, as security for its loans. International Baking, then, is the debtor; and its location governs perfection.

    h. California Secretary of State.

    i. Michigan Secretary of State.

    j. Same.

78. Clearly Ace was not perfected on May 1 because the filing is not in the state whose law governs. However, Ace was perfected on May 2, a time at which the filing would mislead no one and when the literal requirements of the complex of sections governing perfection are satisfied. Note that a financing statement can be filed before any security interest attaches, and the filing remains effective for five years. The Ace/Weaver situation is not substantively different from a transaction in which Ace filed a financing statement and then later sold the goods to Weaver.

Section 13.   Perfection Without Filing (Pledges and the Like)

79. No, generally a pledge must deprive the debtor of possession. There are two exceptions. *See* §9-312(f) & (g).

80. No, the bank will drill the box for Debtor if Debtor signs an affidavit certifying that he has lost the key. Given that policy of safe deposit companies, Finance Co. cannot argue successfully that it has deprived Debtor of possession of the contents of the box.

81. You can't. The account, the general intangible, and the letter of credit rights are intangibles. The concept of possession and the concept of a general intangible are dissonant. One cannot take possession of or deprive another of possession of an intangible. A secured party must file in order to perfect a security interest in accounts and general intangibles. Control is the method for perfecting a security interest in letter-of-credit rights. *See* §§9-312(b)(2), 9-314. Filing or control are methods for perfecting a security interest in electronic chattel paper. *See* §9-314, §9-105. [You should know that we have never witnessed a security interest in electronic chattel paper. In fact, we've never known of a transaction involving electronic chattel paper. One commentator has suggested that there is no such thing as electronic chattel paper. She claims that prospects for its arrival on the commercial scene are not good, so—fuhgedaboudit.]

82.
    a. Delivery of the certificate to Broker is sufficient. *See* §8-301. Since the certificate is investment property, *see* §9-102(a)(49), filing is also sufficient. *See* §9-312(a). Broker may be in possession of the certificate, holding it in a securities account for Debtor. In that case, Broker is a securities intermediary. *See* §8-102(a)(14)(ii). The pledge concept does not fit if Broker is maintaining a securities account. In that case, Broker must obtain a written security agreement from the debtor. Broker will be automatically perfected, by virtue of the fact that it will have control of the security. *See* §§8-106(a) & (b), 9-106, 9-314(c).

    b. The pledge concept does not work well for Uncle. He should perfect by control under §8-106(d)(2). Uncle must obtain a written agreement with Debtor and Broker. *See* §8-106, cmt. 7, example 10.

83.
    a. There is authority, misguided it would seem, holding that the bank is under a duty to manage the debtor's portfolio if the bank is in possession of that portfolio. That burden is heavy and fraught with peril, as this problem illustrates. The debtor should decide when or whether to convert debentures or to sell declining stocks or bonds. It is difficult to reconcile the language of §9-207 with the notion that the pledgee becomes an investment counsellor. The references to chattel paper and instruments in subsection (1) probably refer to factors who undertake to collect the sums due. *Cf.* subsection (d), excusing from those duties the factor that takes without recourse.

    b. The secured party may and often does repledge the collateral, as §9-207(c)(3) anticipates. Brokers take a pledge from their customers as security for margin purchases and then repledge the securities to a bank that finances the brokerage operation. Often, the repledge will create problems for the debtor, if the original pledgee is insolvent. The second pledgee will usually cut off the debtor's interest in the collateral. *See* cmt. 5 to §9-207. If the debtor satisfies the debt and cannot recover its collateral because it is in the hands of such a protected purchaser (§8-303), the original pledgee is liable to the debtor in conversion. The section does not forbid the repledge, however. Thus, debtors must pick their pledgees carefully.

84. Unless the pledge agreement absolves the bank of any duty to collect the note, as some agreements will, yes. The delay in giving the indorser notice of the dishonor caused Debtor loss because, under the law of negotiable instruments, the indorser is discharged if the notice of dishonor is late. *See* §§3-415(c), 3-503(a) and (c).

85. Yes, but the parties might prefer to use control. *See* §8-106, cmt. 4, examples 1 through 3.

86. Seller can grant Second Bank a security interest in its "letter-of-credit rights" in First Bank's letter of credit. Second Bank must perfect its security interest by control. *See* §9-107. Second Bank can effect control by satisfying §5-114, that is, by an assignment of the "proceeds" of the letter of credit and obtaining First Bank's consent to the assignment.

87. The bank doesn't have to do anything. *See* §9-104(a).

88. §9-103(b). While there are some limits on the extent to which consumer goods can be the subject of a cross-collateralization arrangement such as that described in the problem, those restrictions do not apply here. *See* §9-204(b)(1). In order to perfect in the refrigerator, *S* must file. *S* has a purchase money security interest in the video, however; and that security interest is perfected upon attachment, i.e., automatically; and the bank does not have to do anything to perfect. *See* §9-309(1).

89. A consumer neighbor defeats *S*'s security interest under §9-320(b); a merchant loses to *S*.

90. Perfection of the security interest in the antiques is "automatic" under §9-309(a). That is, it is effective upon attachment. The after-acquired antiques would not be subject to the security interest, unless they are acquired within ten days. *See* §9-204(b)(1).

91.   a. On May 3, First Bank held a perfected security interest in the documents and notes Broker received on May 2 because the bank gave new value and was automatically perfected under the rule of §9-312(e). First Bank did not have a perfected security interest in the May 3 documents and instruments, however, because it took only under the security agreement's after-acquired property clause. Thus, the bank never gave new value for the May 3 documents and instruments, as §9-312(e) requires. This problem illustrates the meaning of "new value" as defined in §9-102(a)(57).

      b. First Bank loses its perfected status under §9-312(e) after twenty days, so it may not rely on that section on May 31 to claim a perfected security interest in the May 2 paper. To perfect, First Bank should have at least filed a financing statement. §9-312(a).

92. Yes, First Bank was perfected throughout. While it held the negotiable bill, it

was perfected under §9-313(a). When it released the bill to Importer, it was perfected under §9-312(f) because the release was made to permit Importer to store the goods. §9-312(f)(2). (The receipt is a proceed of the goods under clauses (A) or (B) of §9-102(a)(64).) While the goods and the warehouse receipt were in the hands of Importer, the bank was perfected under §9-315(c) & (d) (which, collectively, mean that security interest in proceeds is "automatically" perfected for 20 days). When the Importer delivered the negotiable warehouse receipt to the bank, the bank was perfected under §9-313(a) again.

Section 14. Multistate Transactions

93.   a. Yes, the filing in State A remains effective even though the goods have moved, the location of Debtor being the fact that determines the place to file. That location has not changed. This is one of the simplifying changes in Revised Article 9.

b. Bank is still perfected. This is the easy answer to what had become a problem under the prior version of Article 9.

c. Same answer.

d. Same answer.

94. The filing in State A is good for all of these scenarios, which posed a headache for law teachers, if not for secured parties, under the prior version of Article 9. Barney is protected because the location of the debtor determines perfection under §9-301(1), and Debtor is always located in State A. §9-316(a)(1).

95. When Ace reincorporated, its location changed to State B. Under §9-316(a)(2), First Bank became unperfected four months later (September 2).

a. The purchaser wins. Because First Bank's perfection lapsed, it is deemed never to have been perfected against a buyer for value. *See* the last sentence of §9-316(b).

b. The lien creditor, not being a purchaser, *see* §1-201(b)(29) & (30) [§1-201(32) & (33)], loses. There is no "retroactive unperfection." *See* §9-316, cmt. 3.

c. Second Bank is a "purchaser" for value and defeats First Bank. §9-316(b). Remember: the term "Purchaser" includes a secured party. §1-201(b)(29) & (30) [§1-201(32) & (33)].

d. We can't find any reason to change the answer. All that §9-316(b) requires is that Second Bank be a purchaser, not a perfected purchaser.

e. First Bank defeats the trustee, who is not a purchaser.

f. Yes. First Bank is unperfected on September 25 under §9-316(a) because it did not file. So on that date the question is one of *priority* under §9-317(a)(2), a section we will study later.

96.   a. The starting point here is §9-303. Under subsection (c), the local law of State *A* governs perfection of First Bank's security interest until the automobile ceases to be covered by the certificate of title issued by State *A*. Under subsection (b), the automobile ceases to be covered by the certificate when the certificate ceases to be effective under State *A*'s law or when the automobile is later covered by a certificate issued by another state. So until another state issues a certificate, State *A*'s certificate, and State *A*'s law, continues to apply, and First Bank is perfected on both dates. §9-316(d) & (e) come into play only when another State issues a certificate.

b. Yes. §9-316(d) provides that First Bank's perfection continues until State *A*'s certificate would have become ineffective. [Remember, we are not deciding priority issues between the bank and a purchaser. We are addressing only the question of the bank's perfection.]

c. Section 9-316(e)(2) provides that First Bank will become unperfected as to purchasers if it fails to "reperfect" by having its security interest noted on the certificate within four months after the State B certificate is issued. If it does not so perfect, §9-317(b) provides that the dealer, as purchaser for value without notice of the security interest, will have priority over First Bank. So, if First Bank "reperfects" on or before October 1, it will have priority over the dealer, whether dealer buys on June 2 or October 2.

d. Yes, in that case the non-dealer/buyer would prevail, whether or not the bank reperfects by causing its lien to be noted on the new certificate.

e. Second Bank primes First Bank no matter when its security interest attaches or is perfected as long as it perfects its security interest under §9-311(2) without knowledge of First Bank's. *See* §9-337(2).

97.   a. This was so complicated and potentially such a trap for the bank under the prior version of Article 9, yet it is so easy under the revised version. File to where the debtor is located—California. §§9-301(1), 9-307.

b. No, Bank should still file where debtor is incorporated. §§9-301(1), 9-307. The location of Debtor's office is not relevant.

98.   This is another fact setting that created problems under the old version of Article 9 but is moderately simple under the revised version.

a. Yes, Tridelt is located in New York.

b. i. Yes, First Bank will be an assignee of a perfected security interest in goods and need not make any filings. *See* §9-310(c).

ii. No, First Bank will have a security interest by virtue of the assignment but must take steps to perfect. The leases are "chattel paper" of Tridelt. §9-102(a)(11).

c. The bank should file a financing statement in the state where Tridelt is located (New York). The financing statement should include mention of "leases" or "chattel paper" of Tridelt.

d. In order to take a perfected security interest in the inventory, First Bank must first obtain a security agreement from Tridelt describing the collateral as "inventory." *See* §9-203(b). The bank will perfect by filing a financing statement in New York, where Tridelt is located.

The bank need not refile if Tridelt moves its chief executive offices to Florida, but it must refile in Oregon if Tridelt reincorporates in that state. §9-316(a)(2).

99.   a.   Old Article 9 did not apply to sales of notes unless the transaction was intended to create a security interest. Now any and all sales are covered. §9-109(a)(3). This conclusion is not affected by the fact that the note is secured by an interest in real estate. §9-103(b). The question then arises how First National Bank should document the transaction to protect its rights.

                  Despite the change in Article 9, a buyer of a note does not have to take any particular steps to perfect its security interest because under §9-309(4) the security interest is perfected upon attachment. For example, in a true sale of a note, the prudent buyer obtains the seller's indorsement on the note and takes possession of the note in exchange for the purchase price. Possession, with the implied-in-law contract created by the indorsement (UCC §3-415), satisfies the attachment condition and therefore perfects the buyer's interest in the note. Fortunately, therefore, prudent buyers did not have to change their procedures to comply with Revised Article 9.

      b.   More specifically, under §9-309(4), Developer's sale of the promissory note is perfected upon attachment. Attachment occurs under §9-203(a) when the security interest becomes enforceable against the collateral. Under §9-203(b), First National's interest in the note will be enforceable if (a) First National gives value by paying the discounted price, (b) Developer had rights in the note (which it did), and (c) either Developer authenticates a security/sale agreement that describes the note (§9-203(b)(3)(A)) or the First National takes possession of the Note pursuant to the debtor's security agreement (§9-203(b)(3)(B)). (Don't take this to mean that the debtor must sign something called a security agreement. We feel that the definition of security agreement in §9-102(a)(73) will cover a sales agreement or the indorsed note, both of which satisfy the requirements of Article 9. Both are authenticated writings and evidence an agreement that creates or provides for a security interest. The buyer of a promissory note holds a security interest under §1-201(b)(35) [§1-201(37)].

                  Of course, the Buyer in our problem can also follow the "normal" Article 9 perfecting step of filing a financing statement.

                  Article 9 *permits* the bank to take a written security agreement from the developer and to file in the state where the debtor is located. *See* §9-312(a). In this transaction, the debtor for Article 9 purposes is the Developer. Thus filing in Illinois would work. Promissory notes are negotiable instruments, however; and many secured parties will be reluctant to perfect a security interest in a negotiable instrument by filing, for a holder in due course who takes the note will cut off the perfected security interest, as we will see below. *See also* §3-306. This is why, absent other business considerations, the bank will take possession of the note.

Whichever course the bank selects will be sufficient to perfect its security interest in the mortgage, for Article 9 provides that by obtaining a security interest in the payment obligations (the note) the bank also obtains a security interest in the collateral that secures the obligation, here, the mortgage. *See* §9-203(g). By perfecting its security interest in the payment obligation (the note) the bank automatically perfects its security interest in collateral securing it. *See* §9-308(e) & cmt. 6.

   c. The standby letter of credit is a "supporting obligation." *See* §9-102(a)(77). Note that the mortgage does not fit the "supporting obligation" definition, however, because the obligor on the mortgage, Buyer, has no obligation directly to First National Bank.

     By taking a security interest in the note, First National Bank has a security interest in the supporting obligation. *See* §9-203(f). Perfection of the security interest in the note operates to perfect the security interest in the supporting obligation. *See* §9-308(d).

100. Because the bank has a purchase money security interest, it is automatically perfected in Georgia. *See* §9-309(1). The debtor's move to Alabama renders the Georgia perfection good for only four months (§9-316(a)(2)), but, assuming that Alabama has also adopted §9-309(1), Alabama would also have an automatic perfection rule for purchase money security interests in consumer goods. The Alabama rule governs once the four-month period expires, and the bank remains perfected.

101. [This is a review question.]

   a. Sam perfected his interest under Kentucky law on November 1 by filing. Because he was perfected on the date of bankruptcy, he defeats the trustee under §9-201(a) and the negative implication of §9-317(a)(2).

   b. Lee, a non-purchaser, obtained its lien at a time when Sam was perfected. Sam will defeat Lee. It would not matter even if Sam failed to refile in Kentucky either before or after the four-month period specified in §9-316(a)(2). If Sam failed to refile and if Lee had obtained its lien after the four months, Lee would prevail. *See* §9-316(b) & cmt. 3. If instead of being a lien creditor, Lee were a buyer or a secured party, both of which are "purchasers" for value, Lee would defeat Sam if Sam failed to reperfect in Kentucky before the four months expired regardless of whether Lee's interest became perfected on June 10 or August 1, because of §9-316(b)'s "retroactive un-perfection" rule.

Section 15. Perfecting the Security Interest in Proceeds

102.   a. Yes, it does on May 1 by virtue of the automatic (twenty-day) perfection rule of §9-315(c) as limited by §9-315(d).

     b. Yes, the central filing is good for the accounts and the chattel paper.

See §9-315(d)(1)(B). The filing is in the office where a filing for those two kinds of collateral would be filed, and the accounts and chattel paper were not acquired with cash proceeds. *See* §9-315(d)(1)(C). It is not necessary that the original filing mention chattel paper and accounts.

    c.   The security interest in the cash continues indefinitely. §9-315(d)(2). This sounds too good to be true. It is. Cash disappears quickly, and the tracing requirements render cash proceeds problematic for the secured party. The secured party only has a security interest in cash proceeds that it can identify, and it is hard to identify cash as coming from the sale of collateral. In any event, the cash is almost always gone when the debtor defaults or becomes insolvent. Commingling will not per se destroy the cash as proceeds because the secured party may be able to trace under some tracing theory. Most courts and writers assume that the lowest intermediate balance method is the preferred method for tracing.

    d.   Yes, for the filing is not good for the inventory nor for the proceeds. If the debtor is located in a state different from the state where the inventory is located, the filing mentioned in the Problem will not be sufficient. Note that the automatic perfection under §9-315(c) applies only if the security interest in the original collateral is perfected. This lender has an unperfected security interest in the inventory and in the proceeds. It is not perfected at all, and certainly not in the proceeds for the twenty-day period.

103.   The word processor is equipment in the hands of Bell, and the filing is insufficient to continue the perfection beyond the twenty days by virtue of the fact that Bell acquired the word processor with cash proceeds. §9-315(d)(1)(c). Had Bell taken the word processor in trade, however, that is, in trade for inventory, the filing would be sufficient because equipment is collateral in which a security interest can be perfected by filing. If the filing described the collateral as "inventory and equipment," it would be sufficient to keep the bank perfected beyond the twenty days. [This answer assumes that Bell is incorporated in Iowa.]

104.   The bank has no claim to proceeds from the sale of inventory that is not its collateral. The name on the account should not be dispositive. If the bank can show that the cash is from the sale of the bank's collateral, the cash is proceeds in which the bank has a security interest. Here, the Grand Rapids furniture inventory is not the collateral of the bank, and the proceeds would not go to the bank.

105.   On May 1, First Bank has a security interest in the certificate of deposit and in the checks. The security interest remains perfected in the checks, which are cash proceeds, beyond the twenty days. A certificate of deposit may or may not be cash proceeds. It is probably an instrument but could conceivably be a deposit account depending on its form and maturity. Thus, as to the certificate, the security interest becomes unperfected after the twenty days unless it is not an instrument. A negotiable certificate of deposit is clearly an instrument, and in order to continue the perfection in the certificate, the bank's financing statement must cover certificates, or the bank must take possession of the certificate. If Bell had deposited the cash and the checks into a bank account, as most business enterprises would quickly, First Bank would remain perfected but might have a tracing problem. [One of us disagrees with this answer and feels that a certificate of deposit, whether negotiable or nonnegotiable, does not qualify as cash proceeds.]

Section 16. Introduction to Priorities

106.   a. Bank defeats *S*, a lien creditor that levied on the equipment after Bank perfected. Under the negative implication of §9-317(a)(2)(A), or under the rule of §9-201(a), Bank defeats lien creditor.

b. Buyers come in two basic types: Buyers in ordinary course and buyers not in ordinary course. The term is defined in §1-201(b)(9) [§1-201(9)]. A buyer not in ordinary course, which is any buyer that does not qualify for the super-protection afforded by §9-320(a), can defeat an unperfected secured party under §9-317(c) only if the buyer takes for value and takes delivery before the secured party perfects. Bank perfected on May 3; and if buyer takes delivery after that date, buyer loses to Bank. If, on the other hand, buyer takes delivery before Bank perfects, buyer will prevail. Note that, in any event, buyer must buy without knowledge of Bank's security interest in order to defeat Bank.

c. The lessee's protection also rests on the taking of delivery. *See* §9-317(c).

d. Buyers and lessees must take delivery. Otherwise, the theory goes, Bank might be deceived by the seller/debtor's possession of the equipment. The avoidance of "secret liens" is a key principle of the law of secured transactions. Secret liens undercut the Article Nine filing system and make lenders uncertain of the value of their collateral. Seeing the equipment on Debtor's premises would lead Bank to think that Debtor had an interest in the equipment. The prepaying buyer or lessee, furthermore, creates suspicion. Is he buying or leasing or is he lending? Commercial buyers and lessees customarily do not prepay unless they are trying to help their seller out of a financial bind. That sounds like lending. Note that §9-317(c) and (d) do not help lenders but buyers. It does not matter whether the bank files early. *B* will defeat Bank if Bank fails to perfect. Bank cannot perfect until its security interest attaches. If *B* takes delivery before Bank obtains its security interest, *B* should prevail.

e. Buyers of intangibles cannot take delivery of the subject of their purchase. Section 9-317(d), therefore, contains no delivery requirement.

107.   Bank should prevail as to the original equipment and as to the after-acquired equipment. In most jurisdictions, a lien creditor such as *S* cannot attach

after-acquired property without levying on the property after the debtor obtains an interest in it. In any event, because Bank is perfected throughout, there is no way that *S* can have priority over Bank.

108. *S* holds a purchase-money security interest, as defined in §9-103. It lent to the buyer in order for the buyer to purchase its goods, and the goods were security for the loan. The twenty-day grace period protects this purchase-money seller. Section 9-317(e) gives the purchase-money lender 20 days after the debtor receives possession of the goods to file. *S* has filed in time. Buyers that receive delivery not in ordinary course also lose here; but, as we see later, buyers in ordinary course win [*see* §9-320(a)]. The priority of buyers is dealt with more fully in Section 18.

Purchase-money security interests are not like ordinary loans. As we shall see, they get superpriority over older loans in the same assets. Here they get the benefit of a twenty-day grace period. Why? The purchase-money financer brings new value to the debtor, which the debtor uses to buy a new asset. The debtor's other creditors thus should not be affected. Article Nine recognizes this by giving the purchase-money financer special rights. Here, the twenty-day grace period gives the purchase-money financer a reasonable time to file after the transaction is complete. The new value created by the purchase money security interest vitiates any problems with secret liens.

109. Here, the secured party is not a purchase-money lender, and the lien creditor has obtained a lien before the secured party perfects. The clear language of §9-317(a)(2)(A) dictates that the lien creditor prevail. The same rule applies for (1) bulk buyers, other buyers not in ordinary course, and lessees, all of whom must take delivery and for value before the secured party perfects; and (2) licensees and buyers of intangibles, all of whom must give value without knowledge before the secured party perfects. *See* §9-317(b), (c) & (d).

110. Lenders that are purchase money secured parties have the same benefits under §9-317(e) that purchase-money sellers have. The bank has a twenty-day grace period within which to file. Here the bank will win.

111. Second Bank prevails here because it filed before First Bank perfected. Under §9-322(a)(1), the first secured party to file or perfect will have priority. This is the core priority rule in Article Nine for conflicts between secured creditors. First Bank could have had priority if it had given value on May 1. But because it did not give value until May 3, it cannot be perfected until May 3. A secured party is not perfected until its security interest attaches. The security interest cannot attach until value is given. *See* §9-203(b)(1).

112. Here, Second Bank has perfected first, but First Bank has filed first. Under §9-322(a)(1), the first to file or perfect wins. First Bank wins. This result is not unfair, because the May 1 filing is theoretically there for Second Bank to see. It should be forewarned, then, not to take a security interest without investigating the circumstances of the First Bank filing. In practice, though, filing offices may take days to process a filing.

113. First Bank gets all of the money. Even without looking at §9-322(b)(1), which

expressly so provides, we should know that First Bank prevails. First Bank perfected first, and §9-322(a)(1) says that the first to perfect has priority. By depriving the debtor of possession, First Bank put the world on notice that the debtor may have sold or encumbered the equipment. Unless it receives a satisfactory explanation, what bank in its right mind would lend against an asset that the debtor does not have in its possession?

114.   The order of lending does not determine priority. The order of filing or perfection determines it. *See* §9-322(a)(1). Second Bank perfected first and filed first. Second Bank prevails.

115.   Under §9-324(a), a purchase-money secured party with a security interest in equipment has twenty days after the debtor receives the equipment to file; and if it does so, it defeats any prior filed secured party. S, then, will defeat Bank. S would not prevail if it filed on May 23 because the twenty-day grace period expired on May 22.

116.   Under a literal reading of §9-324(a)(1), S wins here. Arguably, however, the policy of the purchase money priority rules is best satisfied by prorating the funds received upon the sale of the equipment: 10 percent for the bank, 90 percent for S. The proration approach, which yields the same result no matter who files first, has merit. Section 9-324(g) bars the proration approach, however, and favors S, a purchase-money seller, over the bank, a purchase-money lender. In any event, S must file within the twenty days. Note that in the event there are two purchase-money *lenders*, the first to file or perfect will prevail. No prorating there either. *See* §9-324, cmt. 13.

117.   S benefits from the purchase money priority afforded by §9-324(a). That priority extends to all proceeds. S, therefore, gets the check and defeats the bank.

118.   If the collateral had been beer, which would be the wholesaler's inventory, §9-324(b) would apply; and S would not get the check. Although §9-324(b) gives priority to the purchase-money secured party with a security interest in inventory, that priority narrows when the debtor sells the collateral and holds proceeds. In fact, the only cash proceeds that the purchase money seller of inventory will get are (1) cash proceeds received on or before the resale and delivery of the inventory to the sub-buyer and (2) cash proceeds from chattel paper or an instrument Debtor receives from the sub-buyer. Unless, then, the debtor sells the purchase money seller's collateral for cash, receives a cash down payment, or takes chattel paper or an instrument from the sub-buyer, S will not receive any cash proceeds.

Even for the check, which qualifies as "cash proceeds," S can recover only if S holds a perfected security interest when the debtor receives possession of the inventory—that is, S cannot take advantage of the twenty-day grace period given to non-inventory, purchase-money financers. S must also have given notice to the holders of conflicting security interests. S will also have priority as to the beer S delivers to Debtor and will have priority in the chattel paper and instruments that Debtor takes from his sub-buyers, but S will have no priority in amounts due S from customers to whom Debtor sold on open account, i.e., no priority in Debtor's accounts and no priority in the cash proceeds from those accounts.

119.   a. First Bank holds a purchase-money security interest on the first $50,000 and so prevails as to that. §§9-103, 9-324(a). The second advance is not purchase money and thus is junior to Second Bank's loan because Second Bank was first to file or perfect. §9-322(a). At one time the second non-purchase-money loan called the status of the first loan into question, with some courts saying that the second loan transformed the purchase-money security interest into a non-purchase-money loan and thus stripped it of its superpriority. Section 9-103 rejects that argument. §9-103(f)(1) & cmt. 7a.

b. The priority does not change, even for refinancing, as the substance of the transactions has not changed. §9-103(f)(3). The payments are trickier. Ideally the parties will have allocated them by contract. If not, §9-103(e) uses a first-in-time rule as a default, so the purchase-money portion will be paid off first.

c. Perhaps. Section 9-103(e) and (f) govern non-consumer transactions. The statute is silent on consumer transactions. §9-312(h) & cmt. 8. A good many pre-revision cases found that subsequent loans on consumer goods transformed the old purchase-money security interest into a non-purchase-money security interest. It remains to be seen whether these cases remain good authority.

120. This problem illustrates the curious fact that a farmer's "inventory" is not "inventory" for Code purposes. Animals in a feed lot are farm products. *See* §9-102(a)(34) & (35). The purchase-money priority rule for inventory, §9-324(b), with its five-year notice requirement to inventory lenders, therefore, does not apply to agricultural lenders that take a security interest in a farm debtor's livestock, grain, and the like. Rather, a six-month notice rule applies in this problem. Here, though, the purchase-money security holder can get priority in *all* identifiable proceeds, not merely in identifiable *cash* proceeds.

121. Second will take subject to the badly perfected security interest of First. *See* §9-517, cmt. 2. First Bank did what it had to do to perfect. Someone must initially bear the risk for an error in the filing office. It's time for Second's lawyers to take a close look at the state's tort claims act.

122. First Bank prevails as to the accounts. Second Bank has a perfected security interest in the accounts but only as proceeds, and First Bank filed first and thus wins under §9-322. Second Bank prevails as to the inventory. First Bank's security interest is only in accounts. (This answer assumes the inventory is not proceeds of accounts.) Both First Bank and Second Bank have perfected security interests in the deposit account as proceeds. First Bank filed first, though, so it wins.

    If the inventory lender (Second Bank) had filed first, it would win on all collateral. It would win the inventory for the reasons above, and on the accounts and the deposit account because it would have been first to file. An accounts lender might thus pause before lending in the teeth of a prior inventory loan without getting a subordination agreement with the inventory lender, unless it wants to make essentially an unsecured loan.

123.   a. Yes. First Bank has properly perfected its security interest by control. §§9-104(a)(1) & 9-314(a). It has the right to take the funds in the deposit account which is subject to its control in case of default. §9-604(a)(4)-(5). Its set-off rights are outside of Article Nine, but presumably would be honored as well. *Cf.* §9-340.

b. First Bank's security interest in accounts is junior only if Second has control, an unlikely event. Second Bank would thus claim the deposit account as identifiable cash proceeds of accounts. §9-322. Generally, §9-327(1) or (3) gives First Bank priority over even senior security interests that do not have control over the deposit accounts. This suggests a risk faced by accounts financers. They might do well to enter into control agreements to ensure priority.

c. Still First Bank. It is not first in time, but §9-327(3) makes the bank with which the deposit account is maintained senior to all other security interest holders, even when the deposit account is claimed as proceeds of the bank's security interest. §9-327, cmt. 4. Second Bank could always seek a subordination agreement under §9-339. Alternatively, it could become the bank's customer under §9-104(a)(3), which also would give it priority. §9-327(4).

d. Transferees of money out of a deposit account take free of a security interest in the account. §9-332(b).

e. Tough. Second Bank's security interest does not affect First Bank's rights and duties with regard to the deposit account, unless First Bank and *D* have agreed otherwise. If Second Bank authorized *D* to draw on the account, it has no right to complain when *D* does so. Of course, Second Bank could have forced *D* to give up its checkwriting privileges, though under these facts that might prove unworkable.

Section 17. *Future Advances*

124.   a. All of the money goes to First Bank, which filed first and therefore defeats Second Bank under the rule of §9-322(a)(1) and under the negative implication of §9-323(a). *See* §9-323, cmt. 2.

b. It does not matter that First knew of Second's entry into the picture. Second was forewarned that First had priority. First and Debtor can squeeze Second out. It should not matter that First does not lend until May 3 or even later. Once First files, Second is on notice.

c. None of the altered facts in question b should change First's priority except for the case in which First is perfected temporarily without filing and without possession under the three subsections of §9-312. In those cases, §9-323(a) protects Second Bank as to the later advance.

Quite apart from any priority issue, no collateral stands as security for a debt unless the debtor has granted the creditor a security interest in the collateral to secure that debt. If the security agreement that Debtor executed in favor of First Bank only secures the May 1 advance, the later advances are not secured. Whether a security agreement that does not mention renewals or does not contain a dragnet clause (a clause making it clear that the security agreement covers all loans) would secure the loan once it is renewed is a question on which authorities do not agree. The majority probably favors the view that the security agreement covers the renewal. Note, however, that this is not a question of determining which of two secured parties has priority. The question here is whether with respect to the renewal First Bank is a secured party. See also the answer to the next problem.

d. Yes. On May 3, First Bank can take a new security agreement from Debtor and obtain security for a new advance. Once First Bank makes that advance, it will have a perfected security interest, and it will defeat Second Bank because First Bank filed first. There was some authority to the contrary under pre-revised Article 9, but the plain language of the revised statute indicates that the first to file wins. That is the import of §9-322(a)(1). *See* §9-323, cmt. 3, example 1.

e. Again, there was some pre-revision authority to the effect that the May 3 advance, not being contemplated by the debtor and the bank on May 1, is subordinate to Second Bank's security interest. That holding would be correct if the language of the security agreement and the financing statement did not cover inventory. The problem indicates, however, that the security agreement and the financing statement did cover inventory. The majority of cases, and most of the commentators, would protect First Bank. Remember, Second Bank can see the filing and is warned that First Bank is in the picture. No second lender paying attention will lend in those circumstances without obtaining a subordination agreement or a termination statement from First. In any event, we think the language of §9-322(a)(1) couldn't be much clearer. *See* §9-322, cmt. 4 (last para.).

125. The bank is able to squeeze the lien creditor out of the security interest picture. Because the bank's later advance is within the 45-day period, it is protected against the lien creditor. Advances on May 15 with or without knowledge of the lien and on June 20 without knowledge of the lien would also beat the lien creditor. The June 20 advance is beyond the 45th day, but it is made without knowledge. If the lien creditor notifies the bank on May 2, the bank and the debtor may still squeeze the lien creditor out, if they desire to do so, though they must act within the 45 days. Notice on the 45th day would take that option away from the bank because it no longer has the 45 days' absolute protection and now cannot make a priority advance since it has knowledge.

Advances made pursuant to commitments incurred by the bank date back to the time of the commitment. Thus if the bank commits during the 45 days or commits without knowledge (either within or without the 45 days), the advance pursuant to the commitment is prior to the rights of the lien creditor.

126.   Yes, the bank will defeat the buyer. Either of two events will cut off the ability of the bank to squeeze out this buyer: notice to the bank of the sale to the buyer or running of the 45 days. Unlike §9-323(b), §9-323(d) is solicitous of the buyer's rights.

An advance on May 20 without knowledge of the sale would defeat the buyer. An advance on June 17, with or without knowledge, would lose to the buyer. Advances pursuant to commitment date from the time of the commitment and stand or fall on the lender's state of knowledge at the time it makes the commitment. A commitment on May 1 will protect advances pursuant to that commitment because the commitment is within the 45 days and is without knowledge of the sale. A commitment on May 20 would protect advances pursuant to it only if the commitment is made without knowledge. Any commitment outside the 45 days would not preserve the lender's priority.

Note that the buyer has an incentive, then, to give the lender notice of the sale, for once the lender has notice, it cannot squeeze the buyer out.

Note also that the same rules apply to lessees not in ordinary course. *See* §9-323(f). Buyers in ordinary course and lessees in ordinary course defeat all of the lender's advances. *See* §9-320(a), -321(c). (This buyer is not a buyer in ordinary course because it bought in bulk, which the definition of buyer in ordinary course expressly excludes. §1-201(b)(9) (last sentence) [§1-201(9) (last sentence)].) For further discussion, see the next section.

If *B* is a buyer of accounts, it defeats the later advances under §9-323(c).

Section 18. Purchaser Priorities

127.   a. If *A* has taken delivery, *A* will prevail under §9-320(a) because *A* is a buyer in ordinary course. It does not matter under the definition of that term (§1-201(b)(9) [§1-201(9)]) that *A* knows of the security interest. Just as you and I know that most retailers have granted a security interest in their inventory to a bank or finance company or to a seller, we take free despite that knowledge, which does not prevent us from rising to the level of a buyer in ordinary course. After all, the secured party wants its debtor to sell the inventory, so a buyer should anticipate that a sale is with the secured party's approval.

Section 1-201(b)(9) [§1-201(9)] defines "buyer in ordinary course" in a way that limits the definition to a buyer who has taken possession of the goods or who has the right under Article 2 to receive delivery of the goods. A promise to pay is value. The fact that *A* has not paid does not prevent *A* from becoming a buyer in ordinary course, any more than *A*'s failure to pay bars it from contract remedies. The law protects *B's* expectation interest, the promise to pay being value.

b.   Here, *B* has knowledge that infects him and prevents him from claiming buyer in ordinary course status. Under §1-201(b)(9) [§1-201(9)], *B's* knowledge that the sale is in contravention of the bank's rights is fatal.

The bank's failure to enforce its prohibition of sale has convinced some courts that the bank has waived or is estopped from asserting its rights under the prohibition clause. The cases are not totally convincing. In any case, this could work only if *B* has taken delivery or has a right to recover the goods.

c.   A pawnbroker cannot be a buyer in ordinary course. *See* §1-201(b)(9) (last clause, first sentence) [§1-201(9)].

d.   This horizontal sale is probably in ordinary course. Although it is customary to think of retailers as parties that sell only to vertical customers, in fact, dealers often sell to other dealers. Automobile dealers may need a model that is no longer available from the manufacturer. Such a dealer will seek to obtain the model from another dealer through a service that keeps track on a computer of every dealer's inventory. Courts accept such sales as sales in ordinary course.

e.   *E* is a buyer in bulk and cannot qualify for buyer in ordinary course status. *See* §1-201(b)(9) [§1-201(9)].

f.   *F* sounds like a lender that is taking security in a transaction disguised as a sale. The disguise should not work. Article 9 applies to all secured transactions, no matter the form. *See* §9-109(a)(1). If *F* is a secured party, it must comply with the attachment and perfection rules of the article and will be subject to the priority rule of §9-322(a)(1), which will render *F* subordinate to the bank.

g.   *G* also runs the risk of being characterized as a lender. Prepaying buyers that lend sellers funds to acquire the parts and raw materials or other inventory that is the subject of the sale to the buyer may be able to take advantage of the purchase-money priority rule of §9-324(b). They must, however, comply with the terms of that provision, which requires notice to the bank and the filing of a financing statement. If it is ordinary in the industry to pay early, however, *G* may be a buyer in ordinary course.

h.   *H* may not be a buyer in ordinary course. The combination of a very low price and a family connection suggests a sweetheart deal not available to ordinary buyers. On the other hand, discontinued lines, seasonal goods, and floor models often sell at sharp discounts, and sellers needing quick cash may mark down goods drastically. Whether a sale is suspicious enough to fall outside the definition of buyer in ordinary course is thus a matter of context.

128.   a.   As a buyer in ordinary course, *B* does take free; but note that *B* has created a new interest, which at the moment resides in *D*. If *B* takes free of First Bank's security interest, *C* comes within the shelter of *B* and also takes free of it.

    b.   No. *B* has created a new security interest in favor of *D*.

    c.   No. The assignment makes First Bank a secured party, succeeding to the rights of *D*. Because *B* is probably not a consumer, *D* must file to perfect. Because *D* is perfected, First Bank need not file, as the assignee of a perfected security interest. *See* §9-310(c).

129.   a.   *B* prevails either under §9-315(a)(1) (authorized sale) or under §9-320(a) (protection of buyer in ordinary course).

    b.   *C* cannot avail itself of the protection under either provision, as it is not a buyer and as the facts do not show that First Bank agreed to subordinate its security interest. Clearly, the priority rule of §9-322(a)(1) applies here, and *C* will lose to the bank. This disposition is not authorized.

    c.   *E* cannot use §9-315 and is not a buyer. He cannot, therefore, qualify for protection under §9-320(a). Even though he is a purchaser, nothing in Article 9 protects the donee.

    d.   *F* is a bulk buyer, and the sale to *F* is not authorized. This is not the type of sale that secured lenders authorize. *F*, moreover, being a bulk buyer, does not meet the buyer in ordinary course definition. *See* §1-201(b)(9) [§1-201(9)].

130.   a.   Yes. That is the import of §9-315(a)(1).

    b.   Bank can maintain an action in replevin to recover the goods or an action in conversion to recover their value from *B*.

    c.   No. An innocent donee will take subject to the bank's security interest, which is to say that the donee will also be liable to the bank in replevin or conversion.

    d.   Yes. Section 9-315(a)(2) provides not only that the security interest follows the goods into the hands of the purchaser, it also gives the bank a security interest in the proceeds. The bank, of course, may have only one recovery.

131.   [This question like many in this book, illustrates the operation of sections in Article 9, here, §9-320(a) & (b), but is not commercially realistic. First, mobile homes usually are subject to certificate of title laws. Second, many retail installment contracts involve items that sell for less than a mobile home. The discount department store that sells snow blowers and refrigerators under such contracts almost never files financing statements. A purchase-money security interest in consumer goods requires none, and in any event the filing cost usually exceeds the benefit, given the normal default rate, costs of repossession, and value of the repossessed collateral.]

    a.   This is the same question that we saw in Problem 128 above. The difference here is that this buyer is a consumer. *B* in any event defeats the bank's security interest but creates a new security interest in the dealer.

    b.   Again, *B* does not take free of the security interest *B* created under the installment sales agreement.

    c.   *C* will defeat the bank because *C* comes within the shelter of *B*, who defeats the bank. *C* will take free of *R*'s security interest under the rule of §9-320(b), assuming that *C* does not know of *R*'s security interest. This is a consumer-to-consumer sale, sometimes referred to as the garage sale exception. *R*'s security interest is automatically perfected because it is a purchase money security interest in consumer goods. *See* §9-309(1)

d. If *R* had filed, as it had the option to do under Article 9, *R* would have defeated *C*. §9-320(b)(4). After all, *C* could always search the public records. (Would *C* likely do so?)

132.   a. *Y* does not defeat the security interest because although *Y* is a buyer in ordinary course, *Y* only defeats security interests created by its seller ("the buyer's seller"), *X*. *See* §9-320(a) & cmt. 3. The security interest in this problem was created by *B*, so it survives.

b. No: the bank would stand in *R*'s shoes, and *Y* would take subject to the bank's security interest.

133.   a. Under the Code, *B* will not defeat the PCA, because a buyer of farm products from a farmer does not defeat the secured party even if the buyer is a buyer in ordinary course. §9-320(a) & cmt. 4. Failure of the state to enact one of the options under the Food Security Act of 1985, 7 U.S.C. §1631(d), however, reverses that result, and *B* will defeat the PCA unless the PCA notified the buyer. *See* 7 U.S.C. §1631(e).

b. *K* cannot defeat the PCA under the Code, because *K*, even if it is a buyer in ordinary course, cannot take free and clear of a security interest created by someone other than its seller. *B* did not create the PCA's security interest; *F* did. Under the Food Security Act, however, because *B* defeats the PCA, *K* will come within the shelter of *B* and defeat the PCA.

c. *T*'s rights are the same as those of *K* under the same reasoning set out in the preceding answer.

d. The downstream buyers are potentially liable for conversion of the production credit association's collateral. It is not economical to sue the consumer here. *B* and *K*, however, are tempting targets, liable as they are in conversion to the PCA.

134. Under pre-revised Article 9, the New York Court of Appeals thought so. Some commentators disagreed. Clearly, the crucial fact is that which states that *C* is a buyer in ordinary course. It is difficult to see how a party familiar with bill-and-hold practices could qualify as a buyer in ordinary course when it buys and pays without checking to see that *M* will honor its requests for delivery of the goods. If *B* is a buyer in ordinary course, perhaps the courts should have fashioned an exception to protect *M*, that is, an exception to the rule of §9-320(a) when a secured party is in possession of the goods under §9-313. Revised Article 9 fashions one. *See* §9-320(e). See also the next two problems.

135. The same arguments advanced to protect *M* in the preceding problem should protect the bank here. The bank has done all it can do to protect itself, and there perhaps should be an understanding that §9-320(a) does not operate to defeat a secured party in possession of the goods. This is a very common practice. The bank has taken possession precisely to avoid sales by the debtor. One can also argue, of course, that there can be no sale in ordinary course because a buyer that prepays for a carload of goods it cannot see is barmy, and a barmy buyer is not a buyer in ordinary course. We don't think the language of §9-320(e) covers these facts, but the policy certainly does. *See* §1-103(a) [§1-102(1) & cmt. 1].

136.   This question describes the field warehouse, a once-popular device to deprive the debtor of possession of his collateral to prevent him from selling it. The policy arguments in the preceding two questions apply with equal vigor here. *M*, in the judgment of most writers, should be protected either by holding that the sale is not in ordinary course or by applying §9-320(e), which we think fits this transaction. §9-320, cmt. 8 (last sentence); §9-313(c) & cmt. 4. *M*, through its agent, the field warehouse, is in possession. That possession must, however, satisfy §9-203(b)(3)(B); that is, it must be pursuant to the debtor's security agreement.

Section 19.   Chattel Paper and Accounts

137.   a.   Yes to both. Retailer obtained a security interest in the snow blower by virtue of the installment sales agreement. When Retailer assigned the paper to First Bank on May 2, the bank became an assignee of the security interest in the snow blower. §9-310(c).

b.   Yes. The contract is chattel paper. *See* §9-102(a)(11). By taking possession of the paper, the bank perfected in the paper. *See* §9-313(a).

c.   Yes. Retailer was perfected as to the snow blower under the automatic perfection rule of §9-309(1). When Retailer assigned the paper to First Bank, the bank did not need to file in order to have a perfected security interest in the snow blower. As the assignee of a perfected security interest in the snow blower, the bank was perfected automatically. *See* §9-310(c). The assignment is complete without transfer of possession of the paper. The bank would not have a perfected security interest in the contract (the chattel paper), however, not having taken possession of it and not having filed. First Bank should file in the state where the Retailer is located, and the retailer must sign the financing statement. The retailer is the debtor with respect to the security interest in the contract.

138.   a.   First Bank has no interest in the computers, having taken neither a security agreement in the reversionary interest in the computers nor a security interest in the computer company's inventory.

b.   First Bank has a security interest in the leases themselves and in the stream of payments due under the leases. That interest is perfected by virtue of the bank's filing. §9-312(a). True leases are chattel paper. *See* §9-102(a)(11).

c.   Those leases that cover the credit sales are also chattel paper, and

First Bank has a perfected security interest in them. Computer, Inc. took a security interest in the computers subject to those "leases." Section 2-401(1) stipulates that any attempt by a seller that has delivered goods under a sale to reserve title, as this seller did in the sale disguised as a lease, has a security interest. Computer, Inc., then, had a security interest in the equipment on May 1. When it assigned that interest to First Bank, the bank became a secured party. Note, however, that neither the bank nor the computer company filed as to the equipment. First Bank's interest, therefore, is unperfected.

If, then, Computers, Inc. becomes bankrupt, First Bank will defeat the trustee's claim to the true leases and the disguised credit sales because the bank is perfected. If a lessee becomes bankrupt, however, the bank will not defeat the lessee's trustee's claim to the equipment because the bank does not have a perfected security interest in the equipment. For true leases, the bank never had rights in the equipment; for disguised sales, it held an unperfected security interest, which is defeated by the trustee in bankruptcy. *See* Section 27.

139. This lease is a true lease. *See* §1-203 [§§1-201(37) & 2A-103(1)(j)]. First Bank has a security interest in the lease (chattel paper). Under a true lease, the lessor has a reversionary interest in the equipment. Leasing Co. also granted a security interest to First Bank in the reversionary interest in the equipment.

    a. Second Bank, by virtue of the security interest it takes from Construction Co., the lessee, obtains a security interest in the construction company's leasehold interest in the equipment. The claims of Second Bank and Leasing Co. (and thus of First Bank, its assignee) are not in conflict. Leasing Co. has conveyed away the leasehold interest to the construction company and cannot interfere with the leasehold as long as the construction company or somebody else makes the lease payments. In the event the payments cease, presumably the leasehold comes to an end, Second Bank has no collateral, and the leasing company will assert its reversionary rights under the lease. Second Bank would perfect its security interest by filing a financing statement, signed by the construction company. The filing must be in the state where the construction company is located, New Jersey. §9-301(1).

    b. First Bank can perfect its security interest in the lease by taking possession of it or by filing. *See* §9-312(a), -313(a). If it files, it should take a financing statement from Leasing Co., its debtor and the owner of the interest being conveyed (described in the statement as "lease" or "chattel paper"), and should file in New York, the state where Leasing Co. is located. §9-301(1). First Bank also has a security interest in the equipment, but its interest in the equipment is limited. It derives from and is limited by Leasing Co.'s interest. Leasing Co. only has a reversionary interest, but a reversionary interest in equipment with a useful life of eight years that is subject to a lease for only four years could be quite valuable.

The debtor on First Bank's financing statement covering the equipment should be Leasing Co., and the collateral should be described as "inventory held for lease" or something similar. First should file in New York, the state where Leasing Co. is located. §9-301(1).

c. The trustee in the construction company's bankruptcy will be able to hold the equipment during the term of the lease, provided she elects to make the lease payments. Bankruptcy Code §365(a). In that event, nothing in the transaction permits First Bank to interfere with the trustee's rights. Second Bank, of course, does have rights against the trustee, but the question does not ask about those rights.

d. When Leasing Co. files in bankruptcy, First Bank will defeat the leasing company's trustee's claim to the lease and the payments under it because First Bank has a perfected security interest in the lease payments. Possession of the chattel paper would be sufficient to perfect the bank as to the stream of lease payments. The bank will also defeat the trustee's claim to Leasing Co.'s reversionary rights in the equipment because the bank has filed as to the inventory in the state where the leasing company is located. As we will see, the trustee in bankruptcy is treated for priority purposes largely like a judicial lien creditor as of the time of the bankruptcy petition. Bankruptcy Code §544(a)(1). Under ordinary priority rules, First Bank would be the senior lienholder. On the trustee's rights in bankruptcy, *see* Section 27.

140.   a. No; unless the secured party notifies the account debtor (Buyer), the account debtor may make its payment directly to the assignor of the account instead of to First Bank, the assignee. *See* §9-406(a).

b. Yes, if the notice had been authenticated by the assignor or assignee and also had directed Buyer to pay the bank. *See* §9-406(a).

c. i. Yes. *See* §9-404(a). This preserves the common law of assignment.

ii. It depends on whether the setoff arose prior to or after the notice of assignment. In the former case, yes; in the latter, no. *See* §9-404(a)(2) & cmt. 2.

d. Such a waiver of defense clause is enforceable under §9-403(b) if Buyer is a merchant. FTC rules limit the right of a consumer to waive its defenses, however. *See* Federal Trade Commission, Holder-in-Due-Course-Regulations, 16 C.F.R. Part 433 (2002). *See also* §9-403(d).

141.   Section 9-404(a) renders the assignee subject to "any defense or claim in recoupment." That language does not ordinarily permit this account debtor to argue that the bank took subject to his affirmative claim, as §9-404(b) makes clear. This limit may not apply if Owner is a consumer. *See* §9-404(c) & (d). Also, Owner may be able to reduce any remaining indebtedness through its claim, though Owner cannot actually get any money back.

Section 20. More on Purchasers, This Time of Paper

142.   a. Yes. Even though the bank has a perfected security interest in the lease as proceeds of inventory, Finance Co. wins. The transaction appears to be regular in all respects. The filing of the bank's financing statement covering inventory does not affect the Finance Company's priority. Finance Co.'s state of knowledge is not relevant. There is no stamp on the lease indicating that it has been assigned. *See* §9-330(a)(2).

        This result violates the first to file or perfect priority rule. It can be justified, though, by the importance of chattel paper financing. Strict adherence to the usual rule would cut off this method of financing. Furthermore, inventory financers are interested more in the payments from the sale of collateral than in the collateral itself, and chattel paper financing often facilitates these payments.

    b. Yes. First Bank is claiming the lease as proceeds from the disposition of its inventory collateral. Finance Co. wins. The state of Finance Co.'s knowledge is not relevant. *See* §9-330, cmt. 5.

    c. No. Taking on account of an antecedent loan is not "new" value, though it is value. §9-102(a)(57). Section 9-330 protects the finance company that takes with knowledge only if it gives new value. *See* §9-330(a)(1).

    d. If the bank's security agreement indicates that the bank has a security interest in the lease, which is chattel paper, the bank has a good argument that it is protected from the reach of §9-330. It would not have a security interest "claimed merely as proceeds" for the purposes of §9-330(a). Financing of this sort expressly includes accounts and chattel paper as collateral, allowing the debtor to borrow based in part on the amount of the accounts and chattel paper. *See* PEB Commentary No. 8. If the bank can show that it relied, its argument is that much stronger. These arguments do not avail the bank, however, if Finance Co. takes without knowledge of the bank's interest. *See* §9-330(b).

    e. The promissory note would be proceeds, but it is an instrument, not chattel paper. *See* §9-102(a)(47) & (65). If Finance Co. takes a negotiable instrument properly endorsed and if it gives value and acts without notice and in good faith, it is a holder in due course and will cut off all claims of the bank. *See* §§3-302, 3-306. *See also* §9-331(a) (Article 9 does not limit the rights of a holder in due course). If the finance company does not qualify as a holder in due course, it may benefit from the protection of §9-330(d), which covers the transfer of instruments, that is, a "transfer" rather than a "negotiation."

    f. First Bank might have policed its collateral more sedulously by taking possession of the chattel paper as soon as Dealer leased or sold a golf cart. By taking possession, the bank would have preempted the operation of §9-330, which applies only if the finance company takes possession of the chattel paper. The bank might also have stamped the paper with a legend indicating that it was assigned to the bank, in which case §9-330(a) cannot apply. Section 9-330(b) would also be inapplicable in that case because the stamping of the paper would give the finance company knowledge that the purchase by the finance company violates the rights of the bank. §9-330(f).

143.

a. Under §9-315(a)(1) (if the sale free of the security interest is authorized) or §9-320(a), *B* defeats the security interest the dealer granted to the bank in the dealer's inventory. Of course, because the paper is proceeds from the sale of the bank's collateral, the bank has a security interest in the paper; and the paper includes a security interest in the boat.

b. Well, §9-315(a)(2) says the bank has a security interest in proceeds. The chattel paper (the sales contract) is proceeds and thus falls under the definition of collateral. When the dealer repossesses the boat, the boat is proceeds of the new collateral, and the bank has a security interest in the boat. [This analysis may not be the only way to get the bank a security interest in the boat, but it will suffice. The bank is going to lose anyway.] Dealer's repossession of the boat does not make the boat inventory. Repossession gives Dealer only a possessory interest in the goods; *B* is still the owner. Not until a foreclosure sale might the ownership change. §9-330, cmt. 10(a)(2).

c. Yes. The "sale" of the paper (chattel paper) to the finance company is an Article 9 secured transaction. *See* §9-109(a)(3). It operates to vest in Ace the dealer's rights under the sales agreement.

d. Ace Finance Co. has priority. Section 9-330(c)(2) clearly favors the finance company over the bank as to the boat, even if the finance company would lose to the bank under §9-322(a). This result, giving the finance company the sailboat ahead of the bank, parallels the rule of §9-330(a), which favors the finance company as to the chattel paper.

e. If *B* returned the boat for repairs, Dealer is only a bailee. First Bank gets no rights of any importance in the boat. Ace would thus prevail under §9-330(c). If *B* rejected the boat or revoked its acceptance, then Dealer owns it again. Both Ace and First Bank's rights are, however, subject to any claims *B* may have. §§9-403, 9-404. First Bank's security interest will reattach, as the goods are proceeds of the chattel paper. Ace also has rights in the returned boat as proceeds. If Ace has perfected only by possession, though, its proceeds right will be unperfected after twenty days. So First Bank wins? No. Even an unperfected security interest in chattel paper beats a perfected proceeds security interest. §9-330(c)(2).

144.

a. Yes, under the cited section.

b. Yes. The repo is a secured transaction. *R* is perfected by possession.

c. A security. §8-102(a)(15). It is also investment property. §9-102(a)(49).

d. Under §9-322(a)(1), the first to perfect would prevail. Bank perfected first and would prevail, but the section does not apply, as §9-331(a) hints, if *R* is a protected purchaser.

    e.   Yes. Section 9-322(a), if it applies, limits the rights of *R*, a "protected purchaser" under Article 8. *See* §8-303(b).

    f.   No. Section 9-331(a) prevents that.

145.   a.   Yes. Section 9-312(e) says so.

    b.   Ace has a security interest, and it is perfected under §9-313(a). Section 7-502(1)(a) indicates that Ace also has title to the document, but that would be an extraordinary result. Lenders do not speculate in commodities. They take security interests in them. Commercial banks are forbidden by law from speculating in commodities. We think §7-502(1)(a) is moderately hyperbolic and doubt that any lender would ever expect to realize more than the amount of its loan balance on the sale of the commodity or the receipt. Any excess surely belongs to the debtor or its trustee in bankruptcy. Buyers of soybeans would take title, but lenders against soybeans probably do not.

    c.   Section 9-322(a)(1) would give the note and the receipt to the bank, which perfected first, but the section does not apply.

    d.   Yes.

    e.   Yes. §9-331(a).

    f.   Yes, again. We think this is the proper analysis.

146.   a.   See the answer to Question 145(b) above.

    b.   Possibly when *B* applied for the letter of credit, *B* granted the bank a security interest in any documents and goods covered by them. If that is the case, the bank is perfected by virtue of its possession of the document. *See* §9-312(c). Note, moreover, that under §5-118, the bank has a statutory security interest in the document and that under §9-309(8), that security interest is perfected automatically upon attachment.

    c.   Article 9 does limit the rights of a holder by due negotiation of a document of title. *See* §9-331(a). The issuer in the normal course of a letter-of-credit transaction will take the document by due negotiation, and §9-320(a) cannot limit it.

Section 21. Bailments

147. There are three ways to take a security interest in goods that are not subject to a negotiable document of title. Note that this category includes goods in the hands of a bailee that has issued a nonnegotiable document as well as those in the hands of a bailee that has issued no document. In this problem, the pipeline company's acceptance of the delivery order operates as the issuance of a document of title. An accepted delivery order is the equivalent of a warehouse receipt. *See* §7-102, cmt. 3.

The three ways of perfecting a security interest are: (1) having a document issued in the name of the secured party, (2) notice that the bailee receives rendering it the agent of the secured party rather than of the original bailor, and (3) filing as to the goods. §9-312(d). Note that the notice to the bailee option can be quite efficient. Once the bailee receives the secured party's notice, the bailee, as a matter of bailment law, *see* §7-401(3), must deliver the goods to the secured party. The same is true if the bailee issues a warehouse receipt directly to the bank, as they often do in these cases. In the event of notice received by the bailee or bailee issuance of a nonnegotiable document to the bank, the secured party, the bank, is then in possession of the goods through its agent, the bailee. That possession, of course, can satisfy both the attachment provisions and the perfection provisions of Article 9. *See* §§9-203(b)(3)(B), 9-313(a). Section 9-312(c) does not apply here. Section 9-312(d) governs. The delivery order is nonnegotiable. In this case, if the bank used the second option of §9-312(d), the bank should have taken a security agreement from the buyer/borrower. Under the third option, filing, the bank should also take a security agreement from the buyer. In all probability, the bank will take a security agreement under all three options, because the security agreement covers matters that would otherwise not be covered.

If the bank, then, follows one of these three options in §9-312(d), it will have a perfected security interest in the propane.

148.   a.   Yes. Note the language in §9-312(c)(2) & cmt. 7. Prior to the Code, it was the prevailing view that goods subject to a negotiable document of title were "mere simulacra," that is, merely a shadow, their existence being wrapped up in the commodity paper, the warehouse receipt. The Code alters that view somewhat when it indicates that the bank may take a security interest in the goods themselves and perfect by filing. Note, however, that the security interest so perfected will be subordinate to Second Bank's security interest, as subsection (2) makes clear.

      b.   Yes. This is the preferred method of taking and perfecting a security interest in goods that are in the hands of a bailee that has issued a negotiable document for them. This rule enhances the value of the negotiable document—which passes easily from merchant to merchant in the marketing and financing of commodities.

      c.   Second will prevail, as the language of the subsection suggests. This rule, being more specific than the rule of §9-322(a)(1), will govern and is an exception to the rule of §9-322(a)(1) to the effect that generally the first to perfect will prevail.

149.   a.   All four of them. *See* §7-501.

      b.   Under the stated facts, *T* fails to rise to the level of a holder by due negotiation. The problem does not tell you that the receipt was negotiable. There is no indication that there has been an endorsement or that the receipt was in bearer form. *T* himself does not take in good faith, or for value, or in the ordinary course of business or finance.

150. Any of facts a through g would prevent B from rising to the level of a holder by due negotiation. (One note: in g, it is true that the definition of purchase includes gift. §1-201(b)(29) [§1-201(32)]. However, the value requirement in §7-501(4) effectively removes a donee from the definition of "holder by due negotiation.") Facts h and i, however, would not prevent B from being a holder by due negotiation, because banks in the ordinary course of business and finance take and transfer negotiable warehouse receipts.

151. B would have greater rights than T and greater rights than the producer, P. It does not matter whether B is a lender or a broker, because both entities take negotiable receipts in the ordinary course of their affairs. Note that B will be a holder by due negotiation only if the producer left a receipt in bearer form where a thief could get it or endorsed the receipt in blank and left it where a thief could get it.

152. C takes the same rights that B enjoyed. C comes under B's umbrella. *See* §7-504(1).

153. No. The rights of a person who does not take by due negotiation are strictly derivative of the rights of her transferor. She comes under the *"nemo dat"* rule of §7-504(1); she gets the rights of her transferor. T, the transferor, did not have rights superior to the producer.

154.   a. B qualifies for holder by due negotiation status, but B is subject to the paramount rights rule of §7-503(1). The producer's rights arise before the bailment. *See* cmt. 1 (2d sentence). *Cf.* §2-403.
  b. B will also lose to First Bank because the bank also enjoys paramount rights in the cotton. *Id.*
  c.   If T were a truck driver, his transfer of the receipt to B would not be in the ordinary course of business or finance. Truck drivers do not deal in warehouse receipts. Thus, B, not taking by due negotiation, has only those rights given it under §7-504(1) and loses to the true owner, the producer. The result is the same. The producer wins over the taker of the receipt, but the analysis differs.

155. If the producer entrusts the cotton to T, and if B takes by due negotiation (that is, if T is someone whose business it is to deal in warehouse receipts covering cotton, another cotton producer, for example), B may be able to escape the effect of the paramount rights rule of §7-503(1) under subsection (a) or (b) of that section. Those subsections fashion exceptions to the operation of the paramount rights rule for situations in which the party with the paramount rights clothes the bailor, T in this case, with actual or apparent authority to bail the goods. The facts suggest that the producer has indeed clothed T with such authority, in which case B will prevail over the producer. Once a producer has chosen to place its goods into commerce, it perforce loses some of its protections against relatively more innocent buyers or transferees. Presumably the producer can choose its bailees carefully and reduce its risks.

156. The bank should make an estoppel by deed type of argument under §7-502(1)(c). Under this theory, the late delivery of the ore by W to the carrier "feeds" the earlier issued negotiable bill. This provision codifies a pre-Code case, Baldwin v. Childs, 249 N.Y. 212, 163 N.E. 737 (1928), in which the court invoked the estoppel. The bank would lose, however, had the bill been nonnegotiable. A nonnegotiable bill is like a quitclaim deed; its taker receives only those rights that the transferor possessed. When *W* conveys a nonnegotiable bill to the bank, the bank is not a holder by due negotiation and does not benefit from estoppel rules of §7-502(1)(c), but comes under §7-504(1).

Section 22.   *Fixture Priority Rules*

157.   a.   This question falls into the general rule of Article 9's fixture priorities. That rule appears in §9-334(c). Heating Co. cannot fit itself into subsections (d) through (h), exceptions to the general rule and therefore is subordinate to S&L's mortgage. Under the given facts, Heating Co. cannot qualify for the priority of subsection (d) because the facts tell you that Heating Co. does not have a purchase money security interest. [Most of the time, Heating Co. will have a purchase money security interest, as you suspect; and as we will see below, Heating Co. will prevail over the mortgagee if it satisfies the requirements of subsection (d).]

b.   Mortgage Investment Co. would defeat Heating Co. under the first rule of conveyancing law. Mortgage would succeed to the rights of S&L. Because S&L defeats Heating, Mortgage would defeat Heating. That result is consistent with the rule of subsection (e).

c.   Under the altered facts, which do give the heating company a purchase-money security interest, the heating company would defeat the S&L and Mortgage Investment if Heating Co. files a fixture filing within 20 days of the time installs the furnace. *See* §9-334(d).

158.   a.   S&L will have priority. Generally, to defeat the real estate encumbrance's interest in a fixture, the secured party must make a fixture filing before the encumbrancer records its mortgage. Here, Heating Co. failed to make a fixture filing and cannot qualify for the protection of subsection (e). Thus, the general rule of subsection (c) applies, and the encumbrancer wins.

b.   The answer would be the same even if Heating Co. made a fixture filing during the designated period. Although subsection (d) contains a grace period, the heating company has not satisfied the requirement that its fixture be affixed *after* the encumbrancer obtains its mortgage. Any other rule would mislead the mortgagee. It would be lending against real estate that it thought had a new furnace, when in fact it was going to lose the furnace to the heating company. Subsection (d) requires the purchase-money secured party to show that the rights of the encumbrancer arose when the old furnace was in the building.

159.   a.   Here Heating Co. can avail itself of the purchase money rule of subsection (d), having complied with all of its requirements.

  b.   i.   In the event the mortgage were a construction mortgage, the heating company loses Under subsection (h). Under these facts, the construction mortgagee is not subject to the purchase money rule for reasons adequately set out in Comment 11.

  ii.   Heating Co. loses if it fails to file within 20 days of installation. May 23 is the 20th day.

160.   a.   First Bank wins.

  b.   There is no dispute with a real estate encumbrancer here, so §9-334 does not apply. Section 9-322(a)(1) governs.

  c.   No.

  d.   The banks should be able to defeat a real estate encumbrancer under §9-334(e)(2)(A). This machine fits the notion of a readily removable office machine. A non-fixture filing is sufficient to defeat the real estate encumbrancer who should not reasonably rely on such collateral, whether or not state fixture law deems it a fixture. Note, however, that this exception is available to the banks only if they perfect before the goods are affixed. The exception is not limited in any way by the time that the encumbrancer obtains its mortgage. This is an important rule for equipment lessors, many of whom are really secured parties but who are not in a position to bother with the trouble of making a fixture filing, such filings involving, as they do, a legal description of sorts and a determination whether the debtor has an interest of record in the premises. *See* §9-502(b).

161.   If the collateral were a manufactured home, the readily removable office machine exception would not apply. The bank, then, would have to look for another rule to protect itself. If it made a fixture filing on May 1, before the encumbrancer obtained its mortgage interest on May 3, the bank would win. If it did not file ahead of the mortgagee, the bank could show that it satisfies the purchase money rule of subsection (d). If the home is subject to a certificate of title law, the bank might be able to use subsection (e)(4), a provision that is, perhaps, the easiest to satisfy.

162.   Subsection (e)(3) protects the banks against the trustee if they make a non-fixture filing. Section 544(a)(1) of the Bankruptcy Code gives the trustee in bankruptcy the rights of a lien creditor against the real estate, but §9-334(e)(3) renders the rights of the lien creditor subordinate to the rights of the secured party that perfects by a non-fixture filing. The rights of the trustee as lien creditor are a function of state law. Thus, even though a court finds that the machine is a fixture, if the secured parties have filed centrally, they will defeat the trustee. Note that the Bankruptcy Code anticipates this rule by denying good-faith purchase status for the trustee in fixtures, though it otherwise it does grant the trustee good-faith purchase status as to real estate. *See* Bankruptcy Code §544(a)(3) (giving the trustee the rights of a bona fide purchaser of real estate "other than fixtures").

163.   The S&L will get the window. The exception for consumer goods in subsection (e)(2)(C) only applies to replacements of domestic appliances. Dealer should have made a fixture filing within 20 days of the installation to gain priority over the mortgagee. If, however, the collateral had been a new refrigerator to replace an old one and assuming that the court held it to be a fixture, Dealer would win, having qualified for the protection of subsection (e)(2)(C).

   If the dispute were between the dealer and the debtor's trustee in bankruptcy, the dealer would prevail as to the window because the trustee's rights are limited under subsection (e)(3). This security interest is automatically perfected. Dealer, then, would qualify for the protection of subsection (e)(3). That assumes, of course, as the question states, that the window is a fixture. The court might find that it is ordinary building materials incorporated into the real estate, in which case a secured part such as the dealer cannot obtain a security interest in it. *See* §9-334(a).

164.   This is a review of the purchase-money rule of subsection (d). The non-fixture filing is not good against the mortgagee. The subsection requires a fixture filing. Such a filing on June 9 would be sufficient to give the heating company priority. A filing on June 29 would not. If the mortgage is a construction mortgage, of course, subsection (d) does not apply. *See* §9-334(h).

165.   a.   These facts invoke the general rule of subsection (c). They do not fit into any of the exceptions in subsections (d) through (h). First Bank, the real estate encumbrancer, prevails.

   b.   If First took its mortgage on May 3, the result would differ. This would then be a subsection (e)(1) case. The mortgagee would have a warning that Second Bank was in the picture. Second Bank's filing would be of record before First Bank, the mortgagee, recorded. Mortgagees traditionally do not disburse funds until they have filed their mortgages and run a search to make certain that there are no filings made between the date of the mortgagee's commitment to lend and the date of the recording. If they see a fixture filing, they do not disburse the loan proceeds until matters are ironed out.

166.   St. Paul will defeat the trustee even if the court finds that the personal computers are fixtures. *See* §9-334(e). St Paul will defeat the mortgagee under subsection (e)(2)(A), the computers falling within the definition of readily removable office machines. Note that St. Paul's strategy makes sense. It avoids the expense of a fixture filing, and it avoids the risk that a court might find the computers to be non-fixtures. In that case, a fixture filing in the local real estate records office would not be sufficient to defeat other secured parties or the trustee in bankruptcy of the debtor. Subsections (e)(2) and (3) apply only if the court finds that the goods are fixtures. If the court finds that they are not fixtures but plain, ordinary equipment, the fixture filing in the real estate records will be defective; but a non-fixture filing in the secretary of state's office is good for equipment that is not a fixture. *See* §9-501(a)(2).

Section 23. Further Scope Questions

167. *G* prevails. Note that *G*'s lien has purchase-money features that probably account for this last in time, first in right rule. Note also that if *G* surrenders possession of the car, *G* loses the lien. *G* would lose if the lien were statutory and if the statute provides that the secured party has priority. That exception does not apply if the lien is a common law lien that does not have priority. Section 9-333 reverses that rule for common law liens. *Cf.* §7-209(3)(a) & cmt. 3 (statute rendering possessory lien subordinate to prior-filed security interest).

168.   a.   This is a sale. *See* §1-203(d) [§1-201(37)(d)]. Lessor should file but may designate itself as "lessor" and may designate the buyer as "lessee." *See* §9-505(a) & cmt. 2.

b.   This is a true lease, not a secured transaction. Because it is not clear that the lessee will exercise the option, we cannot say that the lessee will take the goods for the nominal consideration at the end of the second term. No filing, then, is necessary. Were the consideration for exercise of the option nominal, we should assume that the lessee will exercise it. In that case, we have a sale disguised as a lease, the lessor is a secured party, and filing is necessary. While this lease is a true lease during the first term, if the lessee exercises the option, during the second term, it will be a secured transaction—a sale with the "lessor" holding a security interest. Thus, during the second term, filing would be necessary.

c.   This is also a true lease. Were it a sale, the lessee would not agree to return goods to the lessor while they have a useful life.

d.   This is clearly a sale. *See* §1-203(b)(2) [§1-201(37)(b)]. A filing is essential to protect the "lessor."

e.   This is a sale. *See* §1-203(e) [§1-201(37)]. The estimate is as of the date the parties enter into the transaction.

f.   i.   This is a sale. *See* subsection (c).
ii.   One hundred dollars is probably nominal. Most equipment's salvage value would exceed $100.
iii.   While the authority is in conflict, a price that is considerably below market value is nominal. Even if the lessee doesn't want the equipment, at that price she will buy it and resell it in the market at a profit. Thus, a filing is necessary.

g.   In all of these cases it is necessary to know whether the lessee has the right to terminate the lease with short notice. That right in the "lessee" suggests that there is no sale. The lessee is retaining the option of getting out of the deal and putting the goods back on the "lessor." If the market falls, that is exactly what the lessee will do. In a contract of sale, the buyer has to take the goods even if the market falls. Thus the right to terminate is an incident of a true lease and usually no filing is necessary.

169. Whether the consignment is "true" or an inventory financing arrangement no longer matters. This consignment is subject to Article 9. *See* §9-109(a)(4). The definition of "consignment" carves out exceptions to the scope provision. *See* §9-102(a)(20). The definitional exceptions do not apply in this transaction unless the value of the bicycles is less than $1,000.

170.   *B* is either a consignor or a seller of inventory on credit that is trying to retain a security interest. In either case, the Code is willing to give *B* priority over First Bank but only if *B* complies with Article 9 rules for an inventory purchase money priority. *See* §9-324(b).

171.
    a.   Under strict security of property analysis, the trustee has no rights in the cotton because *G* has no rights in it. *G* is only a bailee. *But cf.* §9-319 (providing that consignee has full title to consigned goods). Courts might be concerned, however, that the practice evident here is not commercially harmless.

    b.   This setting is redolent of pre-Code consignment arrangements that misled creditors of the bailee. Under modern credit practices, however, the argument that the bailment creates ostensible ownership in *C* is weak. Few, if any, of *C*'s creditors will rely on its naked possession of inventory. Even *G*'s inventory lender will soon learn, if it is at all sophisticated, that the cotton belongs to the farmers and not to *G*. In any event, it makes no difference that the trustee had knowledge. *Cf.* §9-317(a)(2) (suggesting that lack of knowledge not necessary for trustee to defeat unperfected secured party).

172.
    a.   No. It is not ordinary for a buyer to take goods in satisfaction of a debt. This transaction is out of the ordinary course.

    b.   No. The facts do not indicate that Aussie had a security interest. Aussie is simply a transferee and a creditor of Wool Co.

    c.   Section 2-402(2) refers to common law fraud rules (*Twyne's Case*, 76 Eng. Rep. 809 (Star Chamber 1601)) under which it was a fraudulent conveyance when a buyer paid for goods and left them with the seller. Both the common law rule and §2-402(2) make exception for such arrangements when there is an innocent explanation for them. The facts do not provide such an explanation, and this transaction between Wool and Mill may be a fraud on Aussie, in which case Aussie has a better claim to the wool than Mill.

173.   Generally, if the lease is a true lease, the creditors of the lessee take subject to the terms of the lease. *See* §2A-307(1). It does not matter whether the lease payments are nominal or reasonable. In the facts of this problem, the arrangement may well be a true lease. Note, however, that the lessee might use the equipment up. In other words, it may be that the lessor is selling the equipment or giving the equipment to the lessee. If the lease provides that the lessee must return the equipment if the lessee does not buy strapping from lessor, the arrangement sounds more like the true lease. This may be a case for a cautionary filing designating the parties as lessee and lessor. *See* §9-505(a).

Section 24. The Seller's Right to Reclaim

174.   a.   *B* has a special property, which is to say that it has an interest, the contours of which depend on the rights and remedies of the parties. *See* §2-501(1).

b.   Yes, as the section indicates. In view of *B*'s breach, *S* may withhold delivery and may resell the goods free of *B*'s interest. *See* §2-703(a), (d) & (f).

c.   Almost certainly *B*'s inventory lender will have taken a security interest in *B*'s after-acquired inventory; and once *B* has a property interest in the goods, the inventory lender's security interest will have attached under §9-203(b)(2). Under the first rule of conveyancing law, the lender's interest, however, will stand no higher than *B*'s. Because *S* defeats *B*, *S* will also defeat *B*'s inventory lender.

175.   If it learns that *B* is insolvent, *S* may stop delivery while the goods are in transit. If *B* is in breach, *S* may stop delivery of goods in transit if the goods comprise a carload or container load. *See* §§2-702(1), 2-705(1).

176.   Absent fraud by *B*, once the goods are delivered, *S* has no rights in them. To retain rights, *S* must have *B* execute a security agreement granting *S* a security interest. *B*'s inventory lender and *B*'s trustee in bankruptcy will obtain interests in the goods when *B* obtains an interest. To the extent that *B*'s interest defeats *S* (and *B*'s interest in the goods is supeior to the interest of *S* under the facts of this problem, even if B does not pay), the lender and the trustee will defeat *S*. All of this follows from the first rule of conveyancing, the derivation principle, which holds that a taker (the lender or the trustee) enjoys the same rights as the transferor.

177.   If a buyer fraudulently (either as a matter of fact or a matter of law) induces a seller to deliver goods on credit, the buyer has only voidable title, and the seller has the right to avoid that title, a right to reclaim. The demand required by §2-702(2) is described by some as a perfection feature of the right to reclaim, but it may be more accurate to view it as a limit in the nature of a statute of limitations. In any event, the seller must make it for the right to reclaim to survive. Bear in mind that this right to reclaim is an extraordinary claim against property delivered under the contract of sale. Normally, a seller loses all rights in goods once it delivers them. True, the seller can retain a security interest, but that retention must be pursuant to agreement. (The seller's Article 2 security interest, a security interest that arises not by the agreement of the buyer but by operation of law, *see* §2-505(1), expires on delivery to the buyer of the goods or the negotiable document of title covering them.) The right to reclaim arises by operation of law and is in the nature of a non-possessory lien without notice, i.e., a secret lien—an extraordinary commercial concept. Courts have generally and rightly enforced the demand requirement strictly. Note that the section does away with the demand requirement if the buyer has made written representation of its solvency. Most courts do not consider the check a written representation of solvency, though at least one did. Common law fraud is good enough.

Receiving goods on credit while insolvent, whether buyer knows it or not, is fraud at law. Paying for goods in a cash sale with a check drawn on insufficient funds is also fraud at law. It does not matter that the buyer is unaware that it is overdrawn. Note that §2-702 does not apply to cash sale fraud, because the cash sale is not, by definition, a credit sale.

178.   a. S has a right to reclaim.
   b. No
   c. Comments to §2-507 originally provided that S was required to protect his interest by giving the demand required by the credit sale section (§2-702). The Permanent Editorial Board, in what some view as an inappropriate exercise of its office, changed the comment; and the requirement for the demand is now omitted. (Check your state's version of §2-507.)
   d. It does not matter whether B knew that the check was an overdraft. If the check is post-dated, however, §2-507 does not apply. As §2-511, cmt. 6 indicates, a post-dated check renders the transaction a credit sale, and the governing section is §2-702, not §2-507.

179.   a. The reference in the comment to the effect that the right to reclaim conforms with the policy of the good-faith purchase sections of the Code supports the view that the seller's right to reclaim does not defeat a purchaser for value who takes the goods in good faith from the fraudulent buyer B. A buyer in ordinary course is a good-faith purchaser for value.
   b. A secured party is a good-faith purchaser for value whether or not it is perfected and, therefore, defeats the reclaiming seller. (Note that a lien creditor, not being a good-faith purchaser, will not defeat the reclaiming seller under this analysis.)

180. Not under the current official version of the comments. Under the former version, however, the demand was necessary. *See* your state's version of §2-507, cmt. 3.

181. Traditionalists might call it "the property" or "title."

182. Voidable title. *See* §2-403(1) (2d sentence).

183.   a. Good title. *See* §2-403(1) (2d sentence).
   b. Good title. *See* id.
   c. Good title. *See* id. (A buyer in bulk is not a buyer in ordinary course, but it clearly is a purchaser and it can be a good-faith purchaser for value.)

184. No. The lien creditor is not a purchaser and cannot defeat the right to reclaim. The words "subject to," as courts have construed them, mean that the seller's right to reclaim is subject to the rights of the lien creditor, whatever those rights happen to be. Those rights, moreover, arise not under the Code but under non-Code law. In most jurisdictions, Pennsylvania being an exception, the non-Code law provides (mostly in nineteenth-century cases) that the lien creditor's rights are indeed subordinate to those of the reclaiming seller. The words "subject to" in §2-702(3) should be read not to mean "inferior to" but to mean subject to whatever rights the common law gives the lien creditor.

185. a. It is not clear whether Bankruptcy Code §546(c) is meant to be a provision that excludes the cash seller's right to reclaim fashioned by UCC §2-507 or by the right to reclaim at common law. The cash seller's right to reclaim, of course, arises in bankruptcy much less often than the credit seller's claim. It may be that the omission was unintentional. In that case, the cash seller may retain the right to reclaim against the trustee, a lien creditor, in bankruptcy. If the section is meant to codify the only circumstances in which a seller has a right to reclaim, the cash seller will lose to the trustee, and so will the seller relying on common law fraud for its right to reclaim the goods. Only the credit seller will be able to use the provision against the trustee.

b. Yes, the seller must perfect by making a written demand. The UCC does not require the demand to be in writing. Note also that the timing language in the two sections is different. The UCC says "within ten days after receipt"; the Bankruptcy Code says "before ten days after receipt." Check the cases in your circuit.

c. Clearly, everyone assumes that the words "subject to" in Bankruptcy Code §546(c) mean "subordinate to." That conclusion may be incorrect, however, in light of the cases construing the same terms in UCC §2-702(3) differently. *See* Problem 185. In Pennsylvania, the lien creditor defeated the reclaiming seller at common law. In most other jurisdictions, the lien creditor lost to the reclaiming seller. If the words "subject to" do not mean "inferior to" but mean that the court must determine outside the UCC and the Bankruptcy Code what the rights of the lien creditor against the reclaiming seller are, the result may be in favor of the seller in most jurisdictions and against him in Pennsylvania and perhaps elsewhere. Most writers and courts ignore the history of the meaning of "subject to" in these cases and read Bankruptcy Code §546(c) as giving the seller's right to reclaim priority over the trustee's lien.

d. Such statements protect the seller outside the bankruptcy context under UCC §2-702(2) but do not avail the seller in bankruptcy, Bankruptcy Code §546(c) not having an analogous provision.

186. *S*'s right to reclaim is not a security interest. Historically, it stems from the seller's lien, the notion that a seller wrongfully deprived of the goods by the buyer could get them back. The idea that a seller's lien can exist when the goods are out of the seller's possession is an extraordinary one because it is a secret lien. To extend the secret lien to proceeds from the sale of the goods by the seller would be extraordinary treatment of an extraordinary right. One court has so ruled, however, and raised the question posed in this problem. It is probably best to avoid these questions by refusing to let the reclaiming seller have a claim to the proceeds; but if the reclaiming seller does have a right to the proceeds, that right should be subordinate to other parties claiming proceeds that would defeat the seller. The inventory and account

lenders are good-faith purchasers for value and should have a better claim to the proceeds than the reclaiming seller. The trustee and the lien creditor, on the other hand, would lose the goods to the reclaiming seller and arguably should lose the proceeds to the reclaiming seller.

187.   As the preceding answer suggests, the seller's right to reclaim is neither an Article 9 nor an Article 2 security interest. First, Article 9 applies to consensus secured transactions. The right of the seller to reclaim arises by operation of law. Second, the seller's right to reclaim extends to the full value of the goods. A secured party in Article 9 is entitled to realize on the collateral only to the extent of the debtor's debt. The reclaiming seller's interest is not so limited. The reclaiming seller can take the goods back, sell them for more than what the original buyer agreed to pay, and pocket the difference between the original purchase price and the resale purchase price. Finally, the reclaiming seller need not comply with any of the debtor protection rules of Part 6 of Article 9 and need not perfect its interest.

The right to reclaim is similar to the Article 2 security interest defined in §2-505(1)(a), and it may be that that security interest, which arises by operation of the law of negotiable documents of title and is not subject to any of the strictures that apply to Article 9 security interests, is misnamed. The security interest defined in §2-505 looks much like the seller's right to reclaim. Note, however, that comment 1 to §2-505 states that the security interest of the seller "is restricted to securing payment or performance by the buyer." That language suggests that the seller cannot reclaim the goods, resell them, and pocket the difference between the original contract price and the resale price. There are no cases of which we are aware. The security interest defined in §2-711(3), though it arises by operation of law and not by consensual transfer, clearly sounds like a security interest. Under §2-711(3), the buyer may resort to the goods only to the extent of the sum due from the defaulting seller. After the buyer satisfies that claim against the seller, the buyer must return the goods or any excess value in them to the seller.

Section 25.   Article 9 and the Powers of the Trustee in Bankruptcy

At this point, it would be worthwhile to review UCC §9-317. *See* Problems 106 through 110.

188.   Generally, a perfected secured party such as the bank will defeat the trustee's lien creditor rights, even in after-acquired equipment, though it may have problems with the trustee's power to avoid a preference. Here, however, the debtor acquired the equipment after the date of bankruptcy. In that event, the Bankruptcy Code interdicts application of the UCC. Bankruptcy Code §552 makes it clear that the bank has no rights in equipment acquired after the debtor files in bankruptcy.

189.   No. The DIP's rights in the inventory were subordinate to those of the bank as of the commencement of the bankruptcy case, that is, the filing of the bankruptcy petition. The subsequent sale should not deprive the bank of its

collateral. The section makes it clear that proceeds from the sale of collateral belong to the secured party. *See* Bankruptcy Code §552(b)(1).

190. Normally, the automatic stay section, Bankruptcy Code §362, prevents creditors from taking any action against the debtor's property after the commencement of the case. Here, however, the effect of the stay would be to impair the rights of an innocent purchase-money creditor. The cited sections make it clear that it is not a violation of the automatic stay to file the financing statement. That filing renders Manufacturing Co. perfected as of the time of bankruptcy petition filing. *See* UCC §9-317(e).

191. The automatic stay does not inhibit the giving of the seller's reclamation notice as required by UCC §2-702(2) and Bankruptcy Code §546(c).

192. All of the proposed actions violate the automatic stay. Note that the attempt to file a financing statement after the commencement of the case would be a useless act in any event because the trustee, having the rights of a lien creditor as of December 1, would defeat the secured party under the rule of Bankruptcy Code §544(a)(1) and UCC §9-317(a)(2)(A). This is not a purchase money security interest.

193.

a. As we will see later in the study of the timing provision of the preference section (547(e)(2)(A)), for preference purposes, this transaction occurred on August 30, outside the preference period; the trustee may not set the transaction aside as a preferential transfer voidable in bankruptcy.

b. Yes, Electric Co. will defeat First Bank under UCC §9-317(a)(2), because Electric Co. became a lien creditor prior to the time that the bank perfected. For purposes of UCC §9-317(a)(2), perfection occurred on September 4, which is after the date on which the electric company obtained its lien, September 3. *See* §544(b)(1).

c. Yes, the trustee may set the electric company's lien aside as a preference. It is a transfer of the debtor's property on account of an antecedent debt while the debtor is presumed to be insolvent and during the preference period. The trustee will be able to set aside the electric company's lien.

d. Yes, that is the effect of Bankruptcy Code §551.

e. The answer is that the trustee is limited by the amount of the electric company's lien. The trustee may not upset the secured party's claim entirely. Under the rule of Moore v. Bay, 284 U.S. 4 (1931), a curious rule that almost never applies, the trustee may upset the whole claim, but *Moore* applies only to unsecured bankruptcy claims. *See* §544(b)(1). A lien creditor's claim is, for Bankruptcy Code purposes, a secured claim. *See* Bankruptcy Code §506; and the rule of Moore v. Bay does not apply.

Section 26. Preferences

194. All of these transactions, the payment of money, the creation of a security interest, and the obtaining of a judicial lien are transfers of the debtor's property on account of an antecedent debt during the 90-day period while the debtor is presumed to be insolvent. In virtually every case, such transfers permit the transferee creditor to obtain more from the debtor's estate than the creditor would have obtained in a Chapter 7 liquidation. In short, all three of the transfers are preferences that the trustee may avoid.

195. a. This is probably a preference because the note is a demand note.

b. If, however, the payment were made on a debt that was completely secured, there is no preference because the bank would get no more by virtue of the payment than it would get in a Chapter 7 liquidation. Note, moreover, that when a creditor is completely secured, payment on the debt reduces the debt and frees up collateral. By virtue of the payment, the debtor's "equity" in the collateral increases by the amount of the payment. In such cases, it is difficult to see how the payment satisfies the preference definition. The payment does not deplete the estate. On the debtor's balance sheet the cash account is reduced, but the equity value in the equipment account increases by the same amount.

c. This is a preference. Transfers to insiders are avoidable if they occur within one year of the commencement of the case. The president would be an insider. *See* Bankruptcy Code §101(31)(B)(ii).

d. Unlike the payment under the demand note in Problem (a) above, this regularly scheduled installment payment on the note is protected by the exception in Bankruptcy Code §547(c)(2).

e. If the grant of the security interest and the making of the loan by the secured party are contemporaneous, the trustee will not be able to set the security interest aside. If the transaction is intended by the parties to be contemporaneous and if the transaction is substantially contemporaneous, the exception in Bankruptcy Code §547(c)(1) applies. It is critical, then, for the secured party to be able to show that the loan and the grant of the security interest occurred on the same day or thereabouts. The timing rule of Bankruptcy Code §547(e)(2)(A) indicates that if the secured party perfects its security interest within ten days of the time the interest attaches, the time of the transfer is the time of attachment. (In Bankruptcy Code parlance, "at the time such transfer takes effect between the transferor and the transferee" is the equivalent of the UCC concept of "attachment.") If the secured party does not file until after November 13, the timing rule indicates that the time of the transfer is the time of perfection—November 14, say. In that case, we have a transfer on November 14 of the debtor's collateral to a secured party that made a loan on November 3. That is not a substantially contemporaneous transfer. It is a transfer on account of an antecedent debt and would be a preference that the trustee could avoid.

 f. Yes, it matters because a filing within the ten-day period allowed by the timing rule renders the transfer effective on August 31, a day which falls outside the preference period, while a filing more than ten days after attachment renders the transfer effective on the date of filing, which will fall within the preference period and will be a transfer that meets the other elements of the preference definition.

 g. There are two time periods here. The first is a ten-day period under the timing rule of subsection (e)(A). That period begins to run on the day of attachment. The second is a twenty-day period that arises under the purchase-money exception in subsection (c)(3). That twenty-day period begins to run on the day the goods are delivered and gives the secured party more time within which to file than the timing rule of subsection (e)(A) allows.

 h. This is really an attachment problem. The timing rule governs and says that as long as the secured party perfects within ten days of attachment, the transfer shall be deemed to have occurred at the time of attachment. If perfection is later, the time of the transfer shall be deemed to be the time of perfection. Attachment does not occur until the bank makes a loan on the 10th. Because the bank perfected within ten days of the 10th; the bank's transfer occurs on September 10, and the transfer is contemporaneous with the bank's loan. There is no preference. Note that if the bank had given value on August 15 by making a binding commitment, attachment would have occurred on that date, and the perfection on September 17 would constitute a transfer outside of the ten-day grace period. This result may seem harsh, but it is consistent with the Bankruptcy Code's (and the UCC's) policy of encouraging prompt perfection of security interests. Remember that the secured party that does not file is holding a secret lien.

 i. These facts illustrate the operation of the netting exception in subsection (c)(4). The transfer of the security interest on September 15 is a preference, but the subsequent unsecured loan on October 15 prompts the netting of the two transactions, so that the trustee's avoidance of the September 15 transfer is limited to $30,000, the difference between the $50,000 preferential transfer on September 15 and the unsecured advance on October 15.

 j. The two monthly payments to the trade creditor are precisely the kind of payments that subsection (c)(2) excepts. Otherwise, these payments are clearly transfers that would be voidable under the definition in subsection (2).

196. a. The bank cannot obtain an interest in an account until it arises. When an account arises within the preference period, the bank obtains an interest on that date. Bear in mind, the bank's claim here is not to proceeds from the sale of inventory. This bank is an account lender not an inventory lender

 b. Yes, this is a transfer that fits the definition of a preference. No, there was such an attempt in the pre-revised version of Article 9. *See* pre-revised §9-108. That was an attempt by state legislatures to override bankruptcy law. Bankruptcy Code §547(e)(3) neutered old §9-108.

    c.   Yes, it would be a problem if the Bankruptcy Code did not make allowances. Account lenders typically rely on after-acquired property, and that perfectly legitimate business practice runs afoul of the preference section unless there is an exception for it.

    d.   The Bankruptcy Code does make allowance for account lenders that rely on after-acquired accounts and inventory lenders that rely on after-acquired inventory. The rule is set forth in subsection (c)(5).

    e.   Secured equipment lenders tend to rely on discrete items of collateral and not on after-acquired equipment. Their lending practices will not be seriously offended by a preference rule that says security interests in after acquired equipment that the debtor obtains during the preference period will be voidable. It is true that some working capital lenders rely on after-acquired equipment. The preference section tells them not to rely too heavily.

197.   a.   Under the first set of facts, there is no preference. Subsection (c)(5) is an improvement-in-position test. The secured party that is oversecured on the 90th day cannot improve its position. That secured party, therefore, will not receive a preference by virtue of the debtor's acquisition of additional inventory during the preference period.

    b.   If the secured party is underscored on the 90th day, there may be an improvement in position. Under the modified facts, the secured party was underscored in the amount of $14,000 on the 10th day and was fully secured on the date of bankruptcy. The secured party has improved its position to the extent of $14,000 and will have to return all but $5,000 worth of the inventory to the trustee.

    c.   This is simple math. Under the first example, there is a preference of $2,000; under the second and third there is no preference, there being no improvement in position; the secured party is still $2,000 undersecured.

198.   As long as the parties intended from the time of the loan that it would be a secured loan, the transaction is not a preference. It fits the exception in subsection (c)(1) for substantially contemporaneous transactions. If, however, the bank made the loan and then thought better of it and asked for collateral, there is a preference.

199.   As long as the parties intended from the time of the loan that it would be a secured loan, the transaction is not a preference. It fits the exception in subsection (c)(1) for substantially contemporaneous transactions. If, however, the bank made the loan and then thought better of it and asked for collateral, there is a preference.

Section 27. The Trustee as Lien Creditor

200. Yes. Under the preference section's timing rule, §547(e)(2)(c)(i), the transfer occurs immediately before the commencement of the case and, therefore, falls within the preference period. Note also that this secured party is unperfected at the time of filing and, therefore, will lose to the trustee under Bankruptcy Code §544(a)(1).

201.

    a. The analysis differs, but the trustee still wins. Because the filing occurs after the commencement of the case, the trustee will defeat the secured party under Bankruptcy Code §544(a)(1). In this case the trustee will not be able to attack the transaction as a preference. The grace period in the preference section, Bankruptcy Code §547(e)(2)(C), gives the secured party ten days to perfect. That grace period only protects the secured party from a preference attack, however. The timing rule of subsection (e) applies only "[f]or the purposes of this section," id., that is, the preference section. The secured party may not avail itself of the timing rule when the trustee makes a strong-arm challenge under Bankruptcy Code §544(a)(1).

    b. It would matter that the secured party had a purchase-money security interest. A purchase money secured party is not subject to attack under Bankruptcy Code §544(a)(1) if the purchase money secured party perfects within twenty days of the time the debtor receives the collateral. *See* UCC §9-317(e).

Section 28. Part 5: Default

202.

    a. Yes, Debtor is in violation of the note and the security agreement. The secured party may enforce its rights. *See* §9-609(a)(1).

    b. No. Under §9-201 and §9-317(a)(2), the secured party defeats the rights of the lien creditor whose lien arises after the secured party perfects.

    c. It does not matter that Debtor is current on the note. If she has breached a provision in the security agreement by permitting a lien creditor to assert an interest in the collateral, the secured party may proceed against the collateral. To let a creditor attach one's property is normally the prelude to bad things, and the bank's conduct is quite reasonable.

203. This question fleshes out the meaning of "breach of the peace" in §9-609(b)(2).

    a. This conduct is probably proper. The cases are generally tough on the bank in this setting, but this conduct is probably not a breach of the peace.

    b. This is probably not a breach of the peace. If the employee told Banker not to come into the premises, there might well be a breach.

c.   This conduct is not permissible. It is a breach of the peace even if the security agreement gave Bank the right to go on the premises. The agreement did not give Bank the right to break the lock.

d.   Some courts object to this kind of repossession, but a majority seem to indicate that it is all right absent some additional fact, such as the debtor's brandishing a shotgun. (You were not aware that banking was such an exciting profession.) The consensus seems to have emerged that the bank should not try to repossess the goods in the debtor's presence if the debtor objects. The bank that does not train its repo agents to avoid foul language is asking for trouble, as one bank learned to its dismay.

204.

a.   The fact that in retrospect we know the price was below the market price does not mean that the bank misbehaved. *See* §9-627(a). If the bank can show that it sought purchasers through advertisements and that it made inquiries of used equipment dealers as to the going price for the collateral, the bank has probably satisfied the requirement of §9-610(b). A few courts take the approach that a lower-than-market price indicates that the bank is liable for losses under §9-625(b) & (e).

b.   It is proper to use a dealer if that conduct will fetch (or arguably will fetch) the best price. The deduction for the commission is probably envisioned by the language of §9-627(b).

c.   The timing of the sale is relevant in determining whether the bank acted in a commercially reasonable fashion. The fact that an earlier sale would have yielded a better price is not evidence per se that the bank failed to act properly, but it is an indication that it did so. *See* §9-627(a). In all of these settings, the bank must guard against appearances of commercial unreasonableness and must be able to prove the actions that it took. Experienced bankers, then, log all telephone calls in connection with the preparation for the sale, keep copies of advertisements and correspondence in connection with the sale, and make a record of face-to-face conversations. These practices are tedious, but in litigation such records are valuable.

d.   The secured party may purchase the collateral at a public or a private sale; but if it purchases at a private sale, it must show that it paid a recognized market price. *See* §9-610(c).

205. Yes. *See* §9-617(b).

206.

a.   Note that as a general principle, debtors are liable for any deficiency. *See* §9-608. The issue here is whether the secured party's failure to observe the notice requirements (or other secured party duties under Part 6) prevents the secured party from seeking the deficiency. Pre-revised Article 9 cases were split. Some said that the secured party's failure to comply with the predecessor of §9-611(b) barred the secured party from a deficiency judgment. Others said that the failure merely shifted to the secured party the burden of proving that the secured party got the best price. Section 9-626 provides the answer by creating a presumption that a sale in accordance with Part 6 would have yielded a price leaving no deficiency. The secured party may, however, marshal evidence to overcome that presumption.

b. The debtor's pre-default waiver is ineffective. *See* §9-624(a).

[Note that these answers assume that the debtor is not a consumer.]

207.   a. Yes. The debtor is in default, and the secured party may proceed. Default in an interest payment can be quite innocent, but it can also indicate that the debtor is in trouble. The acceleration clause will probably be enforced, though there was some indication during the heyday of lender liability that courts would examine the secured party's conduct for evidence of bad faith. Generally, however, the secured party can proceed against the collateral. Note that a bank cannot accelerate on the grounds that it deems itself insecure unless it acts in the good-faith belief that it is insecure. *See* §1-309 [§1-208]. The right to accelerate the full debt in the event of default on an installment such as an interest payment, however, is generally not subject to good-faith inquiry.

b. Yes. The debtor is seeking, in effect, to reclaim the collateral, a right that the Code and debtor/creditor law always gives to a debtor. *See* §9-506. Note that the debtor must also pay the secured party's reasonable expenses of repossessing the collateral and its expenses in connection with preparing for the sale.

PART TWO

PAYMENT SYSTEMS

Payment Systems: Problems

1. NEGOTIABLE INSTRUMENTS

This part of the book focuses on negotiable instruments, primarily promissory notes and checks. In the problems that follow, the UCC sections cited without brackets are those of revised Article 1 (2002) and revised Articles 3 and 4 (2002). The sections appearing within brackets are from older versions of the same articles.

The reader may wonder what impact the electronic revolution has had on the law of negotiable instruments. A full discussion of that topic is beyond the scope of this book, which is more narrowly focused on the UCC. We note that neither the Electronic Signatures in Global and National Commerce Act (E-Sign) nor the Uniform Electronic Transactions Act (UETA) applies to transactions that are governed by Articles 3 or 4. One key consequence is that negotiable instruments as defined in revised Article 3 must still be in writing, that is, reduced to tangible form. *See* §§1-201(b)(43) [§1-201(46)], 3-103(a)(8) [§3-103(a)(6)], 3-103(a)(12) [§3-103(a)(9)], 3-104(a). However, revised Articles 3 and 4 have been updated to allow other documents (e.g., a stop payment order under §4-403) to be provided electronically. "Record" is the term used to refer to either information inscribed on a tangible medium, or stored in an electronic or other medium and retrievable in perceivable form. Section 1-201(b)(31). Likewise, although the word "signed" within revised Article 3 generally refers only to writings, *see* §1-201(b)(37), cmt. 37 [§1-201(39)], some sections now incorporate a broader definition that accommodates electronic signatures. *See* §§3-602, 3-604.

Section 29.   The Effect of a Signature on a Negotiable Instrument: The "Contract" Liability Concept

There are three categories of liability in negotiable instruments law: (1) contract, (2) warranty, and (3) tort (usually conversion). "Contract" liability is not a concept of contract law (offer, acceptance, consideration, mutual manifestation of assent, etc.) but of the law merchant. In the law merchant, a merchant's signature on a "specialty," which is an obligation enforceable by itself by mere production of the paper bearing the signature, was a signal event. The merchant's signature entailed liability without any other evidence of a promise or consideration. That concept—liability by virtue of a signature alone—survives in negotiable instruments law under the confusing rubric of "contract" liability.

The following problems deal with that kind of contract liability. The Code fashions these rules presupposing that a person's signature on an instrument signals a legal obligation to pay money. There is a converse rule at work here—the rule that no person has such "contract" liability unless that person signs the instrument.

Problems

208. Thief stole a blank check from Drawer's check book. Thief then forged Drawer's signature on a check that Thief drew for the amount of $1,000. Thief made the check payable to the order of Seller, who took it from Thief, thinking Thief was Drawer, in payment for goods sold to Thief. When Seller presented the check at the counters of First Bank, the drawee bank, First dishonored it.

   a.   Does Drawer have contract liability on the check? §3-401(a).

   b.   Did Drawer "sign" the check? Does his "signature" appear on it? Why is the imprinted name at the top of the check (Dave Drawer, 123 Main Street, Chicago, Illinois) not a signature? §§1-201(b)(37) [§1-201(39)], 3-401(b).

   c.   Is Thief liable on the instrument? What is his engagement? §3-403(a).

   d.   Fashion a set of facts that occurs after Thief forges the instrument that would render Drawer liable. §3-403(a).

209. Assume that Drawer prepared the check in Problem 208, that is, that the drawer's signature on the check is genuine and that First Bank, the drawee bank, dishonored when Seller presented the check for payment.

   a.   Does Seller have a cause of action against the drawee bank on the instrument? §§3-401(a), 3-408.

   b.   Can Seller use principles of law outside the Code to fashion an argument to hold the drawee? Would third-party beneficiary theory help seller? Some tort theory? Can Seller claim that the drawee bank is liable because it certified this check? §3-409(d).

c. In answering Question b, does it matter to you whether, in fact, Drawer had sufficient funds in his account at First Bank to cover the check?

Section 30. The Concepts of Transfer and Negotiation

In negotiable instruments law, there is a measure of literalness that modern lawyers find a bit tedious. Negotiable instruments, as we know them, were fashioned by merchants and lawyers in the seventeenth and eighteenth centuries. To them, the literal rules, some of which survive today, were evidence of regularity. If a party failed to observe the rules, the merchants and lawyers concluded that something was wrong; and if something was irregular or wrong, the negotiable instruments regime did not work. The sections cited in the following problems exemplify some of the literal rules that arose out of those old practices and that still have application in negotiable instruments law.

The more important rules these problems illustrate are the rules of contract liability: the contract liability of the maker of a note, that of the drawer (of a check or a draft), that of the acceptor (a certifying bank if the instrument accepted is a check), and that of the indorser whose signature can appear on any negotiable instrument.

Problems

210. §§3-413, 3-414, 3-415. Assume that Drawer drew a check payable to the order of Seller, and that Seller indorsed the reverse side of it by signing her name and that she then handed it to X.
    a. Is the indorsement special or in blank? §3-205.
    b. Does the nature of the indorsement as special or in blank matter in determining whether X is a holder? §3-205(a) and (b).
    c. Before Seller indorsed, was the check order paper or bearer paper? What kind of paper is it after the indorsement? §3-109.
    d. Assume that X is a holder. What parties are liable to him as a holder? If the drawee bank dishonors, may X enforce the instrument against Seller? Against Drawer?
    e. If Thief forged Drawer's signature, would X have a claim against Seller in the event the bank dishonored? Against Drawer? Against Thief?

211. Assume in the preceding problem that Crook stole the check from Seller after Seller indorsed and that Crook then indorsed and delivered to X. X then indorsed and delivered the check for value to Y, who presented to the drawee bank, which dishonored.
    a. Is Y a holder?

> b. Does *Y* have a cause of action against *X*? (If *X* indorsed specially?) Against Seller? Against Crook? Against Drawer?
>
> c. If *Y* recovers from *X*, can *X* enforce the instrument against anyone? Would *X* be an indorser who paid the instrument under §3-415?

212. **§§1-201(b)(21) [§1-201(20)], 3-403(a).** Assume in Problem 210 that Seller indorsed the check by signing the reverse side under the following words "Pay *X*," and that Crook stole the check, forged *X*'s indorsement, and delivered to *Y*. With these modified facts, answer question 211.

213. Thief stole Drawer's checkbook, forged Drawer's name as drawer, and made the check payable to Seller. Seller indorsed the check and deposited it at Second Bank, which sent it on to First Bank, the drawee bank. First Bank dishonored and returned the check to Second.

> a. Does Second have a cause of action against Drawer on the check? Against Thief? Against First? Against Seller?
>
> b. Who should bear the loss under these facts? Would §1-103(b) [§1-103] prevent use of supplemental principles of law to hold Thief liable to Seller?

214. Ace Corp. has a check-writing machine that imprints Ace's signature on checks payable to Ace's employees and suppliers. *C*, a clerk, used the machine without authorization to write a check to herself for $1,000. *C* indorsed the check to Second Bank, which gave value to *C* and sent the check through to First Bank, the drawee bank, which dishonored.

> a. Does Second have a cause of action against *C*? Against Ace?
>
> b. Would it matter to you that *C* found the check-writing machine in the storeroom next to the company's supply of coffee cups? §3-406.
>
> c. How do you suppose corporations protect themselves from unauthorized use of a check-writing machine?
>
> d. If the law imposes on the drawee bank any losses Ace incurs when First honors a check over a signature of the drawer that is unauthorized, how would the drawee bank protect itself?

215. **§3-402.** Assume that Ace Corp.'s president, Joe Ace, signs four company checks in the following fashion: (1) "Joe Ace"; (2) "Joe Ace, agent"; (3) "Ace Corp., Joe Ace"; and (4) "Ace Corp., by Joe Ace, President." If the drawee bank dishonors one of the checks, will a holder in due course have a cause of action against Joe? Would your answer be different if the instrument were a promissory note and the claimant were the holder of the note?

Section 31. Conditions of Contract Liability

The following problems deal with the conditions of what we have been calling "contract" liability. Those conditions arise rather infrequently, and, in the case of a drawer, it does not make much difference whether the holder trying to enforce the instrument has satisfied them. If you work through the problems, you will be familiar with the few conditions that matter much.

Problem

216. *§§3-414(f), 3-415(e), 3-503(c).*   On May 1, Drawer drew a check in favor of *S*, who took it and indorsed it on that day to *X*, who indorsed it and deposited it for collection on June 15. The drawee bank dishonored on June 20 and gave notice to *X* on that day. *X* gave notice to Drawer on July 30. *X* also did not give notice to *S* until July 30. (Each of the following questions is asking (1) whether the initiation of the collection of the check through the banking system is timely, (2) whether the notice of dishonor is timely, and (3) whether if one or the other, or both, are late, it makes any difference.)
  a.   Can *X* recover from any of the parties?
  b.   Can *S* recover from any of the parties?

Section 32. *Negotiable Instruments and the Underlying Transaction*

The law of payments systems balances two commercial interests when it concerns itself with the underlying transaction. First is the idea that a negotiable instrument travels without baggage, that is, the idea that third parties may deal with the instrument and not worry about the equities of the underlying transaction. The value reflected in this feature of negotiable instruments law is peculiarly commercial. The second concern is one of seeing to it that there not be unjust enrichment in the application of rules fashioned to achieve the first objective.

These problems also continue the investigation of the "contract" liability concept.

Problems

217. *§§3-310(b)(1), 3-602.*   Drawer gave a check to Seller, Seller indorsed to *X* who indorsed to *Y*. *Y* deposited the check at Second Bank, and Second then presented the check through the check collection system to First. If First pays the check,
  a.   Was there ever a party liable on it unconditionally, that is, liable without dishonor by First?
  b.   What happens to the conditional liability of Drawer on the check? Of Seller? Of *X*?
  c.   What happens to the liability of Drawer in the contract under which Seller sold goods to Drawer? Can Seller maintain a cause of action against Drawer for payment on the sales contract?
  d.   What do we call a check that bears the signature of the drawee? §3-409(d). What is the contract of the certifying bank? §3-413(b).

218. *§3-309.*   Drawer, a buyer, gave a check to Seller, and Seller lost it.
  a.   May Seller sue Drawer on the underlying sales contract if Drawer

refuses to give Seller a replacement check? §§3-310(b)(1), 3-310(b)(4). Why might Drawer be reluctant to give Seller a replacement check?

b. Can Seller sue Drawer on the lost check? §3-309. Is Drawer liable on the check absent dishonor? §3-414(b). Has there been dishonor?

Section 33. *Holders in Due Course and Their Rights*

There is a grand bonus in store for the party that takes a negotiable instrument in entirely regular fashion: the bonus of having the right to seek payment on the instrument without regard to the equities of the underlying transaction. But that bonus generally benefits only the party that takes a negotiable instrument in "due course." Note that there are two stages to all of this. First, the "holder" of a negotiable instrument can prove the debt merely by introducing the instrument into evidence. Second, if the obligor on the instrument claims that there are defenses in the underlying transaction, the "due course" issue becomes paramount, since holders in due course cut off most defenses. Also, holders in due course cut off claims, that is, they hold free of any prior owner's claim in conversion, replevin, or the like. Problem 223(d) and the problems under Section 36, Conversion, deal with that feature of holder-in-due-course protection.

Both federal and state laws restrict the operation of the holder-in-due-course doctrine in consumer transactions. *See, e.g.,* Federal Trade Commission Holder-In-Due-Course Regulations, 16 C.F.R. §§433.1 through 433.3. Revised Article 3 is subject to these other laws. *See* §§3-302(g), 3-305(f). Although a full examination of such consumer protection laws is beyond the scope of this book, Problem 229 illustrates how some of these laws intersect with the UCC.

Problems

219. Maker gave a promissory note dated September 1, 2002, in the face amount of $100,000 "payable one year from date to Seller" to cover sums due for the sale by Seller to Maker of earth moving equipment. Maker claims that the equipment is defective and has attempted to revoke his acceptance of the equipment under the Code.

a. If Seller proves that Maker executed the note, has he established a prima facie case under §3-308?

b. Why cannot Seller negotiate this note? §3-104(a)(1).

220. *§§3-302(a), 3-303, 3-305(b).* Maker gave National Sales Corp. a negotiable promissory note dated September 1, 2002, in the face amount of $100,000, payable "to the order of National Sales Corp. 120 days after date" in connection with the sale of goods by National to Maker. National's president signed the back of the note with the company's signature. She then delivered the note to First Bank. First is now attempting to collect the note from Maker, who claims that National sold shabby goods and that he has a defense to National's claim. Will First take subject to the defense if First

    a. promised to pay $100,000 for the note, but has paid only $60,000 at the time it learns of Maker's defense? §3-303(a)(1).

    b. promised to pay a discounted amount for the note ($99,500) but has paid only $60,000 at the time it learns of Maker's defense? §3-302(d).

    c. took the note as security for an antecedent debt that National owed First or in payment of a debt due from National to First? §§3-302(e), 3-303(a)(3).

    d. paid for the note with a cashier's check? §3-303(a)(4).

221. Would your answers to Problem 220 be different if National asked Maker to make the note payable to the order of First Bank?

222. Assume in Problem 220 that the buyer of the goods was a "Drawer" rather than Maker, because it gave National a check for $100,000, rather than a note in that amount. National's president signed the back of the check with the company's signature, and deposited the check in National's account at Second Bank. Drawer stopped payment because he believed the goods were shabby; as a result, the check was dishonored. Second Bank now sues Drawer on its contract liability under §3-414(b). Will Second Bank take subject to Drawer's defense if it:

    a. credited National's account in the amount of $100,000 with the understanding that National had the right to withdraw the entire amount? Does it make any difference whether National did in fact withdraw any of the money? §§4-210(a)(2), 4-211.

    b. credited National's account without granting a right to withdraw, but permitted National to withdraw $500 of the funds?

    c. credited National's account without granting a right to withdraw, but has made loans to National and holds an Article 9 security interest in all negotiable instruments or other proceeds from the sale of National's inventory?

223. *§3-306 (last sentence).* Buyer gave Seller a check payable to the order of Seller in the amount of $1,000. Seller indorsed the check by signing it on the reverse side "Sally Seller." Thief then stole the check from Seller and delivered it to X, who took for value and without any notice that the check was stolen. X deposited the check at Second Bank, which also gave value. Second put the check through the collection chain, and First paid it.

    a. May Seller recover from Buyer on the underlying contract? §§3-309, 3-310.

    b. May Seller recover from Buyer under the stolen instrument section? §3-309.

    c. May Seller recover in conversion against Thief if she can find him? §1-103(b) [§1-103].

    d. May Seller recover from Second in conversion? §3-306 (last sentence). In replevin? On some other common law claim? §1-103(b) [§1-103].

224. *§1-201(b)(21) [§1-201(20)].* Assume in the preceding question that Seller had not yet indorsed the check. Thief stole the check, forged Seller's indorsement, and delivered the check to X. Now answer parts a through d in the preceding Question.

225. Buyer gave Seller a check in the amount of $1,000 as payment for the sale of a used automobile. Seller indorsed the check and deposited it at Second Bank, which sent it through the check collection system to First Bank. Before the check arrived at First, Buyer, angry that the car he bought did not function properly, stopped payment on the check. First dishonored and returned the check to Second.
  a. May Second recover on the check from Buyer under these facts? §3-414(b).
  b. May Second recover from Buyer if Second demonstrates that Second credited Seller's account and that Seller withdrew all of the check's proceeds? Half of the proceeds? §§4-210, 4-211.
  c. Would your answer to (b) differ if Buyer claimed that Seller fraudulently induced Buyer to pay for the car?
  d. Would your answer to (b) differ
    i. if Buyer raised as his defense against Second the allegation that Buyer, being frail and of poor eyesight, thought he was signing a birthday card and not a check when he in fact executed the check? §3-305(a)(1).
    ii. if Buyer raised as his defense the argument that he was only 16 at the time of the transaction with Seller? §3-305(a)(1).

226. Seller, a pipe and pipe fittings distributor, sold pipe to Buyer and asked Buyer to make his check payable to Manufacturer, who had supplied fittings to Seller and remains unpaid.
  a. If the pipe that Seller sold to Buyer is defective and therefore worthless, may Buyer successfully defend against Manufacturer's claim against Buyer when First dishonors the check? §§3-302, cmt. 4, 3-305(b).
  b. Would your answer be any different if Manufacturer had taken the check not in payment for fittings delivered but as a down payment for fittings that are to be delivered next month? §3-303(a)(1).

227. Seller defrauded Buyer by delivering drums loaded with water instead of the linseed oil that he had agreed to sell Buyer. Before learning of the fraud, Buyer had given Seller a $100,000 check as a down payment on the oil. Buyer has stopped payment on the check and has gone to the newspapers with the story of the swindle. Seller indorsed the check for value to X before X heard the news. Thereafter, X indorsed and delivered the check to Y, who knew the story. Y then indorsed the check back to Seller. Could Buyer raise the fraud defense if he had been sued on the instrument by
  a. X? §3-305(b).

b. *Y*? Is *Y* a holder in due course? §3-302(a)(2). Does *Y* have the rights of *X* as a holder in due course? §3-203(b).

c. Seller? Does Seller come within *X*'s or *Y*'s umbrella? §3-203(b) (second clause).

228. *§3-407.* Assume in the preceding question that the goods conform, that Buyer gave Seller a negotiable promissory note in the face amount of $10,000, but that Seller fraudulently raised the note to $100,000.

a. May *X* enforce the instrument? If so, for what amount? §3-407(c).

b. May *Y* enforce the instrument? If so, for what amount?

c. May Seller enforce the instrument? §3-407(b).

229. Using high-pressure sales tactics and fraudulent representations, Seller induced Homeowner to purchase aluminum siding. In exchange, Homeowner executed a promissory note payable to the order of Seller in the amount of $20,000. Seller sold the note to ABC Finance Company, and disappeared with the proceeds.

When the note came due, ABC demanded payment from Homeowner. Homeowner asserted fraud as a defense. ABC responded that payment was due anyway, because it was a holder in due course. Is this true?

230. *§3-602.* On March 1, 2002, Merchant borrowed $10,000 from ABC Finance Company to cover the cost of new equipment for his store. Merchant signed a negotiable promissory note that was due January 5, 2003, and was payable to the order of ABC Finance Company. On October 1, 2002, Merchant inherited some money. On that day, he paid $10,000 to ABC to settle his debt.

On January 5, 2003, XYZ Loan Company telephoned Merchant to demand payment of the note. XYZ told Merchant that it had purchased the note from ABC on September 13, 2002. Merchant protested that he had already paid the note. XYZ said that it didn't care, and that payment was due nevertheless. Upset, Merchant telephoned ABC, only to learn that its phone number had been disconnected and its offices closed. Merchant comes to you for advice.

a. If XYZ sues on the note, does Merchant have any defense?

b. Suppose XYZ had purchased the note in November 2002. Would that make a difference? Would it matter whether XYZ was a holder in due course?

Section 34. The Bank-Customer Relationship

The following eleven problems deal with questions that arise between the bank and its customer. This bank is the drawee (also known as the "payor bank" in Article 4 terms), and the customer is the drawer of the check. The issue here is one of allocating liability when the bank honors a check that it should not honor and when it dishonors a check that it should honor. The bank-customer deposit agreement usually includes some of the rules covering this relationship, but some of them come from cases decided long ago and are alluded to in the Code sections we cite.

Banks have lobbied hard in this area and have garnered a few victories. One of them is in the subrogation rules. Subrogation, you should bear in mind, is equity's response to unjust enrichment. The banks' arguments for subrogation under §4-407 are moderately complicated; but if you keep the unjust enrichment feature of subrogation in mind, you should be able to figure everything out.

Problems

231. *§4-401(a).* Indicate, giving your reasons, which of the following circumstances would render a check not properly payable:

    a. Drawer's signature is forged.

    b. Payee's indorsement is forged.

    c. Holder of bearer instrument forges indorsement.

    d. Payee alters sum payable from $100 to $1,000. §§3-407(c), 4-401(d)(1).

    e. On May 2, Payor Bank receives a check the drawer issued on May 1 but post-dated to May 10. §4-401(c).

    f. Payor Bank negligently fails to dishonor a check drawn on insufficient funds by its midnight deadline, §4-104(a)(10), and debits Drawer's account.

    g. Unbeknownst to Payor Bank, Thief presents a stolen check bearing Payee's authorized indorsement in blank.

    h. Payor Bank pays a check on which Payee's indorsement is missing. Should the Payor Bank be liable to Drawer if it pays this item?

232. If a payor bank pays a check and thereby creates an overdraft, does it matter for purposes of charging the drawer's account that the payor violated its overdraft agreement with the drawer by, for example, creating an overdraft greater in amount than the overdraft agreement allowed? §§4-401(a) and 4-401(b). Does it make a difference if the reason the payor violated its agreement was because it failed to observe reasonable banking practices (i.e., was negligent)? If not, is §4-401 inconsistent with §4-103(a), which states that a bank cannot disclaim liability for failure to exercise ordinary care?

233. *§4-402.* May a customer whose check is wrongfully dishonored recover damages for

    a. mental anguish?

    b. ulcers?

    c. the equity customer enjoyed in an automobile repossessed by the creditor to whom the customer wrote the overdraft?

    d. lost business (that is, lost profits)?

    e. loss of bargain on a real estate transaction that fell through when down payment check bounced?

    f. punitive damages?

234. In cases of wrongful dishonor, what damages are recoverable in a suit by a corporation's president and sole shareholder, when the bank dishonored a corporate check?

235. *§4-103.* Can the bank write a customer-bank deposit agreement that alters the results in the preceding question?

236. *§4-404.* Customer writes a check payable to X on January 1, 2002. X does nothing with the check until August 1, 2002, when he presents it over the counter to Payor Bank. If Payor Bank refuses to pay the check, is it liable for wrongful dishonor?

237. *§4-403.* Suppose a buyer writes a check to seller for goods. In which of the following cases may this buyer recover damages from the bank where he keeps his checking account and is a customer?
   a. The customer proves only that the bank paid his check after receiving timely notice to stop payment.
   b. The customer proves that the bank paid the check over a timely stop order, and that he has rightfully rejected defective merchandise.

238. *§4-407(3).* In case (b) of the preceding question, what should the bank do after it recredits its customer's account?

239. *§4-407(1).* Would your answer to Problem 237(b) differ if the evidence showed that the seller had deposited the check at Second Bank and had withdrawn the funds?

240. *§4-407(2).* In Problem 237(b), how would you change the facts to allow the payor bank to subrogate itself to the rights of the seller?

241. *§1-103(b) [§1-103].* If the payor bank pays over its customer's stop payment order, may the bank recover from the seller in restitution?

Section 35. *Warranties*

In addition to "contract" liability, which makers, drawers, acceptors, and indorsers undertake when they sign a negotiable instrument, indorsers and transferors of a negotiable instrument also make warranties to certain parties that take or pay the instrument. It is the theory of warranties in negotiable instruments law that the party taking or paying an instrument (1) relies on certain unspoken representations of the person delivering the instrument, or (2) relies on the signatures of prior parties. Most scholars are pretty much of the view that there is little, if any, reliance these days. Checks, the instruments that give rise to warranty disputes, usually find their way quite quickly into the banking system, where there is little reliance (though the banks argue to the contrary).

There are two sets of warranty sections, one in Article 3 and one in Article 4. *See* §§3-416, 3-417, 4-207, 4-208. For our purposes and for most warranty issues that arise, the warranties are the same in both articles. The answers to the following problems cite the Article 4 sections. In the new version of Articles 3 and 4, most of the relevant comments are in Article 3. There will be references, then, in the answers and sometimes in the problems to comments in the Article 3 sections.

Problems

In the following problems, assume, unless otherwise indicated, that Buyer (*B*) wrote a check to Seller (*S*), that *S* indorsed and deposited it at Second Bank, and that Second presented it through the bank collection system to First Bank, the payor bank.

242.   If *T*, a thief, stole the check from *S*, forged *S*'s indorsement and deposited the check at Second, and if First Bank, the payor bank, honored the check, can there be any successful claim for breach of a transfer warranty? §4-207. Of a presentment warranty? §4-208. If First dishonored, can there ever be any successful claim for breach of a presentment warranty?

243.   A thief, *F*, stole *B*'s checkbook, forged *B*'s signature, and used the check to pay *S* for goods that *S* delivered under a contract of sale.
    a.   If First Bank honors, does First have a cause of action against *S* for breach of the warranty in either §4-207(a)(2) or §4-208(a)(1)? May First debit *B*'s account? §4-401.
    b.   Do "transfer" warranties run to the payor bank?
    c.   If First dishonors the check, may Second Bank make a successful breach of transfer warranty claim against *S*? If *S* is liable to Second for breach of warranty, how may *S* recoup her loss? May she recover from *B*? May she recover from *F*? On what theory? §§3-403, 3-414.

244.   *§§3-103, 4-207, 4-208.*   Thief steals Consumer's mail and finds her statement from First Bank, where she maintains a checking account. Pretending to be Consumer, Thief telephones Merchant to purchase expensive goods or services. Thief provides Merchant with Consumer's name and bank account number, and fraudulently "authorizes" Merchant to draw a check in her name. Merchant prepares the check, stamps the legend "authorized by your customer" on the signature line of the check, and deposits the check in his account at Second Bank. Second forwards the check to First, which pays the check and charges Consumer's account. If Consumer objects to the charge, who bears the loss? (Assume Thief received the goods or services, but has long since disappeared.)

245.   *B* wrote a check payable to the order of *S*, *T-2* stole it, and forged *S*'s indorsement.
    a.   If First Bank honors the check, has Second Bank breached any transfer warranty? Does Second make transfer warranties? Does it make them to First? §4-207(a).

b. If First honors the check, has Second breached any presentment warranty? §4-208(a)(1). Is Second authorized to obtain payment?

c. Would your answer to Problem (b) above be any different if before the theft, S had indorsed the check by signing her name to it? Would Second breach a warranty of authority in these circumstances? Would Second be a holder?

d. Would your answer be any different if *T-2* had stolen the check from the mails after *B* mailed it? In that case, would *T-2* be able to negotiate the check without forging *S's* indorsement? Why not? §§1-201(b)(21) [§1-201(20)], 3-201(b).

246. *B* drew a check payable to *S* for $100 and delivered it to *S*. *S* raised the check to $1,000, deposited it at Second Bank, and withdrew the provisional credit.

a. If First Bank pays the check according to its altered tenor, may First debit *B's* account? By how much? §4-401(d). May First maintain a breach of warranty action against Second? §4-208(a)(2). If so, what would First's damages be? §4-208(b).

b. If First discovers the alteration and dishonors the check, may Second recover from *B* under §3-414(b) or §3-407(c)? If so, what would Second's recovery be? May Second make a successful claim against *S*? On what theory? Breach of warranty? §4-207(a)(3).

c. If *S* pays Second under §4-207(a)(3) in the preceding Question (b), may *S* enforce the instrument against *B* for the original amount of the check? §3-407(b).

Section 36. Conversion

The third category of liability in negotiable instruments law is tort. When a thief steals a check, the rightful owner has a cause of action lying in tort against the thief. Conversion, the tort most commonly used in commercial transactions, gives the rightful owner a cause of action even against parties acting innocently. It is conversion at common law to intermeddle with the property of another.

Problems

247. *§§1-103(b) [§1-103], 3-420.* Which of the following acts constitute conversion?

a. *T-2* steals the check from *S*, the payee.

b. *T-1* steals the check from *B*, the drawer.

c. *X* maliciously grabs the check from *S* and tears it to shreds.

d. *X* negligently shreds *S's* check in the shredding machine.

e. First honors the check after *T-2* steals it from *S* and forges *S's* indorsement. §3-420(a).

f.   Second cashes the check for *T-2* after *T-2* steals it from *S* and forges *S*'s indorsement. §3-420(c).

g.   Second cashes the check for *T-2* after *T-2* steals it from *S*, who has indorsed the check in blank. Would the answer differ if Second's teller required *T-2* to indorse?

248. *B*, the drawer, delivered a check for $1,000 to *S* as payment for services rendered. *T-2* stole the check, forged *S*'s indorsement, and deposited the check at Second Bank. Later the same day, *T-2* withdrew the $1,000 from the account.

a.   If First, the payor bank, honors the check, may it debit *B*'s account? §4-401.

b.   If First honors the check, may *S* maintain an action against First in conversion? §3-420(a) (2d sentence).

249. By way of further review of conversion, in each of the following cases, indicate whether the check has been converted, name the converter, and identify the person that has the cause of action and the person that is liable in conversion.

a.   *T-2* stole the check from *S*, the payee.

b.   *T-1* stole the check from *B*, the drawer.

c.   Second "cashed" the check for *T-2* after *T-2* forged *S*'s indorsement.

d.   First paid the check after *T-2* stole it from *S* and forged *S*'s indorsement.

250. *F* stole *B*'s checkbook and wrote a check payable to *S* for services *S* rendered to *F*. *F* forged *B*'s signature on the check and mailed it to *S*. *T-2* stole the check, forged *S*'s indorsement, and deposited it at Second Bank. Second sent the check through the check collection system, and First Bank paid it. *T-2* then withdrew the funds from Second. Thereafter, *B* learned of the forgery.

a.   From whom may *B* recover? If First suffers a loss by being forced to recredit *B*'s account, may First recover for breach of presentment warranty against Second? *See* §§4-208(a)(1) and 4-208(a)(3).

b.   From whom may *S* recover?

251. *B* issued a check to *S* payable to the order of *S*, and *S* indorsed it by signing her name on the back of the instrument. *T*, a thief, stole the check and gave it to *X* as payment for goods *X* sold to *T*. Assume that *X* took the check in good faith and without notice that anything was wrong.

a.   Does *S* have a cause of action against *T*? §3-420.

b.   Does *S* have a cause of action against *X*? §3-306.

c.   If *X* transfers the instrument to *Y* after *Y* learns of the theft by *T*, does *S* have a cause of action against *Y*? §§3-203(b), 3-302(c).

d.   Would your answers to any of the preceding questions differ if (1) *S* had indorsed the check "pay *Z*," and (2) *T* had forged *Z*'s signature when *T* delivered the check to *X*?

Section 37. *Preclusion*

After positing three categories of liability ("contract," warranty, and tort), negotiable instruments law finishes the job by denying or limiting the remedies available in each of those three categories to parties whose conduct is commercially blameworthy. Preclusion, a form of strict estoppel that often does not entail any inquiry into reliance and detriment, is the instrument of this last adjustment to negotiable instrument law liability. As a matter of general law, estoppel, which is a creature of equity, is available to a party only if the party relied to its detriment. The Code and other areas of commercial law sometimes ignore the reliance and detriment features of estoppel. In those cases, the law often speaks of "preclusion" rather than estoppel. In some instances, *see* §§3-404(b), 3-405(b), the Code merely says that an unauthorized indorsement is effective, which is another way of saying that a party is estopped or precluded to say that the indorsement is unauthorized.

Article 3 attempts to rationalize the preclusion rules by dividing them among four sections. The first provision, §3-404, deals with the imposter rule and with employees who write checks to fictitious payees (typically by padding the payroll or the payables) or who write a check for the employer to a real payee with the intent from the beginning to intercept the check before it is mailed and to forge the indorsement.

The second provision, §3-405, deals with the faithless employee, who is charged with responsibility for handling checks and who fraudulently forges an indorsement, either of a check that is payable to the employer or a check drawn by the employer payable to another employee or a creditor.

The third provision, §3-406, deals with the general rule that negligence that substantially contributes to a forgery or alteration will preclude the negligent party from asserting the forgery or alteration.

Finally, in a fourth provision, §4-406, the Code deals with the customer who is negligent in examining its checking account statement.

In Article 3, the drafters have fashioned comparative negligence rules for the preclusion sections.

Problems

252. *§3-406(a).* This problem deals with the general negligence provision.

B left his checkbook and a check writing machine in the supply room next to the styrofoam coffee cups. *F*, a truck driver delivering stationery supplies to *B*'s office, was in need of a cup of java. He found the checks and the machine and wrote a check payable to himself. *F* then indorsed the check and deposited it at Second Bank. Second sent the check through to First Bank, which paid it. *F* has withdrawn the funds.

    a. May First charge *B*'s account?

    b. Would your answer differ if First was negligent in paying the check?

253. *§§3-406, 3-407(c)(ii).* This is another general negligence problem.

B wrote a check to *S* in payment for goods that *S* delivered under a contract. *B* forgot the price of the goods, though he knew it was in the neighborhood of $100. He sent the check, which he had signed and dated, to *S* without any amount and told *S* to fill in the amount. *B* added to the check a legend at the bottom as follows: "Not good for more than $125." *S*, needing cash to pay his withholding taxes, inserted $1,000 as the amount on the check and deposited it at Second. Second's operations clerk did not notice the legend at the bottom of the check and encoded it for $1,000. Second sent the check through the system, and First paid it.

    a. May First debit *B*'s account?

    b. Has Second breached a presentment warranty?

254. *§§3-405, 3-406.*

    a. *B* wrote a check to *S*, whose secretary, *T-2*, an employee with no "responsibility" or authority to deal with *B*'s checks or financial affairs, forged *S*'s indorsement and cashed the check at Second, telling Second that *S* needed petty cash at the office. Second forwarded the check to First, which paid it. *T-2* had been engaging in this fraud for over two years and had cashed more than $3,000 in checks in this fashion. Does *S* have a cause of action in conversion against Second? Against First? Does it matter whether Second or First failed to observe reasonable banking practices?

    b. Would your answer to any of these questions differ if this were the first time *T-2* had fraudulently indorsed one of *S*'s checks? Would the answer differ if *T-2* did have responsibility to handle checks? §3-405(a)(3) and (b).

255. *§§3-404, 3-405.* *F*, the human resources manager of ABC Co., padded the payroll, that is, he gave the payroll clerk names and addresses of fictitious parties and instructed the clerk to draw checks for the fictitious employees. The clerk, unaware of the manager's fraud, drew the checks and put them in envelopes addressed to the fictitious parties at addresses supplied by *F*. Before the mail messenger took the checks out of the clerk's tray, *F* surreptitiously removed the checks, indorsed them in the names of the fictitious parties and deposited them at his account at Second. Second sent the checks through to First, which paid them. *F* has withdrawn the proceeds of the checks.

    a. May First debit ABC's account? In the alternative, may it recover from Second for breach of the presentment warranty of authority? §§4-208(a)(1), 4-208(c).

    b. If First had dishonored the checks and returned them to Second, could Second recover from ABC? Under these facts would Second be a person entitled to enforce the check? Would it do ABC any good in this setting to stop payment on the checks? §§3-404, 3-414.

    c. Has Second done anything negligent in crediting *F*'s account with payroll checks made payable to third parties? §3-405, cmt. 4 (illustration of depositary bank conduct that would probably constitute lack of due care). If so, would Second's negligence result in a comparative negligence rule? §3-404(d).

   d. Would your answers to any of the foregoing questions differ if, rather than an innocent clerk, F himself had signed the checks on behalf of ABC?

   e. Would your answers to parts (a) through (c) differ if the clerk who drew the checks knew they were payable to fictitious suppliers of ABC? To real suppliers, but for materials that had in fact not been supplied?

   f. Would your answers differ in parts (a) through (c) if the clerk made the checks payable to real employees of ABC but as overtime paychecks, which had in fact been earned?

256. *§4-406.* On May 1, A wrote a check in the amount of $1,000 to L, its landlord, who altered the check by raising it to $10,000. L deposited the check at Second, which gave L value ($5,000 in cash and $5,000 credit on a loan balance) and forwarded the check to First, which paid it in the normal course on May 5. On May 10, A received a bank statement, including the altered item, from First. Because A's bookkeeper was away on business, A did not reconcile the statement until June 15, when the book keeper discovered the alteration.

   a. Did A satisfy the duty required under §4-406(c)? If not, may First properly refuse to recredit A's account in the amount of $9,000?

   b. *§4-406(d)(2).* If on June 5, A wrote a second rent check to L in the face amount of $1,000 and if L again altered the item, deposited the check at Second, and obtained payment through the banking system on June 14, may First properly refuse to recredit A's account for the second $9,000? May First, instead of debiting A's account, recover from Second for breach of the presentment warranty under §4-208(a)(2)? §4-406(f) (last sentence).

   c. Would your answer to Questions (a) or (b) differ if, instead of an altered item, the problem involved L's forgery of A's signature? Or if the problem involved the forgery of the payee's indorsement of a check A had written to the payee? §4-406(d).

   d. Would your answer to Question (a) differ if L maintained his account at First and did not withdraw the $9,000 until June 14?

   e. Would your answers to any of the foregoing questions differ if you decided that First had not observed reasonable care in paying the check?

   f. How long does a customer have to assert against the payor bank a claim for
      i. paying a check with a forged drawer's signature or a material alteration? §4-406(f)?
      ii. paying a check bearing a forged indorsement? §4-111.

257. *§3-404(a).* B, sitting on the terrace of a seaside resort, met I, an imposter, who passed himself off as Baron de Richi and claimed to own the yacht that was anchored just offshore. After ample drinks and insufficient investigation, B gave I a check payable to de Richi in the amount of $100,000, to be used as

a down payment on the yacht. The next morning, when *B* arrived at the appointed place to close the deal with *I*, *B* learned of the fraud. In the meantime, *I*, whose name was Smith, indorsed the check by signing "Baron de Richi" to the reverse side and cashed it at First Bank, the drawee-payor.

    a.   Can First charge *B*'s account? §3-404(a).

    b.   Would your answer to the prior question differ if First failed to observe reasonable banking practices? §3-404(d).

258.   *§3-404(b).*

    a.   *O*, a dishonest officer of ABC Corp. who had no authority to write checks, drew checks in the amount of $1,000 payable as indicated below and signed them with fraudulent intent. After drawing the checks, *O* indorsed them in the name of the payee and deposited them in various accounts to his own name. Thereafter, First Bank, the payor bank, paid the checks. May First charge ABC's account?

       i.   A check payable to a fictitious payee. §3-404(b).

      ii.   A check payable to a real company to which ABC owed money but with the intent that the real payee never receive the check. §3-404(b). Would it matter that *O* was not an employee of ABC? §3-404, cmt. 2, Case #4.

     iii.   A check payable to a real company to which ABC was not indebted.

    b.   In any of the foregoing Problems, would the depositary bank breach a warranty to the payor bank if the payor paid the check?

Section 38. *Final Payment*

The doctrine of final payment is designed to determine the point at which a drawee-payor bank loses the right to invoke restitutionary concepts or the law of mistake in order to recover a payment it has made to a payee or other person enforcing the instrument.

The problems in this section deal with checks because it is in the check setting, once again, that the issue has arisen. Generally, the rule is simple enough: The payor bank may recover the payment if the party holding the proceeds is unjustly enriched or if the payment was by mistake. If the potential defendant gave value in good faith for the check or changed its position in reliance on the payor's payment, the Code invokes the final payment doctrine and forbids restitution and the law of mistake.

Bear in mind, however, that the final payment doctrine does not displace Article 4 claims for breach of warranty or subrogation. If a depositary bank, for example, gives value for a check bearing a forged indorsement, it will be able, under the final payment doctrine, to resist the payor's claim for restitution; but it will not be able to resist the payor's claim that the depositary bank has breached the presentment warranty of authority.

Problems

259. *§3-418.* Seller entered into a contract to sell grain to Buyer for $100,000, payment against Seller's delivery of a negotiable bill of lading to Buyer. On May 1, Seller gave Buyer a negotiable bill covering the grain, and Buyer gave Seller a check for the contract amount. Later that same day, Buyer learned that the grain was moldy and insect-infested. Buyer stopped payment on the check. The next day, Seller took the check to Second Bank, which, acting in good faith, gave Seller value. Second presented the check to First, the drawee-payor bank, which inadvertently paid it over the stop payment order.

    a. May First recover the payment from Second?

    b. Would the answer be the same if Second had given Seller provisional credit for the check but had not permitted Seller to withdraw the funds?

    c. Would your answer in part (a) differ if *T*, a thief, stole the check from Seller, forged Seller's indorsement, and deposited the check at Second?

    d. Would the answer to part (a) differ if, instead of paying over a stop payment order, First had paid the check out of an account that had insufficient funds?

    e. If the final payment doctrine prevents First from recovering from Second, may First pursue Seller under §4-407?

    f. What effect, if any, does the care or lack of care of First have on the analysis of the preceding questions?

260. Seller entered into a contract to sell grain to Buyer for $100,000, delivery against Buyer's payment. On May 1, Buyer gave Seller a check for the contract amount, and Seller took it directly to First Bank and asked for payment. First paid Seller the $100,000 that same day, and Seller released the grain to Buyer. Subsequently, First learned that Buyer's account was overdrawn, and First is now seeking to recover the funds from Seller on the grounds that First paid the check by mistake.

    a. May First recover from Seller?

    b. Would your answer differ if buyer claimed that the grain was partly moldy and insect infested?

    c. Would your answer to part (a) differ if *T*, a thief, stole the check from Seller, forged Seller's signature, and obtained payment from First?

    d. Would your answers to the preceding questions differ if First's mistake had been one of paying over Buyer's unauthorized signature, that is, would the results differ if *T-2* obtained Buyer's checkbook and wrote the check to Seller signing with Buyer's name?

2. DOCUMENTS OF TITLE

Section 39. *The Documentary Draft Transaction*

The documentary draft transaction was a staple of domestic sales until the advent of reliable credit reporting and the open account sale that largely displaced the documentary sale in domestic commerce. The transaction survives in international trade, sometimes with a letter of credit as an adjunct.

We study the documentary draft transaction in part because it remains an important component of international trade but more importantly because it is instructive. The draft, bill of lading, and letter of credit, all of which are still part of the payments system, developed out of the documentary draft transaction. That transaction illustrates their features.

Problems

261. In which of the following contracts does the buyer have the right to examine the merchandise prior to payment?
  a. In general. §§2-512, 2-513.
  b. FOB vessel or FAS. §§2-319(4), 2-513(3)(b).
  c. CIF or C&F. §2-320(4).
  d. COD. §2-513(3)(a).

262. Seller and Buyer agreed to a contract for the sale of diamonds. Seller drew on Buyer, that is, Seller drew an order payable to itself for the amount of the purchase price designating the buyer as the drawee. (Assume that the draft is payable at sight.) When Second Bank takes the draft for collection from Seller, does Second become a holder in due course if
  a. Second Bank takes the draft as collateral for a pre-existing debt incurred by Seller? In payment of a pre-existing note? Would it matter whether the bank makes bookkeeping entries, that is, would the bank become a holder as soon as the draft, properly indorsed, comes into the bank's possession, or does the bank need to take some additional action? §3-303(a)(3).
  b. Second Bank issues a cashier's check to Seller that Seller has yet to cash or deposit? §3-303(4).

263. *§3-305(b).* In the preceding question, assume that Buyer bargained with Seller for credit terms and that the parties used a time draft, that is, a draft drawn by Seller on Buyer that called for Buyer to accept it by signing its face and to pay it 60 days after the date of that acceptance. If Buyer accepted the time draft and if Second Bank is a holder in due course of that draft, may Buyer assert underlying contract defenses against Second Bank when Second presents the draft (now called an acceptance) for payment?

264. *§3-502(b)(2).* If Buyer refused to accept the time draft, has Buyer dishonored the draft? §3-502(b)(3). Does Buyer dishonor an accepted time draft by refusing to pay it when it comes due? How does a Buyer dishonor a sight or demand draft?

265. *§3-305(a).* If Buyer accepts a time draft, and if Second Bank is not a holder in due course because it gave value after it learned of Buyer's underlying contract defenses or after it learned that Buyer dishonored by refusing to pay the draft when it came due, may Buyer assert against Second Bank

   a. recoupment, that is, one-half of the contract price of the diamonds on the grounds that the diamonds are defective and worth only one-half of the contract price or the value as?

   b. setoff, that is, sums due Buyer from Seller for returns in connection with this contract? §3-305(a)(3), cmt. 3 (fifth paragraph). With other contracts? §2-717.

   c. payment, that is, Buyer's cash payment of the contract purchase price? §3-305(a)(2).

   d. the defense that Seller never delivered the merchandise or that Seller delivered nonconforming merchandise and the Buyer rejected it? §3-305(a)(2).

Section 40. The Bill of Lading

Traditionally, the bill of lading was the merchants' device for incorporating goods, while they were being transported, into a piece of paper that merchants could transfer from one to another and use as collateral with their bankers. Traditionally, the bill was always negotiable, and the negotiable bill (sometimes "order bill") stood for the goods. The rules that developed for the negotiable bill reflect the merchants' need to use possession of paper as a substitute for possession of the goods.

In U.S. domestic commerce and recently in international trade, the nonnegotiable bill (sometimes "way bill" or "straight bill") made its appearance. The rules for the nonnegotiable bill differ from those for the negotiable bill in that the nonnegotiable bill does not stand for the goods but is largely a contract of carriage.

Problems

266. *§7-403.* If a seller shipped goods under an order bill of lading, is the carrier liable to the seller if the carrier

   a. delivers the goods to the holder of the bill but fails to require the holder to surrender it?

   b. delivers to a non-holder, that is,

      i. a thief's transferee of a bill bearing a forged indorsement?

ii.   a party in possession to whom the indorsements do not run?

267.   *§7-403.*   If the seller ships under an order bill and the carrier delivers to *X*, a stranger and not the holder, does the holder of the bill have a cause of action against the carrier? Against the seller?

268.   *§§2-514, 4-503.*   Seller delivered to its own bank, Second Bank, a negotiable bill of lading and a negotiable draft drawn on the buyer in the sum of $25,000 payable at sight. Second forwarded the documents to Third Bank, which delivered the documents to the buyer before the buyer paid Third. In such a case, could the seller recover damages from Third? What damages could the seller recover?

269.   A seller desiring to protect against losses is considering the following courses of action. What are the advantages and disadvantages to the seller in each case?
a.   Using a nonnegotiable bill of lading and consigning the goods to seller itself.
b.   Using a nonnegotiable bill, consigning the goods to the buyer, and changing shipping instructions after shipment but before delivery to the buyer-consignee, if the buyer becomes insolvent or otherwise loses its credit standing.
c.   Causing a negotiable bill to issue to seller's order and refusing to indorse the bill.

Section 41.   *The Warehouse Receipt*

The negotiable warehouse receipt, much like its negotiable bill of lading counterpart, stands for the goods. By virtue of that feature, the negotiable receipt can play the traditional document-of-title role in the documentary draft transaction, and sometimes does.

The chief value of the negotiable receipt is the ability of merchants to transfer interests (usually title and security interests) in the goods without disturbing their storage. The merchants simply deliver the negotiable receipt much as they delivered the negotiable bill.

The nonnegotiable receipt does not stand for the goods and is largely a contract for the storage of the goods.

Problems

270.   If a warehouse receives goods and redelivers them to a stranger by mistake,
a.   does §7-204 apply? (If not, when does it apply?)
b.   does §7-404 apply?
c.   does §7-403 apply?

271.   *§7-403.*   To whom should a grain elevator deliver grain if

    a. the elevator issued a nonnegotiable receipt to X, the bailor?

    b. the elevator took the grain from X but issued him no receipt?

    c. in Questions (a) and (b), X instructs the elevator to deliver the grain to Y?

    d. in Questions (a) through (c), if the elevator had issued a negotiable receipt to X?

    e. the elevator issued a negotiable receipt to X, which X negotiated to Y, but X told the elevator not to deliver to Y?

272. Thief stole grain from O and bailed the grain with the elevator, which issued Thief a negotiable receipt. Later, Thief presented the receipt to the elevator, and the elevator redelivered the grain to Thief.

    a. At common law, has the elevator converted O's grain?

    b. Is the elevator liable to O in conversion under the Code? §7-404.

Section 42. More on the Documentary Draft Transaction

Problems

273. In a documentary draft transaction, the seller ships goods under a negotiable bill of lading and draws a time draft on the buyer for the purchase price of the goods. Seller then discounts the draft at Second Bank, which sends the draft and the bill through the banking system for presentation to Buyer in Buyer's city. If the buyer dishonors the draft (either by refusing to accept it when it is first presented or refusing to pay it when it comes due), the seller must reimburse any advance it received from Second Bank in which of the following cases?

    a. The seller drew the draft with Second as payee. §3-414(b).

    b. The seller drew the draft payable to itself and indorsed it without recourse to Second. §3-415(b).

    c. The seller drew the draft without recourse payable to itself and indorsed to Second. §3-414(e).

    d. The seller drew and indorsed the draft "without recourse." §§3-414(e), 3-315(b).

274. Seller brought two drafts to Second Bank. The first was accompanied by a negotiable bill of lading; the second by a nonnegotiable bill of lading. Why might Second take the first draft but not the second? Why might the drawee, the buyer, honor the first draft but not the second?

275. *§§7-403(4), 7-502(1)(b), 9-312(c).* Assume that in the preceding problem that (1) Second took both drafts for value, (2) the buyer dishonored both of them, and (3) the seller is insolvent. Will Second be able to get the goods covered by the bills?

276. *§2-705.* If a seller consigns a shipment of goods to a buyer and if the seller

has grounds that would otherwise permit stoppage of goods in transit, may the seller cause the carrier to stop delivery after
  a. the buyer receives the nonnegotiable bill?
  b. the buyer indorses the nonnegotiable bill to a sub-buyer?
  c. the buyer pays the seller for the goods?
  d. the carrier acknowledges that it holds the goods for the buyer?

277. If the seller consigns goods to the buyer under a nonnegotiable bill of lading and if the buyer loses the bill, what happens? Would your answer differ if the shipment were under a negotiable bill?

278. §7-301, cf. §7-203 (*similar rule for nonreceipt or misdescription in the case of a warehouse receipt*). Assuming that the document contains no disclaimer such as "shipper's load and count," if a bill of lading includes a misdescription of the goods shipped or if the cartons are empty so that the carrier never received any goods, which of the following parties may recover from the carrier?
  a. Second Bank that gives value to the seller and that takes a straight (nonnegotiable) bill designating the buyer as consignee.
  b. A buyer that takes a straight bill designating the buyer as consignee after the buyer gives value to the seller.
  c. A bank that takes an order (negotiable) bill for value.
  d. A buyer that takes an order bill for value.

Section 43. Negotiation and Transfer of Documents of Title

The distinction between negotiation and transfer in document of title law is sharp. Note that commercial parties might transfer a negotiable document. If the conveyance does not meet all of the requirements for due negotiation, it is a transfer even though the document may be in negotiable form.

The effect of transfer is pretty hollow; the transferee gets what the transferor had (the first rule of conveyancing law, *nemo dat*). The benefits of negotiation are considerable, however.

Problems

279. §7-501(4). Which of the following parties is a good-faith purchaser of a negotiable document of title?
  a. A bank that takes the bill from Seller if the bill is to the order of the seller and is indorsed by Seller, or if the bill is to the order of the bank.
  b. *B*, a chemical company, that purchases from a grain broker negotiable warehouse receipts indorsed in blank covering corn.
  c. A bank that lends to a grain broker and takes possession of negotiable warehouse receipts that the broker has indorsed. Would

it matter that the broker failed to indorse the receipts? Would it matter that the bank knew that the broker held the grain subject to the security interest of another bank? Would it matter that the bank took the receipts in satisfaction of the broker's debt?

    d. A cereal manufacturer that takes negotiable warehouse receipts, indorsed in blank,

        i. from a homeless person.

        ii. from a law teacher.

280. *§7-102, cmt. 3.* Chicago Buyer entered into a contract with St. Louis Seller for 100,000 bushels of soybeans. Seller has advised Buyer that the beans are in an elevator in Ainsworth, Iowa. Buyer would like to pay for the beans but wants assurance of delivery. Seller is unwilling to ship until Buyer pays. Devise a method whereby the parties can conclude their transaction using a document of title, not a bill of lading and not a warehouse receipt.

281. Brown is a tenant farmer on the old Wilson farm that is now owned by Doc Wilson, who practices medicine in Cleveland. The farm is in Tennessee. Each year Brown harvests the crop and markets it. This year, as in the past, Brown stored the crop, hoping that the price would rise. The elevator with which he stored it gave him a negotiable receipt, which he later used to sell the crop to National Chemical Corp. Every year, except this one, Brown would send half of the sales proceeds to Wilson under their oral lease arrangement. This year, however, Brown found himself in a cash bind and used all of the proceeds for his own purposes. Tennessee law gives farm landlords a lien for crop rent on the crop and on the proceeds from the sale of the crop, and Wilson now sues National for conversion.

    a. What result? *See* Cleveland v. McNabb, 312 F. Supp. 155 (W.D. Tenn. 1970) (similar fact setting in which court ruled for farm landlord). Is the holding consistent with the policy or letter of §7503(1)(a) and (b)?

    b. Would the result differ if this were the first year that Brown farmed Wilson's land? Id.

    c. What would the result be if Brown sold the crop in the ordinary course of business without using a receipt? *See* §9-320(a); Food Security Act of 1985, 7 U.S.C. §1631 (1985).

    d. Should the result differ depending on whether Brown uses a negotiable document of title? In Hext v. United States, 444 F.2d 804 (5th Cir. 1971), the court held that it does.

282. Foreign Seller and domestic Buyer agreed that Seller would ship goods under a negotiable bill of lading, payment under a commercial letter of credit. Seller shipped the goods and presented the bill of lading along with a draft drawn on the bank that issued the credit. The bank paid the draft at sight and took the bill. When the goods arrived, the bank took possession of them and stored them under negotiable warehouse receipts. In the meantime, Buyer had entered into a contract to resell the goods to a sub-buyer. The sub-buyer paid Buyer, which is now insolvent and which never reimbursed the bank for the advance the bank made when it paid the foreign seller under the letter of credit.

a. When the bank honored Seller's draft, what interest did the bank have in the goods? §§2-506, 7-502(1), 9-312(c).
b. Are the bank's rights determined by Article 9? §9-330.
c. Can the sub-buyer argue that it is a buyer in ordinary course that defeats the bank's security interest under §9-320(a)?

3. LETTERS OF CREDIT

Section 44. *Letter of Credit Transactions*

Article 5 is skeletal. It provides a basic legal framework for letters of credit but leaves much to the courts and to banking practice and custom. No commonly used commercial device is as sensitive to merchant innovation as the letter of credit. When the Code drafters prepared the original version of Article 5, the standby credit was sufficiently undeveloped that they ignored it. They may have been unaware of it, this despite the fact that bankers and bank lawyers were intimately involved as advisers to the reporter for Article 5, Professor Soia Mentschikoff. Yet, the standby has grown to prominence as a commercial device. Original Article 5 provided the legal framework for it.

Since the 1960s when Article 5 was first adopted, there have been other innovations in letter of credit practice. Revised Article 5 accommodates many of those innovations, but even revised Article 5 remains skeletal, and with good reason.

Familiarity with transactions involving letters of credit is rather helpful in understanding the rules. It is beyond the scope of this problems book to explain those transactions fully, but it might help a bit here to note that the commercial letter of credit is the type used in international trade. When a foreign seller agrees to ship goods to a domestic buyer, the seller will often want a letter of credit to secure payment. Once the goods begin their way across the ocean, it is costly for the seller to control them. He would at that point like to have his money or at least a bank obligation in place of the obligation of a U.S. buyer that he does not know. The buyer, at the same time, is reluctant to pay unless she has the right to the goods.

The commercial letter of credit protects both parties. It permits the seller to ship and secure the bank obligation he desires. It also permits the buyer to allow her bank to undertake that obligation, secure in the knowledge that the ocean carrier will deliver the goods to the bank or the buyer herself.

The standby letter of credit, the credit you are bound to meet in practice, is largely domestic. It operates to substitute the bank's credit standing for that of a weaker commercial party. A borrower, for example, may enhance the acceptability of his obligations (notes or bonds) by securing them with a standby. Under the terms of the standby, if the obligor does not pay, the holder may draw on the bank for payment.

From a pedagogical standpoint, the letter of credit is a lovely subject. It often involves an underlying contract of sale (Article 2); it frequently calls for a draft (Article 3) and a bill of lading (Article 7); the draft and bill usually wend their way through the bank collection system (Article 4) and the parties usually avail themselves of one or more security interests (Article 9). Finally, banks will make payment under a credit and often reimburse themselves by wire (Article 4A). Study of letters of credit is therefore a fitting capstone for Code study, providing an opportunity for review of much that we learn in the courses on Payment Systems and Secured Transactions.

The electronic revolution has had an impact on letters of credit. A letter of credit, confirmation, advice, transfer, amendment, or cancellation may be issued in any form that is a "record" (*see* §5-102(a)(14)), and is authenticated by a signature or in accordance with the agreement of the parties or standard practice. §5-104. This means that letters of credit can be issued electronically. §5-104, cmt. 3. Moreover, although a beneficiary usually presents paper documents to the issuer when requesting payment under the credit, Article 5 also provides that facsimiles and other electronic or nonpaper media can be presented as "documents" if expressly permitted by the credit or standard practice. *See* §5-102(a)(6) & cmt. 2.

Note that the Electronic Signatures in Global and National Commerce Act (E-Sign) and the Uniform Electronic Transactions Act (UETA) do not apply to transactions that are governed by Article 5.

Problems

283. U.S. Seller entered into a contract for the sale of goods with Thai Buyer. The terms of the agreement call for payment by letter of credit. Buyer caused the Hong Kong Bank to issue a letter of credit directly to Seller.
    a. Under the Code, has Buyer complied with the sales contract? §2-325(3). Should the seller want an advice (from a bank local to seller) to the effect that the credit has been issued? How should the lawyer for the seller draft the letter-of-credit term in the sales contract to provide more protection for the seller? Why, moreover, would seller want a confirmed credit? §5-107(a).
    b. How does the seller in these circumstances know that in fact Hong Kong Bank issued the credit? Do you suppose that sellers normally have signature books for foreign bank officers? A code book for foreign bank communications sent by telex equipment? Access to SWIFT (Society for Worldwide Interbank Financial Telecommunications)?

284. Assume in the foregoing problem that the seller insisted on and got a credit confirmed by First Bank. In that case, identify
    a. the credit issuer.
    b. the adviser (advising bank).
    c. the confirming bank.
    d. the applicant (account party) (customer).
    e. the beneficiary.

f. the bank and place at which the beneficiary seller must present his documents to have payment under the credit.

g. the typical documents that a commercial letter of credit such as the one in this transaction might call for.

285. Your client, a small savings and loan association, is arranging to lend money to a borrower on the borrower's note secured by a mortgage. The S&L is asking the borrower to arrange to have its commercial bank issue a letter of credit in favor of the S&L for 10 percent of the face amount of the note. This arrangement is in lieu of a down payment by the borrower. The S&L officer wants to be able to draw in the event of a default on the note. The commercial bank has proposed a letter of credit containing language indicating that the S&L may draw on the bank issuer and that the draw must be accompanied by "all documents causing this credit to be called upon." Your client would prefer the language "documentation of the borrower's default." One of your client's colleagues wants the language to read "upon borrower's default." What do you tell your client?

286. There is authority in contract law to the effect that courts should construe a contract so that it will have effect and will not be rendered a nullity. In an ambiguous credit, should courts construe the credit to promote payment to the beneficiary as an instance of this contract rule of construction?

287. In contract law, it is a general rule of construction that an ambiguous contract should be construed against its drafter. Who do you suppose drafts most of the terms of the letter of credit? In government contract cases, the government usually provides the bank with the language that must be incorporated into the letter of credit issued in favor of the government agency. Should these credits be construed against the government, if they are ambiguous? Do you agree with the view announced by the U.S. Court of Appeals for the First Circuit that letters of credit should be construed strongly against the issuer? *See* Banco Espanol de Credito v. State Street Bank & Trust Co., 385 F.2d 230 (1st Cir. 1967), *cert. denied*, 390 U.S. 1013 (1968).

288. The International Chamber of Commerce (ICC), a trade group of enterprises engaged in international trade that has its headquarters in Paris, through its Commission on Banking Technique and Practice has fashioned a set of rules that apply to letters of credit, primarily to documents that are traditionally submitted under commercial letters of credit. The ICC revises these rules, the Uniform Customs and Practice for Documentary Credits (UCP), every ten years or so. There is no warranty under UCP 500, the latest version of the UCP. Should courts invoke §5-110, a warranty rule, to an issuer's claim that the beneficiary received payment under the credit by presenting fraudulent documents if the credit is subject to UCP 500? Does it matter that the Uniform Customs do not contain a presentment warranty?

289. a. First Bank's letter of credit in favor of Seller Corp. stipulates that Seller must present, among other documents, an invoice in duplicate evidencing shipment of "approximately 100 Tons ¼-inch specialty steel rods at $142 per Ton (length not less than 6 feet, nor more than 8 feet)." If First Bank's document examiner receives an invoice describing the goods as "steel rods," should the bank honor the seller's draft? If the issuer dishonors, will it be liable to the beneficiary for wrongful dishonor of its credit obligation? *See* UCP 500 art. 37(c).[1]

    b.   Would your answer differ if the credit had not been subject to the UCP?

    c.   If you were the lawyer for the seller, how would you draft the description of the goods in the invoice?

Section 45. Duties of the Credit Issuer

The key to the success of the letter of credit is the integrity of the credit issuer's obligation to pay the beneficiary quickly and without regard to the equities of the underlying transaction. The independence principle teaches that the issuer must pay against facially conforming documents. While bank bad faith can subvert that principle, banks generally pay promptly, even when they have lost their right of reimbursement against the applicant for the credit.

Sections 5-108 and 5-109 define the independence principle first as to the applicant and then as to the beneficiary. Note that the latter section contains an exception for fraud. At times that exception has occupied much of letter-of-credit law.

Problems

290. *§5-108(a)*. If the documents conform on their face, but the letter-of-credit issuer pays the wrong beneficiary, that is, the draft is forged and a fraudulent party is presenting the documents for payment, may the issuer obtain reimbursement from the applicant? How might an issuer protect itself from losses of this kind?

291. *§5-108*. A letter of credit calls for a bill of lading with an "on board" stamp, that is, a certification by the carrier that the goods are not only received for shipment but have been loaded on board the vessel. The stamp is important to many buyers and banks because marine insurance does not cover the goods until they pass the ship's rail. The on-board stamp on the bill accompanied by an insurance certificate certifying that the seller obtained marine insurance will give the buyer and the banks comfort when they pay the seller's draft that the goods, if destroyed, will be covered by the insurance. Assume that the beneficiary presents to the issuer a bill of lading that does not bear the stamp,

---

1. "The description of the goods in the commercial invoice must correspond with the description in the Credit." ICC Uniform Customs and Practice for Documentary Credits (ICC Pub. No. 500) art. 37(c) (1993).

    a.   Should the issuer pay the beneficiary's draft?

    b.   Would your answer differ if the credit called for an ocean bill of lading, and the beneficiary presented an air bill?

    c.   Would your answer differ if the credit called for a bill of lading with a clause requiring the carrier to notify "Mohammed Sofan" of the shipment if the bill presented directed the carrier to notify "Mohammed Soran"?

292. *§5-108(a).* Assume in part (a) of the preceding question that the document checker missed the fact that the on-board stamp was missing from the face of the bill but that the goods were in fact on board. Based on its error, the bank paid the beneficiary. Now the bank seeks reimbursement from its customer, the applicant, who is claiming that the bank erred by paying the beneficiary and should not obtain reimbursement.

    a.   May the issuer have reimbursement from the applicant?

    b.   Would your answer differ if the goods were not on board but on the dock, and were then destroyed by fire and not covered by insurance?

293. *§5-108(b).* First Bank issued a letter of credit in favor of Mortgage Co. to secure 10 percent of the mortgage loan that Mortgage Co. made to First's customer, the applicant for the credit. Under its terms, the credit expired on May 1, a Thursday. Mortgage Co. mailed its draft and conforming documents under the credit on April 22, but because of a delay in the mails, the documents did not arrive at First Bank until May 2.

    a.   Must First pay Mortgage Co.'s draft?

    b.   Would your answer differ if the draft arrived with the documents on Wednesday, April 30, and the credit expired while the bank was examining the documents under the reasonable time rule of §5-108(b)?

    c.   Suppose the draft and documents arrived on April 23, and one of the documents, a certificate of default, was unsigned. If the bank waits until May 2 to give notice of the defect, can the bank argue successfully that the credit has expired and it is not liable to the beneficiary?

    d.   Would your answer to (c) differ if the bank could show that its delay did not cause detriment to the beneficiary, that is, that the beneficiary could not have cured the defect if the bank had given notice on April 26?

294. *§5-109(a).* An issuer received documents that conformed on their face with the terms of the credit but learned from an independent source that the goods were, in fact, not up to industry standards.

    a.   May the issuer refuse to honor the beneficiary's draft?

    b.   Would your answer differ if the bank was relying on the goods as security for the advance it made when it paid the beneficiary's draft?

    c.   Would your answer differ if the documents included a certificate reciting that the goods satisfied industry standards and if the bank learned from another source that the goods were defective?

Section 46. The Exception for Fraud

Because fraud is a serious problem for commerce, courts have felt that they cannot ignore it, even though an exception to the independence principle for fraud creates serious problems for the letter of credit. Litigation over the fraud exception has yielded a judicial balancing of the equities of the defrauded party against the integrity of the letter of credit as a commercial product. Once the courts established the fraud exception, §5-109(b) being a codification of those cases, they strained to cabin it. They did so primarily in two rather ingenious ways. First, they defined fraud narrowly, so that only egregious fraud would satisfy the exception. Second, they vigorously invoked equity prerequisites for injunctive relief, requiring the applicant to show that it had no adequate remedy at law and that it had a strong likelihood of success on the merits. The net effect of these judicially confected limits on the judicially confected fraud exception has been to guard the credit's integrity but to allow injunctions against payment in the most compelling cases, but not as a matter of course. The solution is not always successful but is largely a happy one. Note that §5-109(b) codifies these judicial rules.

Problems

295. *§5-109(b).* Seller and Buyer entered into a contract for the sale of diodes with payment to be made under a letter of credit. Seller presented facially conforming documents to the letter of credit issuer, but Buyer alleged that the bill of lading was fraudulent in that Seller had shipped rubbish in the cartons instead of diodes.

    a. Is this an example of the kind of fraud that will justify court interference with the independence principle?

    b. If it is such a case, should the court issue an injunction against payment of the credit? What further demonstration would you as trial judge want before you would issue the injunction?

296. First Bank (FB) issued a standby letter of credit in favor of Saudi Bank (SB), which had issued an international bank guaranty in favor of a Saudi buyer of goods manufactured by a U.S. seller. If SB certifies to FB that SB has paid under the guaranty and if that certification is all that FB's letter of credit calls for, is there any way that the U.S. seller can prevent payment under the credit? If it cannot stop payment, is all lost?

297. In which of the following cases do you think that a court might issue a preliminary injunction?

    a. The letter of credit calls for a certificate from the beneficiary, a landlord, to the effect that the tenant has not paid its rent. The landlord presents the certificate with a demand for payment under the credit. The tenant claims that because the landlord has breached a covenant in the lease, the rent is not due; that the certification is, therefore, false; and that an injunction forbidding payment under the credit should issue.

b. The credit calls for beneficiary-seller's certificate that its invoices to the applicant-buyer have not been paid. Buyer alleges that the goods were defective, that it does not owe the money covered by the invoices, that the seller's certification is therefore fraudulent, and that an injunction should issue.

298.

a. Applicant for a credit issued in favor of a large corporation has learned that the documents that the corporation is submitting under the credit contain false assertions. If Applicant pleads these facts, should a court issue a temporary restraining order against payment under the credit?

b. Would your answer to the preceding question differ if payment under the credit and the issuer's subsequent charge against Applicant's account would render Applicant insolvent? Would it matter that the payment would not render Applicant insolvent but, according to Applicant, would embarrass Applicant in the trade by having industry members learn that its standby had been drawn against?

c. Applicant for a credit issued by First Bank, a large money center bank, has learned that the beneficiary of the credit has supplied the bank with documents that are facially nonconforming. Applicant fears, however, that the bank is about to honor the beneficiary's draft. If applicant pleads these facts, should the court enter a temporary restraining order?

299. Applicant is a limited partner in a venture that was to construct a gambling casino. Under the terms of the partnership agreement, Applicant gave the partnership $1 00,000 and a promissory note for $400,000. Applicant secured the note by a letter of credit payable to Lending Bank. Lending Bank took the note from the partnership as security for a loan to the partnership. The partnership has defaulted on the loan, the bank has called Applicant's note, and Applicant has refused to pay the bank. Applicant has learned that the general partner of the partnership who sold the limited partnership interest to Applicant made false and seriously misleading statements to Applicant. These fraudulent statements are in violation of state and federal securities laws. If Applicant pleads these facts, should a court issue a temporary restraining order against Lending Bank preventing it from drawing on the letter of credit?

Section 47. Transferring Interests in Letters of Credit

It is an oversimplification but nonetheless helpful to think of letters of credit as obligations that are generally not transferable. *See* §5-112. There are exceptions. First, the parties can agree to the contrary by stipulating in the credit that the credit is transferable. Second, some transfers occur by operation of law. *See* §5-113. Third, the fact that a credit is not transferable does not prevent the beneficiary from assigning the credit's proceeds. Transfer entails the right to substitute beneficiaries, that is, the right to let a third party draw on the credit. Assignment does not entail that substitution, and thus is permitted. Although not every assignment of proceeds is for security, when the beneficiary does grant a security interest in proceeds, the rules of Article 9 govern such matters as the creation and perfection of that interest. *See* §5-114(f). The fourth method of transferring the benefit of the credit is to have the issuer issue a negotiation credit. Under the negotiation credit, which the following problems describe, the beneficiary takes its documents to a bank that negotiates them. That bank thereby wins rather extensive rights against the credit issuer under the credit. Credits come in two varieties: negotiation credits and straight credits; and a bank cannot become a "negotiating bank" under a straight credit, even though it negotiates the beneficiary's draft. In order to rise to the level of a negotiating bank, the bank must be nominated to negotiate. *See* §5-102(a)(11).

Problems

300. *§§3-308, 5-109(a)(1)(i).* FNB issued a negotiation letter of credit in favor of Seller calling for a draft payable 60 days after sight. Seller discounted its draft at Second Bank, which now seeks acceptance of the draft by the issuer.

    a. Is it necessary for Second to prove that it is a holder in due course to enforce the credit?

    b. If the buyer-applicant alleges that the seller defrauded the buyer and delivered fraudulent documents to Second, may the buyer obtain an injunction against acceptance or payment of the draft when Second presents them to FNB? In this setting, does Second's status as a holder in due course become relevant? If so, who has the burden of proof regarding that status?

    c. If the buyer seeks an injunction in this case on the grounds that the bill of lading is fraudulent, should buyer's petition allege that Second is not a holder in due course? Absent that allegation, is the complaint deficient? May a court issue an injunction if the petitioner fails to demonstrate the likelihood of success on the merits? Would the buyer have a likelihood of success on the merits in this case if Second is a holder in due course?

    d. Would your answers to the foregoing questions differ if the credit was a straight credit?

    e. Under either a straight or a negotiation credit that calls for time drafts, may the applicant buyer obtain an injunction after the time drafts have been accepted by the issuer?

301. *§5-113.* If corporate planners decide to merge a subsidiary into its parent, why might they be interested to know whether the subsidiary is a beneficiary of a letter of credit?

302. May the trustee in bankruptcy of the beneficiary draw on a credit issued to the beneficiary before bankruptcy? May the personal representative of a decedent draw on a credit issued to the decedent? What might issuers do to avoid problems in these cases?

303. FNB issued a letter of credit in favor of Second Bank, which is now insolvent. FDIC is the receiver of Second and by operation of law succeeds to all of Second's assets. May it draw on the credit? If FDIC as receiver transfers the credit voluntarily to itself as insurer of Second's deposits, may FDIC (now in its corporate capacity, that is, for itself and not for the estate of Second) draw on the credit?

304. *§§5-114(c), 9-107, 9-312, 9-314.*
   a. Exporter Co. has entered into a contract with a Ukrainian buyer for 100,000 bushels of hops. The buyer caused a German bank to issue a nontransferable letter of credit in favor of the Exporter, and a New York bank has confirmed the credit. Exporter is now seeking to purchase the hops from a Seattle broker and needs credit to induce its own bank, Exporter's bank, to (1) issue a back-to-back credit in favor of the Seattle broker, or (2) lend Exporter the funds to pay the Seattle broker. How should the parties proceed?
   b. If Exporter effectively assigns his letter-of-credit rights to his bank, who will draw the draft under the credit, Exporter or his bank?

305. Gas Distributor Co. (GDC) sells on open account to customers throughout the country. Some of his accounts do not have triple A credit ratings, and he threatened to terminate sales to them unless they had their banks issue standby letters of credit securing the open accounts. Under the credits, which the low-rated customers' banks issued, if a GDC's invoice to the respective customer is unpaid after 60 days, GDC may present to the standby issuer a copy of the invoice, a draft for the face amount of the invoice, and a certificate reciting that the invoice is unpaid. Upon presentation of those documents, the issuer will honor the draft.

GDC is financing its receivables with First Bank and grants First a security interest in all of its "accounts." First perfects by filing a financing statement that covers all of GDC's accounts.
   a. *§§9-102(a)(77), 9-308(d).* How does First obtain a security interest in the letter-of-credit rights under the credits that secure the accounts?
   b. Who must draw the drafts and the certificates in order to satisfy the documentary conditions of the credits?

Section 48. Issuer Insolvency

When the issuer becomes insolvent, the beneficiary's expectations are surely frustrated. Whether the law should protect a beneficiary that takes a letter of credit from a bank that soon thereafter becomes insolvent is an interesting policy question, the kind of question that this book does not address. To some extent the Code, however, does address the problem, and there has been some litigation. The following problem attempts to clarify some of the moderately confusing issues that arose during the bank insolvency crisis of the 1980s.

Problem

306. First Bank issued a credit for $90,000 to Seller Co. When Seller Co. was about to present its documents and draft under the credit, Seller learned that First was insolvent.

    a. Is Seller an insured depositor under the Federal Deposit Insurance Act?

    b. Would it be a preference in violation of the policy of that Act for the receiver (the FDIC) to pay seller 100 percent of his claim and to pay other creditors less than 100 percent?

    c. If Buyer, the applicant for the credit, had deposited funds with the specific purpose of providing for the payment of the credit, can the receiver keep the funds and dishonor the credit?

4. WIRE TRANSFERS

Section 49. Wire Transfers

It would leave a law teacher with a guilty conscience to teach a course in payments systems and not cover wire transfers. After all, electronic payments systems transfer more funds, more quickly, with more reliability than all of the other systems put together.

Yet, one cannot fault tepid interest in the *law* of wire transfers. It is simply not very exciting at the moment. In fact, it's rather stodgy. Primarily the domain of large business corporations, government agencies, and financial institutions, electronic transfers outside of the debit and credit card system have yielded little litigation, well-established principles, a few fireworks in the legislative process, and a disgruntled law professor here and there; but otherwise not much more than a big yawn.

The net effect of the situation is something of a disappointment to lawyers and law teachers—the system works well, and there is little controversy and less litigation. For the student, the challenge here may be more one of understanding the transactions than understanding the law. These problems illustrate the few questions that have arisen and that might be the subject of class study.

The diagram illustrates a simple wire transfer over, in this case, Fedwire. Note the terminology developed by the industry and recognized by Article

4A and the regulations of the Federal Reserve Board, including Reg J, which govern Fedwire transactions. Note also that a bank will usually play two roles. It is a receiving bank when it receives a payment order (hereafter "p/o"); and it is a sender when it retransmits the order to the next receiving bank.

Buyer (Originator) — p/o → (Receiving Bank) Buyer's Bank (Sender) — p/o → (Receiving Bank) Federal Reserve Bank of San Francisco (Sender) — p/o → (Receiving Bank) Federal Reserve Bank of Atlanta (Sender) — p/o → (Receiving Bank) Seller's Bank — funds → Seller (Beneficiary)

Problems

307. In the foregoing illustration, an Atlanta insurance company and its San Francisco customer agreed that on May 1, the customer would pay its monthly premium by wiring $1 million to the insurance company's account at Second Bank of Atlanta. The customer's financial officer authorized the payment and caused the payment order to be sent by wire from a computer terminal at the customer's offices to a wire transfer terminal at First Bank in San Francisco. Thus the customer became an originator.

   a. When First Bank sends the order (p/o) to the Federal Reserve Bank of San Francisco, the Federal Reserve Bank will forward the funds to Atlanta's Federal Reserve Bank. How does the San Francisco Federal Reserve Bank reimburse itself? Federal Reserve Reg. J, 12 C.F.R. §210.28(a) (2002).

   b. If the payment order misnames the beneficiary's bank but contains the correct number for that bank, what might the Federal Reserve Bank of Atlanta do? Id. §210 27(a). *See also* Problem 309 below.

   c. When does acceptance of the p/o occur between First Bank and the San Francisco Fed?

   d. When does the payment of the insurance premium occur? UCC §4A-209(b).

   e. Under the Code, must Second Bank of Atlanta take action to accept the p/o? UCC §4A-209, cmt. 8; Reg. J, 12 C.F.R. §210.31(a) (2002).

308. *§§4A-201, 4A-202(b), 4A-203.* If a dishonest employee of a bank's customer manages to initiate a funds transfer through a funds transfer system, who will bear the loss? §4A-202. Will the result depend on the fact that the buyer's bank has made available to its customers a commercially reasonable security procedure?

309. *§4A-207.* Crook obtained Widow's investment identification number with Mutual Fund, Inc. Crook used that information to request Mutual Fund to sell Widow's $750,000 interest in the fund and to wire the proceeds to Widow's account at Third Bank in Dallas, account No. 12345. In fact, that account is not in Widow's name but in the name of Coin Store, Inc., a legitimate coin dealer. Crook has selected $750,000 in rare coins with the dealer and will pick them up when Third Bank informs the innocent dealer that $750,000 has been wired to the dealer's account.

What should Third Bank do when it receives a wire transfer payment order designating payment to an account that does not bear the name of the beneficiary listed on the payment order? (This problem illustrates a fraudulent scheme that worked more than once.)

310. On May 1, Insured originated a funds transfer to Insurance Co. in Atlanta. At 1:00 P.M. on that day, Third Bank, the beneficiary's bank in Atlanta, received a payment order from the Federal Reserve Bank of Atlanta.

     a. May Insured cancel the order before Third Bank accepts it? §§4A-209, 4A-211.

     b. May Insured cancel the order after Third Bank has notified the insurance company of the payment? §4A-209(b)(1).

311. *§4A-303.* Insured originated an order for payment to Insurance Co. of $1 million. Through a data entry clerk's error on the premises of Insured's bank, the bank issued a payment order to the Federal Reserve Bank of San Francisco in the amount of $10 million instead of $1 million. How are the losses allocated?

312. *§4A-305.* Insured issued a payment order to Insurance Co. on May 1, the day the premium was due. Through the negligence of Insured's bank, the payment was not received until May 2; Insurance Co. canceled the policy; and Insured's sustained a $25 million uninsured loss. Is the bank liable for Insured's consequential damages?

Payment Systems: Answers

1. NEGOTIABLE INSTRUMENTS

Section 29. The Effect of a Signature on a Negotiable Instrument: The "Contract" Liability Concept

208.

a. No. As a general rule, no party is liable on an instrument unless he signs it. *See* §3-401(a). If the signature were authorized, of course, Drawer would be liable because the drawer of a check or overdraft engages to pay the instrument if it is dishonored. *See* §3-414(b).

b. Because the drawer did not intend the imprinted name to operate as a signature, that is, as an authentication of the check, the imprint does not operate as a signature. *See* §§1-201(b)(37) [§1-201(39)], 3-401(b).

c. Under the fiction of §3-403(a), Thief has signed the instrument and engaged to pay a subsequent party that takes it for value if the instrument is not paid by the drawee bank, First Bank. If First pays the instrument to Seller or some other holder to whom Seller negotiates it, Thief is liable to the bank.

d. If Thief is a relative of Drawer or perhaps an employee, Drawer may be inclined to ratify the signature. If, for example, First Bank is suspicious of the signature and calls Drawer, Drawer might tell First to pay. In that case, Drawer would not be able to say subsequently that the signature is not his. Drawer would have ratified it. *See* §3-403(a) (last sentence).

209.   a.   No. A draft is not an assignment under the Code. Seller may not argue, therefore, that the bank is obliged to honor the drawer's order. This rule is consistent with the general rule that no person is liable on an instrument unless he signs it. The bank has not signed. *See* §§3-401(a), 3-408.

        b.   The cases go against Seller. Section 1-103(b) [§1-103] incorporates extra-Code law only to the extent that the Code does not displace that law. The sections cited in Answer (a) probably displace any extra-Code theories. There have been cases holding the dishonoring drawee bank liable to Seller, but only if Seller can show that she exacted an explicit promise from the bank to pay the instrument.

           Note also that the Code does provide a procedure for imposing instrument liability on the drawee bank that certifies a check. *See* §§3-409(a) and (d), 3-413(a). However, First Bank has not placed its signature on the check, nor has it indicated in writing on the check that the check is certified.

        c.   No. However, even if First Bank is not liable to Seller, it may be liable to its customer, the drawer, if it dishonors a check when funds are sufficient. §4-402.

Section 30. *The Concepts of Transfer and Negotiation*

210.   a.   This is a blank indorsement. It renders the check bearer paper and permits subsequent negotiation of it by delivery alone. *See* §§3-109(a), 3-201(a), 3-205(b).

        b.   No. Seller can indorse the check in blank, by signing only her name, or specially, by writing "Pay X" and signing her name. Either way, X will become a holder. However, whether a subsequent party who takes the check from X is a holder will depend on the way Seller indorses. If Seller indorses in blank, as she did in the problem, subsequent parties can become holders by mere delivery of the check. *See* §3-305(a). If Seller indorses specially, subsequent parties cannot be holders unless X indorses. *See* §3-205(a). The nature of X's indorsement will determine the status of parties subsequent to him as holders, as the analysis starts all over again. Note that once a holder indorses in blank, all subsequent negotiations may be effected by delivery without indorsement. If a holder indorses specially, however, there can be no negotiation without the endorsement of the party to whom the instrument is specially indorsed.

        c.   It was order paper before Seller indorsed and bearer paper after the blank indorsement. *See* §3-205(b).

        d.   X is an indorsee-holder and, therefore, is entitled to enforce the instrument. *See* §3-301. X may enforce the instrument against Seller under §3-415. Assuming that Drawer's signature is genuine, X may enforce the instrument against Drawer under §3-414. Thus X will often have a choice and will select the party most amenable to service or most creditworthy as the target defendant or may sue both parties in the same suit if that is possible. X, of course, must satisfy conditions to recover from these parties and will have only one recovery. Note that if Seller satisfies her indorser obligation to X, Seller will be an indorser who "paid the draft under Section 3-415" and can enforce the check against Drawer under §3-414(b).

    e.   X may recover from Seller under §3-415(a) and, because he is liable as a drawer, from Thief under §3-414(b). X cannot recover against Drawer, whose authorized signature does not appear on the instrument.

211. The following is a diagram of the transaction:

Drawer → Seller → [Crook] → X → Y → First Bank

    a.   Y is a holder because the indorsement is not unauthorized; it is a good indorsement by Seller. *See* §1-201(b)(21) [§1-201(20)].

    b.   As a holder, Y may enforce the contract liability of X, an indorser; of Seller, also an indorser; of Crook, also an indorser; and of Drawer, as a drawer. It does not matter whether X indorsed specially or in blank. X's indorsement gives rise to indorser liability. *See* §3-415(a).

    c.   In these circumstances, X can enforce the instrument against both Crook and Drawer. Crook is liable to X, a subsequent indorser who paid the instrument. *See* §3-415(a) (last sentence). Drawer is liable to X, an indorser who "paid the draft under Section 3-415." §3-414(a) (last sentence).

212. Under the modified facts, Y is not a holder. Because Crook's signing of X's name does not operate as X's signature, *see* §3-403(a), X's indorsement is missing. Unless Y obtains X's indorsement, Y is not a holder, *see* §1-201(b)(21) [§1-201(20)]; and Y cannot enforce the instrument.

213. The following diagram illustrates the transaction:

[Thief] → Seller → Second Bank → First Bank

    a.   Second may not recover from Drawer who, in this case, is not the drawer, not having signed the instrument. Thief's forgery operates as Thief's signature and renders Thief a drawer, *see* §3-403(a); Second may enforce Thief's liability as drawer. First is not liable on the instrument to anyone, not having signed it. *See* §3-401(a). Second, despite the forged drawer's signature, is a holder; Seller is liable as an indorser to Second. *See* §3-415(a).

    b.   Thief should bear the loss but is usually insolvent or missing. Generally Seller, having dealt with Thief, was in the best position to avoid the fraud and will bear the loss. There is no reason to prevent Seller's use of supplemental rules of tort [fraud] or equity [unjust enrichment] to permit Seller to recover from Thief. But remember that Thief is liable to Seller on the instrument because Thief's forgery of Drawer's signature acts as Thief's own signature and makes him liable, being a drawer, to Seller, as an indorser who pays the instrument.

214.   a. As an indorser and as a drawer, C is liable to Second, the holder. *See* §§3-414(b), 3-415(a). Unless one of the estoppel rules applies (and one of them may, namely §3-406), Ace is not liable because its signature is not on the instrument. *See* §3-401(a).

    b. Yes. These facts establish an estoppel under §3-406. Ace's negligence has substantially contributed to C's forgery.

    c. They keep it under lock and key.

    d. Under the doctrine of Price v. Neal, 3 Burr. 1354 (K.B. 1762), the law does impose on the drawee bank losses for payment over a forged drawer's signature. *See* §§4-401(a), 4-208(a)(3). The drawee bank may be able to avoid that liability by invoking the estoppel of §3-406, but most banks avoid it in this setting by telling Ace that they will not accept a facsimile signature machine signature unless Ace agrees to hold the bank harmless from Price v. Neal liability when an unauthorized person uses the machine. The courts have been willing to enforce those agreements, and the Code anticipates them. *See* §3-404, cmt. 2, case #4.

215.   Preprinted checks will bear the name of the Company. This should show unambiguously to any holder that Joe is signing only for the company. Article 3 makes that result explicit. *See* §3-402(c). It is probably best in other cases for officers of corporations always to sign "Ace Corp., by Joe Ace, President." The results are more serious to Joe in the case of a promissory note. Many lenders to closely held companies rely on the credit of the individual officers and stockholders of the company; the name of the company will not appear on the note as a matter of course, as it does on a preprinted check; and Joe will have to argue that the signatures unambiguously show that he signed in a representative capacity. *See* §3-402(b). In the fourth case, he will surely prevail.

Section 31.   Conditions of Contract Liability

216.   a. X has "contract" rights against S as an indorser and against Drawer as drawer. *See* §§3-414, 3-415. To hold the indorser, however, X must get the check into the banking system within 30 days of the date of the indorsement and must give notice of dishonor within 30 days of the day X receives notice of dishonor. X can hold the drawer even if the initiation of collection is late and even if the notice of dishonor is late. As long as the delays do not cause the drawer to lose its deposit, the drawer is not discharged. *See* §3-414(f). Thus, X loses S because X did not deposit the check within 30 days of S's indorsement and did not notify S within 30 days of the time the bank notified X of the dishonor. *See* §§3-415(e), 3-503(a), 3-503(c).

X is late as against Drawer in depositing the check, but the delay does not discharge Drawer. *See* §3-414(f).

b.   *S* does not need to hold anyone, because she is not liable on the instrument. The party that can enforce contract liability against *S* is *X*, *see* §3-415(a); but *X* has lost his rights by virtue of the delays. *S*, then, does not need to enforce the instrument against anyone.

Section 32.   *Negotiable Instruments and the Underlying Transaction*

217.   a.   No. First, not having accepted the check by certifying it, *see* §§3-408, 3-409, was never liable on the instrument; and the other parties that signed, the drawer and the two indorsers, were liable only in the event of dishonor.

b.   When the check is paid, Drawer is discharged on the underlying obligation. *See* §3-310(b)(1). Moreover, since the check was paid, Drawer, Seller, and *X* are discharged on the check. *See* §3-602(a) and (c) [§3-602(a)].

c.   Drawer is discharged. *See* §3-310(b)(1).

d.   A certified check. *See* §3-409(d). The certifying bank undertakes to honor the check when presented. *See* §3-413(a). If the bank includes the amount in its certification, its obligation is limited to that amount. *See* §3-413(b).

218.   a.   The rule of §3-310(b)(1) that issuance of the check to the seller suspends the drawer's liability on the underlying contract must be read together with §3-309. Seller may not sue on the underlying contract, *see* §3-310(b)(4), but must sue on the lost check and satisfy the bond requirements of §3-309(b). Drawer is reluctant to draw a replacement check because if the first check finds its way into the hands of a holder in due course, that person can enforce it against Drawer, even though Drawer has paid Seller via the replacement check. A holder in due course takes the instrument free from that kind of defense.

b.   Seller must sue on the check under §3-309. Seller will have to post a bond or other security to protect Drawer against the eventuality that the check turns up in the hands of a holder in due course who can enforce it.

Since presentment of the lost or stolen check is impossible, it is excused. *See* §3-504(a). Dishonor occurs without presentment if the check is not paid, *see* §3-502(e), thus triggering Drawer's obligation under §3-414(b). *See* §3-310, cmt. 4.

Section 33. Holders in Due Course and Their Rights

219.   a.   No. Note how much easier it would be for Seller to prove a prima facie case on a negotiable instrument under §3-308.

        b.   This note is not negotiable because, in order to be negotiable, a note must be payable either to order or to bearer. *See* §§3-104(a)(1), 3-109. Only negotiable instruments may be negotiated.

220.   a.   A promise is value only to the extent it has been performed. *See* §3-303(a)(1). First Bank gave value only to the extent of $60,000, and can qualify as a holder in due course only to that extent. It is too late for First to qualify as a holder in due course as to the remaining $40,000, because it now has notice of Maker's defense. *See* §3-302. First can recover only $60,000 from Maker. *See* §3-305.

        b.   Here, the parties have agreed on a discounted purchase price that reflects the present value of the note. If First Bank had paid the entire price ($99,500), it would have been a holder in due course of the entire note ($100,000). However, where only partial payment has been made ($60,000), the calculation is more complex. Section 3-302(d) provides the formula. First is a holder in due course to this extent: $100,000 x ($60,000/$99,500).

        c.   First Bank has given value. *See* §3-303(a)(3). However, if First holds only a security interest, its enforcement rights are limited to the amount of the unpaid obligation secured. *See* §3-302(e).

        d.   First Bank has given value, because the note was transferred in exchange for a cashier's check, which is a negotiable instrument. *See* §3-303(a)(4).

221.   No. Even though First Bank is now a payee, it can be a holder in due course, so long as it meets the basic requirements of taking for value, in good faith, and without notice. §3-302, cmt. 4.

222.   a.   Second Bank is a collecting bank. It has a security interest in the check in the amount of $100,000, *see* §4-210(a)(2); thus, it has given value in that amount pursuant to §4-211, and can qualify as a holder in due course. So long as National had a right to withdraw the money, whether it did so is irrelevant.

        b.   Second Bank has a security interest in the check and is a holder for value only to the extent the deposited funds have been withdrawn—that is, to the extent of $500. §4-210(a)(1).

        c.   Second Bank has an Article 9 security interest in the check and is a holder for value to the extent of $100,000 under §4-211.

223.   a.   Seller may not recover. When the drawee bank, First, paid Second, it paid a holder and thereby discharged the liability of the drawer and the indorsers on the check. §3-602(a) and (c) [§3-602(a)]. Moreover, when the check was paid, Buyer was discharged on the underlying contract as well. *See* §3-310(b)(1). Note that this rule puts the loss on Seller, who should not have indorsed the check in blank thereby permitting the thief to make subsequent parties holders.

b. No. Buyer is discharged. *See* §3-602(a) and (c) [§3-602(a).]

c. It makes sense.

d. No. As a holder in due course, Second has the protection of §3-306, which shields it from all claims. Replevin and conversion are claims.

224. Under the revised facts, we have a forged indorsement by Thief. Seller, by not indorsing, has protected herself. Now, the subsequent parties are not holders. *See* §1-201(b)(21) [§1-201(20)].

a. Buyer, therefore, is not discharged. Payment must be to a "party entitled to enforce the instrument," that is, a holder. §3-602(a) [§3-602(a)]. Payment to a person who is not a holder does not discharge anybody. As the drawer of the check, Buyer still is liable on the check, and Seller can enforce his liability pursuant to §3-309. However, Seller may not sue Buyer on the underlying contract. §3-310(b)(4) (last sentence).

b. Seller may recover on the stolen instrument pursuant to §3-309.

c. Again, yes.

d. Seller has a claim for conversion against not only Second, but also X and First Bank. *See* §3-420. There are some limitations, which the problems in Section 36 discuss.

225. a. Yes, for the instrument has been dishonored, and Buyer is liable as drawer. *See* §3-414(b). (This part of the question is strictly review.)

b. Whether Second gave value is not an issue until Buyer establishes a defense. Assuming Buyer does have a defense based on the malfunction of the car (e.g., breach of warranty), we would want to know the extent of the value that the collecting bank has given. *See* §§4-210, 4-211. To that extent, Second could qualify as a holder in due course and overcome "personal" defenses, including breach of warranty. §3-305(b).

c. The question of value remains critical. Fraud in the inducement is also a personal defense, and a holder in due course can overcome it.

d. Yes. A holder in due course is subject to "real" defenses. Fraud in the execution of a negotiable instrument is a "real" defense. Infancy is also a real defense to the extent it is recognized as a defense in contract law. *See* §3-305(a)(1). Note that the defenses the holder in due course is subject to under §3-305(a)(1) are commercially unimportant. Failure of consideration and fraud in the inducement are the two most frequent commercial defenses, and the holder in due course takes free of them.

226. a. No. Manufacturer is a holder in due course, even though it is a payee. *See* §3-302, cmt. 4. Manufacturer is not subject to Buyer's recoupment defense in Buyer's transaction with Seller. *See* §3-305(a)(3).

b. Now Manufacturer fails the value test of Article 3. An unexecuted promise is not value in negotiable instruments law under §3-303(a)(1), though it would be consideration in contract law and in some other articles of the Code. *See* §1-204 [§1-201(44)]. In contract law we are dealing with only two parties, and it is generally fair to hold Seller to his promise if Manufacturer has made a return promise. In negotiable instruments law we are dealing with three parties. The Code is not trying to hold Seller, but rather Buyer, and is trying to hold Buyer when he has a defense. If, therefore, Manufacturer has not performed, the Code will deprive him of his expectation; but if he has performed, it will not deprive him of his reliance damages measured by the contract price.

227. a. No. *X* is a holder in due course who takes free of the defense. *See* §3-305(b).

b. No. Even though *Y* is not a holder in due course, having taken with notice, *see* §3-302(a)(2), he has the rights of a holder in due course. *See* §3-203(b). The law gives him those rights to protect *X*'s market for the check.

c. The law does not protect *X*, however, to the extent of letting the fraudulent seller come within the umbrella of *X*'s holder-in-due-course status. *See* §3-203(b) (2d clause).

228. a. *X* may enforce the note but for the amount originally drawn only. The law assumes that *X* is in a better position to prevent Seller's fraud than Buyer is. *See* §3-407(c)(i). (This answer assumes, of course, that Buyer's conduct does not contribute to Seller's fraud. If Buyer is negligent and somehow makes it easy for Seller to raise the note, Buyer may run afoul of an estoppel rule. *See* §3-406.)

b. *Y* comes within the shelter of *X*'s holder-in-due-course status and thus can recover, but only according to the original tenor of the item. *See* §3-203(b).

c. Under §3-407(b), Seller may not enforce the instrument at all. This is a rare instance of moral outrage in the normally amoral Code. Here, Buyer enjoys a windfall, and the Code punishes Seller for her fraud.

229. No. Pursuant to federal law (16 C.F.R. §§433.1 through 433.3), the promissory note should have included the following notice:

ANY HOLDER OF THIS CONSUMER CREDIT CONTRACT IS SUBJECT TO ALL CLAIMS AND DEFENSES WHICH THE DEBTOR COULD ASSERT AGAINST THE SELLER OF GOODS OR SERVICES OBTAINED PURSUANT HERETO OR WITH THE PROCEEDS HEREOF. RECOVERY HEREUNDER BY THE DEBTOR SHALL NOT EXCEED AMOUNTS PAID BY THE DEBTOR HEREUNDER.

Although this notice would not destroy the negotiability of the note, there could be no holder in due course of the note, *see* §3-106(d), and ABC Company would be subject to Homeowner's fraud defense. Even if the Seller failed to include the required notice in the note, the outcome would be the same. Section 3-305(e) provides that, when the required notice is omitted, the instrument shall have the same effect as if the notice were included. The issuer (Homeowner) can still assert against the holder (ABC Company) all claims and defenses that would have been available if the instrument included the notice.

230.   a.   The answer to this problem depends on which version of Article 3 applies. As originally written and updated in 1990, Article 3 provided a discharge defense only when payment was made to the holder of the instrument. [§3-602(a).] Under this rule, when Merchant paid ABC Finance Company, ABC was no longer the holder, because it had already sold and negotiated the note to XYZ Loan Company. Thus, Merchant has no discharge defense and must pay XYZ. (Of course, Merchant can sue ABC to recover the $10,000—if it can find any of ABC's assets.)

As revised in 2002, Article 3 provides that a party obliged to pay the note (Merchant) *is* discharged if (1) he pays a person formerly entitled to enforce the note (ABC); and (2) at the time of payment, he has not received adequate notice (as defined in the statute) that the note has been transferred and that payment must be made to the transferee (XYZ). Since Merchant did *not* receive notice of transfer, he has a discharge defense under §3-602(b) and (c). This change in §3-602 renders Article 3 consistent with other law. *See* §9-406(a); Restatement (Second) of Contracts §338(1); Restatement (Third) of Property (Mortgages) §5.5. The change also provides a strong incentive to inform obligors about transfers (which is good business practice but increases transaction costs).

One important lesson you should learn from this problem is to check the law of your state before giving legal advice to clients. Even if the Code sponsors have approved changes to the official text of the Code, that doesn't mean that the legislature in your state has enacted those changes. Different legislatures act at different speeds, and some reject or modify Code provisions to meet the needs and demands of their constituents, including the bank lobby.

b.   The change in the facts is a significant one. If XYZ purchased the note in November 2002, then ABC was still the holder of the note when Merchant paid in October 2002. Therefore, under either the original [§3-602(a)] or updated version of Article 3 (§3-602(a) and (c)), Merchant has a discharge defense.

However, if XYZ qualifies as a holder in due course, it may cut off this defense. Discharge is not effective against a person who acquires holder-in-due-course rights without notice of the discharge. §3-601(b). XYZ may have taken the note without notice that Merchant had paid early and was discharged. To protect himself against this risk, Merchant should have demanded return of the note when he paid ABC.

Section 34. The Bank-Customer Relationship

231.
    a.   Not properly payable. If the Payor Bank pays this item, it will not be obeying the order of its depositor. The depositor never gave an order, so the payment is improper.

    b.   Not properly payable. The Drawer ordered the bank to pay to the order of Payee. Bank paid to the order of forger.

    c.   This forged indorsement is dispensable. §3-201(b). A party taking the instrument would be a holder with or without the indorsement, and the Payor Bank may pay the holder because that payment would be consistent with the drawer's instructions.

    d.   The check is properly payable only according to its original tenor $100. *See* §§3-407(c), 4-401(d)(1). Note that this rule puts the risk of alterations on the Payor Bank, not on the Drawer. This is a general rule subject to an estoppel exception. *See* §3-406. The general rule is based on the assumption that the party taking after the alteration is better able to prevent the fraud than the party issuing the check before the alteration.

    e.   Under the old version of Article 4, most courts considered a postdated check not properly payable. In the check collection industry it is currently the fact, however, that bank reader-sorter equipment is incapable of reading the date. On all but the largest checks, which banks intercept and handle manually, the bank's equipment pays the check without regard to its date. For banks (or those who perform outsourcing services for them) to look at every date on the checks, most of which are handled by machine, would increase check collection costs prohibitively. Evolving image processing technology may give bank equipment that capacity in the future. Current banking practices are efficient, and the old rule was inconsistent with them. Revised Article 4 permits customers to use the postdated check and hold the bank to the date, but only if the customer notifies the bank and, presumably, if the customer pays the bank's reasonable charges. *See* §4-401, cmt. 3. In view of customary bank practices of examining only in the largest denominations, new Article 3 and revised Article 4 define "ordinary care" in a way to relieve a bank from the responsibility of examining checks unless the bank's internal practices require it. *See* §3-103(a)(9) [§3-103(a)(7)]; *cf.* §4-104(c) (incorporating Article 3 definition of "ordinary care").

    f.   A check drawn on insufficient funds is not for that reason alone improperly payable. *See* §4-401(a). The bank-customer deposit agreement usually disposes of the question. *See* §4-401, cmt. 1. *See also* Problem 232 (dealing with the same question).

    g.   This check is properly payable. If Thief is gone with the funds, the Code puts the loss for this fraud on the Payee, who should not have left a check with a blank indorsement lying around. Careful payees do not indorse checks until they are about to deposit them. If they choose to indorse them earlier, they can indorse them restrictively, *see* §3-206(c), and protect themselves; or they can indorse in blank and take the risk of loss.

  h. On the one hand, this check may be properly payable if Payee deposited it in a depositary bank and simply forgot to indorse. Section 4-205 treats the depositary bank as a holder in such cases.

    On the other hand, if the Payee transferred the check to some other third party, but failed to indorse, no one can be a holder, and the check is not properly payable. Nevertheless, the Drawer cannot complain about the irregular payment. The Drawer has sustained no damages; the Payee did receive the funds. Under §4-401(b) and the cases, a customer cannot complain when the bank pays a check that is improperly payable if the funds go to satisfy the customer's debt. *Cf.* §4-401(b) (excusing customer from liability when customer did not sign check and did not benefit from proceeds of check).

232. Under the revised version of Article 4, the bank may not create an overdraft in excess of that permitted by the customer's agreement with the bank. *See* §4-401(a) (2d sentence). However, the customer will have a difficult time showing any loss by virtue of the bank's breach of the overdraft agreement. If the bank paid the customer's creditor, the customer has benefited from the payment and probably will not be able to recover in a breach of contract action. *Cf.* §4-401(b) (relieving customer of liability to bank if bank pays an instrument the customer did not sign provided customer does not benefit from payment).

  Whether the bank was negligent makes no difference. Article 4 (including §4-401) does not impose a duty of ordinary care on payor banks. *Cf.* §4-202 (imposing duty on collecting banks to exercise ordinary care in performing certain actions). Moreover, §4-401 is not inconsistent with §4-103(a). Under that section, a bank can vary the effect of the provisions of Article 4 by agreement, but cannot disclaim responsibility for lack of good faith or failure to exercise ordinary care. Since §4-401 does not impose a duty of ordinary care, there is nothing for a payor bank to disclaim in violation of §4-103(a).

  The basis for these apparently loose rules is the assumption that payor banks will normally act competently and that fact finders (usually a jury) should not be charged with the duty to review bank operations. Only in fairy tales do juries always reach the fair and just result. In some counties and circuits of the real world, banks have a hard time obtaining a fair and just verdict from a jury deciding a due care question.

  Some of your teachers will quarrel with this answer. Also, one of your authors cautions that a court sympathetic to the plaintiff in a bank negligence case might rule that common law principles of negligence supplement the Code pursuant to §1-103(b) [§1-103]. Only in fairy tales do all courts understand and respect the Code.

233. a. Yes.

  b. Yes, if he can prove that the payment caused them. Section 4-402 limits liability for wrongful dishonor to actual damages proved.

  c. No. The question assumes that the automobile's fair market value exceeds the debt. In that case, a sale in accord with the rules of Article 9 would yield a surplus that the creditor would have to pay to the customer. *See* §9-608(a)(4). However, the customer might be able to recover the costs of the sale and any other damages proximately caused when his car was unexpectedly and improperly repossessed.

d. Yes, but remember, §4-402 limits liability to actual damages proved. Lost profits are notoriously difficult to prove, as are mental anguish damages and the fact that a bounced check caused ulcers. Of course, there are witnesses that will testify to anything, and judges and jurors that will believe anything.

Note that Article 4 eliminates the "trader rule," which once allowed a person in business to recover substantial damages for wrongful dishonor without having to prove actual damages. §4-402, cmt. 1.

e. Sometimes checks bounce for quite honest reasons. When they do, drawers replace them. Often the process of replacing them is inconvenient to both the payee and the drawer; but it is difficult to imagine that the sole fact that a check was wrongfully dishonored will cause a customer to lose the benefit of his bargain under a contract. Of course, there are witnesses that will testify . . .

f. Section 4-402 does not provide for punitive damages. To recover them, the customer must resort to supplemental principles of common law. *See* §§1-103(b) [§1-103], 1-305(a) [§1-106(1)], 4-402, cmt. 1.

234. Under a strict reading of the Code, the corporation is the "customer." Technically, the president and sole shareholder is not the "customer" and does not have a cause of action for wrongful dishonor under §4-402. (However, some courts have interpreted §4-402 more flexibly, holding that individuals who owned or operated a business could sue as "customers" in those rare cases where the individuals and the business were essentially one and the same.) Even if the president and sole shareholder cannot recover under §4-402, he may be able to recover under supplemental principles of common law. *See* §4-402, cmt. 5.

235. We think that such an attempt would fail. It would violate the spirit if not the letter of §4-103(a), and courts would not enforce the agreement.

236. No. The check is more than six months old and is considered stale. Payor Bank is under no obligation to Customer to pay the check; however, if it does so, it can charge Customer's account. *See* §4-404.

237.
a. Arguably there should be no recovery because the customer has not proved any damages. *See* §4-403(c).

b. Here, the customer has shown the damages. Having rejected the defective goods, customer should not have to pay for them. *See* §§2-601, 2-711. The bank should recredit his account in the amount of the check. Note that the bank is not liable for other damages suffered by reason of the seller's breach of the sales agreement. *See, e.g.*, §§2-712, 2-713, 2-715. The buyer is going to suffer those damages whether the bank stops payment or not. They are a consequence of the seller's breach, not of the bank's wrongful payment over the stop payment order.

238. As subrogee of the buyer's rights in the underlying sales contract between the seller and the buyer, the bank should proceed against the seller and assert the damage claim that Article 2 affords the disappointed buyer under §2-711. *See* §4-407(3).

239. Yes. Under these facts, Second Bank is a holder in due course. The payor bank is subrogated to the rights of Second, which would have been able to enforce the check against the buyer if the payor had dishonored. Thus the payor bank's failure to honor the stop payment order has not damaged the buyer. To recredit buyer's account would be to enrich buyer unjustly. Under these facts, the payor bank is under no duty to recredit buyer's account. *See* §4-407(1).

240. Suppose that the goods were not defective and that the buyer wrongfully rejected the goods. Then, bank could defend by asserting the rights of seller against buyer on the underlying sales contract pursuant to §4-407(2).

241. The answer depends on whether the court will read §4-407 as displacing non-Code law. Comment 5 to that section indicates that an action in restitution will lie.

Section 35. Warranties

242. If First Bank honors after *T* forged *S*'s indorsement, First may assert a breach of presentment warranty under §4-208(a)(1) against Second, which in turn may assert a breach of transfer warranty under §4-207(a)(1) against a prior party that has made such a warranty. Thus, if Thief steals the check from *S* and forges *S*'s indorsement, Second Bank will breach its presentment warranty to the effect that it is authorized to obtain payment. A party holding an instrument through a forged indorsement is not a holder and is not entitled to enforce the instrument. Thief will have breached its transfer warranty of authority to Second. If First dishonors, there can be no breach of a presentment warranty because the beneficiary of the presentment warranty, First, has not parted with funds. Second, however, will have a breach of the transfer warranty claim against Thief. In either case, Second, the first person to deal with the wrongdoer, takes the loss.

243.   a.   If First honors, it will bear the loss under the doctrine of Price v. Neal, 3 Burr. 1354 (K.B. 1762), a Lord Mansfield decision that held payors liable for paying against the forged signature of the drawer—*B* in our model transaction. Price v. Neal is at the bottom of the warranty rules. If your interpretation of a warranty section conflicts with this simple rule of *Price*, your interpretation is wrong. *Price* is an anti-bank rule with which banks are quite comfortable.

To read the warranty sections to conflict with *Price* is inconsistent with everyone's understanding of what they mean. The §4-207(a)(2) warranty that all signatures are good is a transfer warranty that does not run to First, the payor. First does benefit from the §4-208(a)(3) presentment warranty that *S* does not know of any forgery of the drawer's signature. Seldom, however, will *S*, the victim of Forger's fraud, know of the forgery. First may not debit *B*'s account because the item, bearing a forged drawer's signature, is not properly payable. It is not *B*'s order. These results may not be crystal clear from the language of the respective provisions, but they are clearly dictated by the Price v. Neal rule. *See* §3-417, cmt. 3.

 b. No. An affirmative answer would give the payor bank a breach of warranty action when the drawer's signature is forged and thus overturn *Price*, a result we know from the comment that the drafters did not intend.

 c. *S* is liable to Second for breaching the transfer warranty that all signatures are genuine. *See* §4-207(a)(2). *S* may not recover from *B* because *B* did not sign the check. *S* may recover from the forger, if she can find him. By signing *B*'s name to the check, the forger is liable as a drawer. *See* §§3-403(a), 3-414(b).

244. If Consumer complains, First Bank must recredit her account, because her signature was unauthorized and the check was not properly payable. §4-401. As you learned in the preceding problem, when the drawer's signature on a check is unauthorized, ordinarily the payor bank bears the loss under the rule of Price v. Neal. However, revised Article 3 includes new warranties to deal with fraud of this kind. With respect to this "remotely-created consumer item," *see* §3-103(a)(16), Second Bank warranted to First Bank that Consumer authorized the issuance of the check in the amount for which it was drawn. *See* §4-208(a)(4). Since Consumer did not authorize issuance of the check, First can shift the loss back to Second. Second, in turn, can shift the loss back to Merchant, who violated a corresponding transfer warranty that Consumer authorized issuance of the check in the amount for which it was drawn. §4-207(a)(6). These new warranties rest on the premise that depositary banks can control this type of fraud more effectively than payor banks. §3-416, cmt. 8.

245. a. Second makes transfer warranties to subsequent banks in the collection chain (if any), but not to First.

 b. Second has breached the presentment warranty of authority, *see* §4-208(a)(1), which it does make to First. Second does not have authority, because a necessary indorsement, that of *S*, is missing.

 c. If the thief steals the check after *S* indorses in blank, Second is a holder. As such, it is entitled to enforce the check and does not breach the presentment warranty. *S* will probably end up bearing the loss here by virtue of having indorsed in blank. *B* is not liable to *S* on the check, which is paid to a holder, thereby discharging *B* on the check and on the underlying sales contract. *See* Problem 217.

 d. If the thief steals the check from the mail before *S* receives it, the thief will have to forge the indorsement before any bank will take the instrument. Once there is a forgery, Second will probably bear the loss because the thief will be gone or insolvent; and Second will breach its presentment warranty of authority if First Bank pays. Note that if First pays, it will not be able to charge B's account because the check, bearing a forged indorsement, is not properly payable. §4-401. Since S never received the check, the underlying obligation was never suspended. §3-310. That means B must still pay S for the goods or services S provided. S, then, will not bear any loss if the thief steals the check before S receives and indorses it.

246.
   a. First may debit B's account only according to the original tenor of the item. *See* §§3-407(c), 4-401(d)(1). First may then recover $900 from Second for breach of the §4-208(a)(2) presentment warranty.

   b. In the event First dishonors the check entirely, Second, if it has given value to the thief, in good faith and without notice of the alteration, would be able to recover from B according to the original tenor of the item ($100). *See* §3-407(c). Second could recover $900 from S for breach of the transfer warranty in §4-207(a)(3).

   c. No. This is the case in which the Code in effect imposes a penalty and permits B to enjoy a windfall. B will get the goods or services from S without paying for them, for S cannot enforce the instrument, even according to its original tenor against B. *See* §3-407(b). S, of course, is usually not present or is financially irresponsible and cannot answer to Second's breach of warranty claim. Query, furthermore, whether S might not argue successfully that in the event Second makes a claim for breach of the transfer warranty that the amount of Second's recovery should be only $900, because Second has a good claim against B for $100 under §3-407(c). In that case, would B have a claim against S for the $100? (We do not know.)

Section 36. Conversion

247.
   a. This is common law conversion. Note that it is not one of the enumerated acts of conversion in §3-420(a) but is an instance of conversion of personal property, which is, by the language of the section, applicable to instruments (first sentence).

   b. This is not conversion under Article 3. *See* §3-420(a) (last sentence). B is an "issuer" and cannot bring an action for conversion of the instrument.

   c. This is also conversion as a matter of personal property law and, therefore, is conversion under §3-420(a) (first sentence).

   d. This is also conversion. Bear in mind that in tort law, conversion is a matter of strict liability. It matters not whether the converter is careful or acting in good faith. Any interference with a person's property rights is conversion.

e.   This is conversion under §3-420(a) (2d sentence).

f.   This is conversion at common law and also is conversion for which Second will be liable under §3-420(a) (2d sentence). It is not relevant that Second "cashed" the check or that Second no longer holds any proceeds. *See* §3-420, cmt. 3.

g.   Since the check was indorsed in blank, Second can be a holder and most likely is also a holder in due course. As such, it has the superior claim to the check, *see* §3-306, and is not liable for conversion under the common law or §3-420(a). Moreover, the addition of *T-2*'s unnecessary indorsement is not conversion, nor is the payment by the drawer of a check bearing such a forgery, nor is the handling of such a check by a bank in the collection chain.

248.   a.   This is a classic case. First cannot charge the account of its customer because the check, bearing a forged indorsement, is not properly payable. *See* Answer 231(b).

b.   *S* may sue First in conversion. *See* §3-420(a). Ultimately, *B* and *S*, unless she is negligent in such fashion to contribute to the forgery, *see* §3-406(a), or unless she has ratified it, will shift the loss to First. Note, however, that First has recourse against Second, which breached its presentment warranty of authority, *see* §4-208(a)(1). Second, in turn, has a breach of transfer warranty claim against *T-2*, if Second can find him. *See* §4-207(a)(1). Note also, to complete the picture in this little review, that *S* could have sued Second in conversion under Article 3. *See* Answer 247(f).

249.   a.   *T-2* has converted the property of *S*, and *S* may recover from *T-2*.

b.   Under Article 3, *B*, issuer of the check, may not sue in conversion. *See* §3-420(a) (last sentence).

c.   The answer is clear. Second is liable and it does not matter whether it does not have the proceeds of the check, observed reasonable banking practices, or "cashed" the check. [Those facts did bear on the issue in some jurisdictions under old Article 3.]

d.   First has converted the check and is therefore liable to *S*. *See* §3-420(a) (2d sentence).

250.   a.   *B* can force First to recredit his account. The check was not properly payable. *See* Answer 231(a). Moreover, First cannot recover this loss from Second. Under Price v. Neal, and §4-208(a)(3), First should bear the loss because it paid over a forged drawer's signature. However, First may argue that it should be able to recover because *S*'s indorsement was forged, meaning that Second breached its presentment warranty of authority under §4-208(a)(1). The few cases that have confronted this "double forgery" problem consider this to be a case of a forged drawer's signature and place the loss on First, consistent with the rule in Price v. Neal.

b.   *S* may recover in conversion from First, which has paid over a forged indorsement. *See* §3-420(a). *S* may also recover in conversion from *T-2* and from Second. *See* §3-420(c). The Code presumes liability to be the amount payable on the check. *See* §3-420(b).

However, in a case like this one, where the check was not payable from *B*'s account and the drawer was a thief, First and/or Second may be able to rebut the presumption and show that the check was worthless.

251.
    a. *S* has a cause of action against *T* at common law for conversion of the check and under §3-420(a) (first sentence).

    b. *S*'s attempt to recover from *X* on a conversion theory will fail. *X* is a holder in due course. Conversion is a claim, and §3-306 provides that the holder in due course takes free of all claims.

    c. *S* will not recover from *Y* because *Y* comes within the shelter of *X*. *See* §3-203(b).

    d. If the indorsement is forged, the answers to (b) and (c) are different. In the case of a forged indorsement, *X* is not a holder and, therefore, is not a holder in due course. *X* then, takes subject to the claims of *S*; and *Y* has no shelter.

Section 37. Preclusion

252.
    a. Probably yes, even though First paid over a forged drawer's signature. The facts indicate that the negligence of the customer substantially contributed to the forgery, thereby precluding the customer under §3-406 from asserting that the signature is not genuine. There remains, however, the matter of First's conduct, which part (b) of this answer addresses.

    b. Note that under subsection 3-406(b), the bank's negligence renders the liability comparative. If First did not examine the drawer's signature on the check, some courts might take the position that the bank has not observed reasonable banking practices, even though everyone knows that banks cannot examine all signatures and even though we do not want them examining all of the signatures. There are more than four billion checks that run through the banking system each month. If banks examine all of the drawers' signatures, they will solve the nation's unemployment problems, but they probably will not catch many forgeries. Under Article 3, a bank that does not examine the signature is not negligent if it has observed its own practices, as long as those practices are not unusually at variance from general banking usage. *See* §§3-103(a)(9) [§3-103(a)(7)], 4-104(c). If it is the bank's practice to examine signatures on checks above a certain amount, failure to observe that practice would render the bank negligent with attendant consequences.

253.
    a. Arguably, First may debit the account because the negligence of *B* substantially contributed to the unauthorized completion. *See* §3-406(a). Article 3 treats an unauthorized completion as if it were an alteration. *See* §§3-115(c), 3-407(c)(ii). Some courts have held that it is a violation of reasonable standards of the bank collection industry

for the payor to pay the check without looking at it, a look that in this case would have revealed the limitation in the legend. In fact, the bank collection industry rarely, if ever, looks at a check in this amount; and it would cost us all a lot more to have our checks collected if it did. If the court finds, however, that First did not exercise due care, the loss will be apportioned under the comparative negligence rule as Article 3 provides. §3-406(b).

b. Because this unauthorized completion is the same as an alteration, Second Bank has breached its presentment warranty. *See* §4-208(a)(2). In that case, First Bank would be able to recover from Second. The loss, then, would fall on Second (as it probably should if a bank is to take the loss) because Second is much more likely to examine the instrument than First. Second's encoding clerk will handle the check. At First Bank, only machinery will handle it. However, §4-208(c) permits Second to defend the warranty action by proving that *B* is precluded under §3-406 from asserting the alteration against First.

254. a. There is a good argument that *S* has been negligent and that his negligence will preclude his conversion claim under §3-406. Employers should keep track of their financial affairs, and their failure to do so is probably an instance of negligence. *T-2* had been engaging in this misconduct for a long enough period that *S* should have discovered it. The length of time, moreover, would have lulled Second into thinking that the practice was surely authorized. It is also possible, though the facts of the question are incomplete, that *S* is negligent under §4-406. See generally Problem 256. If either First or Second failed to observe reasonable banking practices (i.e., were negligent), the loss would be allocated according to comparative negligence principles. *See* §3-406(b).

b. If this were the first time that *T-2* had misbehaved, *S* probably would not be negligent; there would be no preclusion under §3-406; and both banks would be liable in conversion to *S*. However, if *T-2* had "responsibility" for checks, *S* would be bound by *T-2*'s indorsements, *S*'s care or lack of care notwithstanding, and the banks would not be liable in conversion. This outcome would be subject to a comparative-negligence-type allocation of damages in the event the banks were guilty of failure to exercise due care. *See* §3-405(b).

255. a. The forged indorsements are treated as effective under §3-404(b). Thus, the items are properly payable, and First can debit ABC's account. However, First cannot shift the loss from its negligent customer to Second. If First recredits ABC's account, and sues Second for breach of presentment warranty, Second can defend by proving the indorsements are effective under §3-404(b). *See* §4-208(c).

b. Second could recover. The indorsements are effective under §3-404(b). Second would be a holder and a person entitled to enforce the check, *see* §§3-301, 3-414(b). It would not benefit ABC to stop payment because Second would be able to enforce the instrument against ABC, whose obligation to pay Second in the event of dishonor is codified in §3-414(b).

    c.   There is authority that Second's conduct violates reasonable banking practices. Under Article 3, that negligence will result in allocation of the loss in accordance with comparative-negligence principles. *See* §3-404(d).

    d.   No. *See* §3-404, cmt. 2, Case #1.

    e.   The answers do not change. If the checks are written to fictitious suppliers, the clerk had the requisite fraudulent intent when he drew the checks. Section 3-404(b) renders the indorsements effective; therefore, ABC may not contest their validity as against First or Second. Similarly, if the checks are payable to real parties who have not supplied anything to ABC, the clerk had the requisite fraudulent intent at the time he drew the checks, and §3-404(b) prevents ABC from contesting the indorsements. *See* §3-404, cmt. 2, Case #2.

    f.   The answers do not change. If it is clear, as it is in problem (e), that the clerk was acting fraudulently and intended from the start that the payees would not have any interest in the checks, §3-404(b) governs, and the indorsements are effective. If the clerk formulates his fraudulent intent after he draws the check, §3-405 applies, and renders the indorsements effective. *See* §3-405, cmt. 3, Case #6.

256.   a.   *A* has probably failed to examine the bank statement and report the alteration promptly as §4-406(c) requires, but the failure did not cause the bank any loss. *See* §4-406(d)(1). First gave *L* the money on May 5 before the statement and the check were available to *A*. First must recredit the account because the check was properly payable only according to its original tenor. *See* §4-401(d). Note that the time limit in §4-406(d)(2) applies to multiple alteration or multiple forgery cases and does not apply to single alteration or single forgery cases.

    b.   The clear language of §4-406(d)(2) supports the bank's position that *A* is precluded here and cannot claim that the second check was not properly payable. First may recover from Second only if First cannot recover from *A*. *See* §4-406(f) (last sentence).

    c.   Subsection (d) only applies to forgeries of the drawer's signature and alterations. There is no preclusion under §4-406 when a customer fails to detect a forged indorsement. There is no duty under the section for the customer to look for forged indorsements.

    d.   If *L* maintained an account at First and did not withdraw the funds until a date after the time that *A* should have reported the alteration, First can satisfy the requirements of subsection (d)(1); it can show that the customer's failure to examine the statement and report the alteration caused the bank loss. Had *A* notified First in time, First could have charged *L*'s account and avoided the loss.

    e.   If First does not observe ordinary standards of care, §4-406(e) allocates the loss in accordance with standard comparative-negligence principles.

f.   i. one year; *see* §4-406(f).

ii. three years; *see* §4-111.

[Note that these rules are statutes of limitations and apply irrespective of due care or absence thereof by the bank.]

257.   a. First may charge *B*'s account because *B* is precluded from asserting that the indorsement is forged. *See* §3-404(a).

b. The preceding answer assumes that the bank exercised ordinary care. If it did not, the comparative fault rules apply. *See* §3-404(d).

258.   a. i. First may charge the company's account if §3-406 or §4-406 applies to the unauthorized drawer signature. The facts on that issue are incomplete. The indorsement, whether or not the drawer's signature is authorized, operates as an effective indorsement. §3-404(b).

ii. Again, §3-404 does not address the question of the unauthorized drawer's signature, but does make the indorsement effective. If O is not an employee of the company, §3-404 would still apply, as the comment indicates, but the bank will have to deal with the unauthorized drawer signature issue under other provisions.

iii. Because this is an instance of an employee's drawing a check with fraudulent intent (i.e., that the payee not have any interest in the check), §3-404 applies; and the bank may charge the employer's account.

b. In all of the cases, as the sections and comments indicate, the depositary banks have not breached any warranty because §3-404(b) makes them persons entitled to enforce the checks. In other words, because the forged indorsements are effective, the depositary banks do not breach the warranty of authority in §4-208(a)(1).

Section 38. Final Payment

259.   a. The final payment doctrine applies here, and First may not recover from Second. *See* §3-418(c).

b. The answer would be different. Under these facts, Second is unjustly enriched (and Seller will soon be if First does not recover the payment) because it has not parted with value. Id.

c. The final payment doctrine does not prevent First from enforcing Second's presentment warranty of authority, a warranty that it has breached by virtue of the forged indorsement. *See* §§3-418(c) (2d sentence), 4-208(a)(1).

d. No, the answer would be the same. The final payment doctrine applies when the payor's mistake consists of paying an overdraft. *See* §3-418(b).

e. Yes. The final payment doctrine protects Second, a party that has given value in good faith. It does not protect the seller in these circumstances. *See* §3-418(c) (last sentence). For a case in which a seller is protected, see Problem 260.

f. The final payment doctrine applies irrespective of the bank's care or lack of care. *See* §3-418(a) (last sentence).

260. a. No, the final payment doctrine applies. Seller changed its position in reliance on the payment. *See* §3-418(c).

b. No. The final payment doctrine would still apply, but the bank might have a partial recovery by subrogating itself to the recoupment rights of the buyer against the seller in the underlying transaction. *See* §4-407(3).

c. *T* is not one of the parties protected by the final payment doctrine, and First could recover the payment from *T*.

d. The answer would be the same. First has paid by mistake and will not be able to charge Buyer's account, but First will be able to recover from a payee that has not given value or changed its position in reliance on payment.

2. DOCUMENTS OF TITLE

Section 39. *The Documentary Draft Transaction*

261. a. Generally the buyer has the right to examine the goods unless he agrees to pay "against documents" or otherwise expressly agrees that he will pay before inspecting the goods. *See* §§2-512, 2-513(1).

b. In these contracts, which traditionally appear in international trade, the buyer has agreed, in effect, that it will not have the right to examine the goods before payment. These contracts assume that the document of title covering the goods will arrive in the buyer's country before the goods do and that the buyer must honor the draft that accompanies the document of title at the time the documents arrive.

c. The CIF and C&F sale are still relatively common in international trade. These contracts are similar to the FOB contract in that they assume that the documents will arrive before the goods do and that the buyer will honor the draft when the buyer receives the document of title.

d. The cash on delivery sale also assumes, under Article 2, that the buyer will pay before examining the goods.

262. a. In both of these events, Second has given value. It is not necessary for the bank to make any bookkeeping entries. Delivery of a properly indorsed draft to the bank in satisfaction of a pre-existing

debt or as security for a debt is sufficient to satisfy the value requirement of §3-302(a)(2). *See* §3-303(a)(3).

    b.   Under §3-303(a)(4), the bank has given value.

263.   No. Under this scenario, when Seller delivers the draft to Second for collection, Second forwards the draft to a bank (Third Bank) in Buyer's city. That bank presents the draft to Buyer for acceptance. In the normal course, Buyer will accept the draft by signing it on its face and returning it to Third. Third will hold for Second or will buy the draft from Second. In either case, the bank holding the item will be a holder in due course and will have the power under §3-305(b) to cut off Buyer's underlying contract defenses.

264.   Buyer dishonors the time draft either by refusing to accept the draft when it is presented by Third Bank for acceptance or by refusing to pay the draft when it comes due 60 days after acceptance. *See* §3-502(b)(3). Buyer dishonors a sight draft by refusing to pay it when it is first presented. *See* §3-502(b)(2). A sight draft need not be presented for acceptance but is presented for payment, unless presentment is excused.

265.   a.   Yes. *See* §3-305(a)(3). The failure of Second to be a holder in due course renders it subject to all defenses that are good in the underlying contract.

    b.   Yes, as to the first setoff defense, but no, as to the second. The first setoff is a valid defense under contract law. The second is not because it would not be valid against Seller. *See* §2-717, cmt. 1.

    c.   Payment is a defense in the underlying contract. It is folly, of course, for the obligor on a negotiable instrument to pay the underlying obligation without obtaining surrender of the instrument, for if the instrument finds its way into the hands of a holder in due course, the obligor will have to pay the holder. In this problem, the acceptor got lucky. The acceptance did not find its way into the hands of a holder in due course.

    d.   These facts constitute failure of consideration. *See* §3-305(a)(2).

Section 40. *The Bill of Lading*

266.   a.   No. *See* §7-403(4). The carrier has erred, but the error has not caused the shipper any loss. The error may cause the carrier loss, however, if the bill finds its way into the hands of a holder by due negotiation. In that case, the holder will be able to recover losses from the carrier when the carrier cannot deliver the goods to the holder. Because the buyer received the goods, under the facts of this problem, the seller, the shipper of the goods, will be unable to show that the carrier caused the seller any damages.

    b.   Yes. In these settings the carrier has violated its duty under §7-403(1) to deliver the goods to the person entitled as defined in §7-403(4). Seller must still show damages, however. Presumably it could do so because the misdelivery to a stranger will prevent the buyer from obtaining the goods and will render the seller/shipper in breach of the sales contract.

267. The holder does indeed have a cause of action against the carrier under §7-403. The carrier has an obligation to deliver to the holder. Also, the holder, if he is the buyer, may have a cause of action against the seller for failing to deliver and thereby breaching the underlying contract.

268. Here, Third has failed in its duty as a collecting bank. Although it is not clear from the section, in law and in fact, Third has not observed due care in the presentment of the item, has not observed its duties as a presenting bank of a documentary draft, and is liable. *See* §§2-514, 4-202(a)(1), 4-503. A bank that presents an item (the draft) should not permit the drawee to have the document of title until the drawee honors. The issue here is one of determining the liability that attends that failure. Unless there are mitigating circumstances, Third is liable for the face amount of the item. *See* §4-103(e). Note, however, that there is no notion in Article 4 supporting recovery of consequential damages in the event the collecting bank is negligent. That is an important principle.

269.   a. The problem with this arrangement is that is forces the seller to have an agent at the point of delivery to take the goods from the carrier or to give the carrier instructions changing the name of the party entitled to receive the goods under §7-403(4).

        b. If the seller changes the designation of the consignee, the buyer would no longer be the person entitled under §7-403(4), and the carrier should not deliver to the buyer. The problem with the arrangement is obvious. The seller may not learn of the buyer's credit problems in time to change the consignee designation. Essentially, this is a sale on open account, and sellers should not use the arrangement unless they are confident of the buyer's credit-worthiness or are willing to assume the risk.

        c. Until the seller indorses the bill, no one but the seller can take delivery because the holder of the bill is the person entitled under §7-403(4). Thus, the seller or her agent will have to be at the destination to take the goods from the carrier.

Section 41. *The Warehouse Receipt*

270.   a. No. Section 7-204 applies when a bailor delivers goods to a warehouse and the warehouse loses them or the goods are destroyed, in which cases, of course, the warehouse cannot redeliver when the bailor requests the goods. Section 7-204 is a lost goods section, not a misdelivery section.

        b. Section 7-404 is confusing and has quite limited application. It is a legislative attempt to protect warehouses from conversion liability when they take goods from one not entitled to them and return the goods to that person at the end of the bailment. If a thief, for example, bails stolen goods, the warehouse that returns the goods to the thief will be liable in conversion at common law to the true owner. This provision, §7-404, alters that common law rule. That is its sole purpose.

c. Yes, this is the section that governs when the warehouse misdelivers the goods.

271.   a. X.
b. X.
c. Y.
d. The holder of the receipt.
e. Y.

272.   a. Yes.
b. No. *See* §7-404.

Section 42. More on the Documentary Draft Transaction

273.   a. Seller must reimburse under its engagement as drawer to pay the person entitled to enforce the instrument (the holder) in the event of dishonor. *See* §3-414(b). Seller avoided indorser liability by making the draft payable to the bank and thereby avoiding the need to indorse, but Seller drew the draft and thereby engaged to pay the holder in the event of dishonor.

b. By endorsing without recourse, Seller avoided indorser liability, *see* §3-415(b), but it is still the drawer and must pay the holder of the dishonored draft.

c. By drawing without recourse, Seller avoided drawer liability, *see* §3-414(e), but by indorsing has incurred indorser liability. *See* §3-415(a).

d. Second has no right of recourse, Seller having avoided both drawer and indorser engagements. *See* §§3-414(e), 3-315(b).

274. The first draft, being accompanied by a negotiable bill of lading, is more valuable than the second draft, which is accompanied by a nonnegotiable bill. If Second Bank takes the first draft and gives value for it, Second will have an Article 4 security interest in the bill and the goods it represents. *See* §4-210(a). If Buyer honors the first draft, it will have the right to insist on a properly indorsed bill and will then hold the bill by due negotiation. *See* §§4-503, 7-501. A holder by due negotiation takes title to the bill and to the goods it represents. *See* §7-502(1). Takers of the nonnegotiable document do not enjoy these rights. *See* §7-504(1). If Second discounts the second draft, it will hold a nonnegotiable bill and arguably will have a security interest in it, for whatever a security interest in a nonnegotiable bill is worth. It is worth very little because the nonnegotiable bill does not represent the goods. Similarly, if Buyer honors the second draft and takes the nonnegotiable bill, Buyer will not be a holder by due negotiation because only the holder of a negotiable bill can rise to that level. *See* §7-501(4). Buyer's rights under the bill, then, will be no greater than his transferor's rights. *See* §7-504(1). The bank, having only a worthless security interest, can only transfer that worthless interest to Buyer.

275. Second will be able to get the goods covered by the negotiable bill because, as the holder of the negotiable bill, it is the person entitled. *See* §7-403(4). It will also be protected in Seller's bankruptcy by virtue of a perfected security interest under Article 9. *See* §9-312(c). All of this is verified by the rule of Article 7 to the effect that the taker by due negotiation of the bill holds "title" to the goods. *See* §7-502(1)(a). Whether Second has rights under the goods covered by the nonnegotiable bill depends on the seller's instructions to the carrier and on the Bankruptcy Code. In all probability, Second will have an unsecured claim in Seller's bankruptcy.

276.
    a. Yes, none of the events listed in Article 2 that prevent the seller from exercising the right have occurred. *See* §2-705(2).
    b. Yes. Indorsement of a nonnegotiable document of title is meaningless.
    c. Yes. The buyer that does not trust the seller does not pay against a nonnegotiable bill.
    d. Yes. Note that acknowledgment by the carrier, which would be quite unusual, does not cut off the seller's right to stop shipment. *See* §2-705(2)(b).

       For further instances of Buyer jeopardy when it is purchasing goods under a nonnegotiable bill, *see* §7-504(2).

277. The carrier will deliver the goods to the consignee under a nonnegotiable bill without surrender of the bill because the consignee is the person entitled under §7-403(4). The carrier will not deliver the goods to a party that has lost the negotiable bill unless someone indemnifies the carrier against liability for misdelivery under §7-403. When the seller is shipping on open account, that is, when there is no documentary draft transaction, it will not ship under a negotiable bill. Most truck and rail bills in the United States are nonnegotiable.

278. This problem is a warning that not all parties may rely on the description of goods in a bill of lading. First, even if the carrier does not disclaim liability, as it may under §7-301(1), only certain takers are protected, as the problem and the answer indicate. Most of the time, the carrier will disclaim. Carriers are not inspectors of the packages and containers they receive from the shipper. If the banks and the buyer want protection of this kind, they usually must pay for it by having an independent inspector open the packages. The rules under the Carriage of Goods by Sea Act differ, however, making it more difficult for the carrier to disclaim. *See* 46 U.S.C.A. Appx. §1303 (West Supp. 2002).

       With the advent of containerization, many commercial parties began the practice of arranging for inspection of the container at the seller's facility as the seller "stuffs" the container. After inspection, the seller and the inspector seal the container. The buyer relies on this procedure rather than on the description of the goods in the bill of lading.

a. No recovery because, with respect to nonnegotiable bills, only the consignee of the nonnegotiable bill that takes for value in good faith may rely on the description in the bill. The buyer, not the bank, is the consignee under this bill. *See* §7-301(1).

b. This buyer, assuming it is named in the bill as the consignee and that it takes in good faith, will be able to recover. Id.

c. The bank takes by due negotiation and will be able to recover under the section. Id.

d. This buyer is also a holder by due negotiation and will be able to recover from the carrier for misdescription under §7-301(1).

Section 43. *Negotiation and Transfer of Documents of Title*

279.
a. If the bank gives value and otherwise satisfies the requisites for due negotiation in §7-501(4), it is a good-faith purchaser of the bill, that is, it is "a holder to whom a negotiable document of title is duly negotiated." §7-502(1). The key point here is that this bank is taking in the ordinary course of financing—a requirement of due negotiation. *See* §7-501(4).

b. Assuming that it acts in good faith, *B* is acquiring the receipt in the regular course of business and would take by due negotiation under the section.

c. Under the first set of facts, and assuming that it acted in good faith, the bank is taking in the regular course of financing and would benefit from status as a holder by due negotiation. If the broker fails to indorse, however, the bank would not be a holder and would not qualify for good-faith purchase protection. The law is moderately tough here. Indorsements matter. Failure to obtain the indorsement may mean that something was fishy. It would also matter if the bank knew of a prior interest in the grain or if the bank took the receipts in satisfaction of a debt. In both of those cases, the bank would not take by due negotiation. *See* §7-501(4).

d. The manufacturer does not satisfy the requirements for due negotiation. *See* §7-501, cmt. 1 (2d paragraph).

280. The documentary draft does not appear to work here because the seller is not willing to ship the product until he receives payment. If the buyer pays, of course, he loses some leverage and may even lose the goods if the seller is dishonest or files in bankruptcy. Note, however, that the banking system might still be able to serve the parties by using a check, probably certified, and a delivery order. Buyer can ask his bank to initiate the delivery of the check on the condition that the bank in Seller's community not deliver it until the seller obtains the elevator's acceptance of the delivery order. Should the delivery order be in negotiable form? Yes, so that the resulting accepted delivery order, the equivalent of a warehouse receipt (*see* §7-102, cmt. 3) will be negotiable.

281.   a. Arguably, the *McNabb* case is contrary to the purpose of §7 503(1)(a) and (b). *See* §7-503, cmt. 1 (third and fourth sentences).

   b. Yes, because in this event, Wilson is less culpable. It is more difficult to consider this conduct as clothing Brown with actual or apparent authority to bail the goods or as acquiescing in the bailment. Id.

   c. If the landlord's lien is comparable to a security interest, under the Code, National Chemical will lose to Wilson if Brown sells without a receipt because the buyer in ordinary course rule of §9-320(a) does not defeat a security interest created by this farmer. The landlord's lien, however, is not created by the farmer but by operation of law. It is an "agricultural lien," a rather rare creature under the laws of most states. *See* §9-102(a)(5). Agricultural liens must be perfected by filing. *See* §9-308(b). If the lien is unperfected, Wilson loses. *See* §9-317(b) & cmt. 7. Section 9-320 does not govern this dispute. We think §9-331 sends us to Article 7 to determine the result. *See* cmt. 3. If this state of affairs is not confusing enough, the Food Security Act confuses it royally. But that is a matter for further Article 9 study.

282.   a. The bank is loaded with rights. Under §2-506, it has the rights of the seller. Under §7-502(1), it appears to have "title" to the document and to the goods it represents. Under §9-312(c), -313(a), it has a perfected security interest in the document and in the goods. The Code's protection of the bank is limited, however, by the reality that the bank is not a buyer here but a lender. Banks do not buy and sell commodities; they take security interests in them. This is a secured transaction; and if the value of the goods exceeds the bank's loan, the bank must account to the seller or the buyer or their respective trustees in bankruptcy for the excess. *See* §9-615(d).

   b. Section 9-331 says that nothing in Article 9 diminishes the rights of a holder by due negotiation who has rights under Article 7. Literal application of that rule would prevent the court from requiring the bank to disgorge the excess referred to in Answer (a). That literal reading is not tenable.

   c. Here, literal application of §9-331 makes sense. The bank has behaved in commercially reasonable fashion. It has taken steps to protect its security interest by depriving Buyer of possession of the goods. Sub-buyer has behaved quite irresponsibly by paying for goods it cannot see. Sub-buyer may as well have bought the Brooklyn Bridge. There was authority, however, protecting Sub-buyer if it could show that the sub-purchase was in the ordinary course of business. There are not many industries in which parties pay for goods before they receive them or before they receive a document of title covering them. In those cases where buyers prepay, they may be lending the seller money. They are certainly relying on the seller's trustworthiness. If the seller is not trustworthy or creditworthy, the buyers should take the loss, not the banks that have acted with commercial punctilio. Section 9-320(e) quite sensibly overturns that authority.

3. LETTERS OF CREDIT

Section 44. Letter of Credit Transactions

283.   a.   Buyer has complied with the underlying contract. Sellers expect that banks local to them will advise the credit in order to provide the seller with verification of the credit. Issuers do not need to be told of this requirement. It is so common that everyone will assume that the foreign issuer will ask a bank in seller's market to advise. There is no assumption, however, that the credit will be confirmed. The seller has to ask for that. Note that §2-325(3) does not require a "confirmed" credit unless the contract speaks of a "confirmed" credit. Sellers want the credit confirmed so that they can present their documents at a local bank and so that they have the commitment of a local bank that they know and trust.

b.   Traditionally, banks did have signature books to verify signatures on letters they received through the mails. They also had telex codes, "keys" that identified the sender of a telex message. Now, most banks use SWIFT, which is a form of electronic data interchange (EDI), computerized transmission that permits banks to communicate over a dedicated communications network provided by a cooperative that the banks themselves own. SWIFT permits the banks to identify each other, to verify that messages are accurate and authentic, and to communicate quickly, all with a minimum of data.

284.   a.   Hong Kong Bank is the issuer. *See* §5-102(a)(9).

b.   First Bank is the adviser. *See* §5-102(a)(1). An adviser will be a confirmer if it adds its confirmation to the advice. An advice could and sometimes does contain a recital to the effect that: "This is only an advice. The undersigned assumes no obligation under this advice beyond the authenticity of the information in this advice."

c.   Because it added its confirmation, First Bank is a confirming bank as well as an advising bank. Typically a confirmation will appear in the advice in language such as the following: "The undersigned hereby advises and confirms the attached credit (of Hong Kong Bank) and undertakes to honor your drafts accompanied by the designated documents if presented at our counters on or before the expiry date specified above."

d.   The buyer applied for the credit for its account and is most often referred to as the applicant, but sometimes as the account party, and sometimes as the customer (of the issuing bank). *See* §5-102(a)(2).

e.   Seller is the beneficiary of the credit. *See* §5-102(a)(3).

f.   In a confirmed-credit transaction, almost always the beneficiary must submit his documents at the confirmer's place of business and must do so on or before the expiry.

g.   Typically, a commercial letter of credit such as this one will call for a draft, a negotiable bill of lading describing the goods, a commercial invoice, evidence of insurance (usually an insurance certificate), perhaps an inspection certificate, and, if necessary, official documents needed to bring the goods through customs.

285.   Credits should not contain this kind of language, which, unfortunately comes from real cases. Experienced letter-of-credit bankers will refuse to issue, advise, or confirm such credits. Letters of credit are supposed to be payable against the presentation by the beneficiary of specified documents. A standby credit can serve the function the parties in this transaction want it to serve, but the credit should call for the S&L to prepare and present a document certifying that the borrower has defaulted on the note. The language of the certificate should be specified in the credit.

Bankers are not investigators. They will not know whether default has occurred and cannot determine whether to pay the beneficiary unless their task is confined to one of examining specified documents. They should not be required by the terms of the credit or by credit law to decide what documents are sufficient to show a default in the underlying transaction. Nor should they have to decide whether default has, in fact, occurred. Letters of credit, then, even standby letters of credit, should only call for documents and should not be payable against factual conditions. Some courts have wisely refused to apply letter-of-credit law to undertakings that the parties style as letters of credit but that call for factual determinations. Such undertakings are bonds or secondary guaranties, not letters of credit.

286.   When an issuer refuses to pay a beneficiary, the letter of credit is working. Letters of credit are not nullities when the issuer does not pay. Letters of credit are binary: pay or no pay. Thus this contract rule of construction does not suit letters of credit. A letter-of-credit issuer that refuses to pay against nonconforming documents has observed the credit's terms in a valid, commercial sense. It has protected its customer as it promised to do when it entered into the application agreement when the customer applied for the credit.

287.   It might make sense to construe a credit against the drafter, but not against the issuer. Why construe a vague credit drafted by the beneficiary against the issuer and thereby force the applicant to suffer a loss resulting from the beneficiary's vague language? Rules of contract law should supplement the law of letters of credit only if contract rules do not harm the unique features of the credit. The notion of substantial compliance, a common theme in contract law, does not mesh well in the document examination process, nor do rules on course of dealing or performance. Some courts have invoked these rules in the credit context, however, as the *Banco Espanol* court did.

288.   State and federal courts are common-law courts that can fashion the common law in a way that supplements the UCP without altering it. Just as the UCC is skeletal, so the UCP leaves many matters to the law that governs the credit. The warranty issue is one area. Fraud, a critical issue in letter-of-credit law is another. The UCP addresses neither. Thus, if the UCC creates a warranty that will permit the issuer to recover payment from the beneficiary who presents fraudulent documents, there being no conflicting rule in the UCP, the UCC can supplement the UCP. Note that there are some rules in UCC Article 5 that cannot be varied, however. *See* §5-103(c).

289. a. The invoice is not complying under Article 37(c) of UCP 500, which requires the description of the goods in the invoice to "correspond" to that of the credit. Most courts, commentators, and bankers read that article as requiring the invoice to contain an *in haec verba* repetition of the description in the credit.

b. Who knows? The benefit of the UCP is that it answers this kind of nitty gritty, often recurring, question.

c. A cautious seller will insist that his invoice procedures result in a word-for-word repetition in the invoice of the description in the credit.

Section 45.   *Duties of the Credit Issuer*

290. The issuer that pays a stranger has not honored the credit and therefore is not discharged of its liability to the true beneficiary. *See* §5-108(i)(5). Whether the issuer should be entitled to reimbursement is a question on which commentators disagree. Banks might include language in the reimbursement agreement requiring the applicant to reimburse even when the bank pays the wrong party. Courts might hold such clauses unenforceable as unconscionable or as an attempt to contract away liability for lack of due care, *see* §4-103(a), unless there are obvious risks that the applicant willingly undertakes.

291. a. The issuer should not pay. Under standard practice and the language of §5-108(a) the issuer should pay the beneficiary only if his documents comply strictly with the terms of the credit. The bill of lading is discrepant or noncomplying.

b. The air bill is also nonconforming. This is from an actual case. The court held that it was not up to the bank to figure out whether shipment of the goods by air rather than by sea was detrimental to the goods.

c. In this case, the court held that it was not up to the bank to determine whether this defect was material and that the bank was justified in dishonoring the beneficiary's draft. Since this case was decided, Article 5 has been revised. New comments suggest that strict compliance does not demand "oppressive perfectionism," and that documents addressed to "Jeneral Motors" are complying. *See* §5-108, cmt. 1. We believe that the substitution of "Soran" for "Sofan" was not an obvious misspelling, and that the court's holding in the case should still be good. Others may disagree.

292. a. If the documentary defect is inconsequential, i.e., the goods were loaded and arrived safely, then the applicant should reimburse the issuer. The reimbursement context and the reimbursement relationship are arguably different from the payment context and the issuer-beneficiary relationship, where the parties (the document examiners) do not know whether the defect matters and cannot take time to find out. Thus, even though §5-108(e) requires the issuer to observe banking practice when it examines documents, and even though general banking practice is that the bank should not pay over a defective bill of lading such as this one, most courts will not permit the applicant to avoid reimbursement. A smart issuer will make it easier to rule in its favor by including in its contract with the applicant a term providing for reimbursement so long as documents substantially comply.

A separate but related question is whether an applicant can recover damages against an issuer that honors a demand for payment in breach of its obligation to applicant. §5-111(b). The answer is yes, but only when the breach has caused the damage. For example, in this problem, if the market has fallen and applicant no longer wants the goods, that is her problem. Market risks belong on commercial parties, not banks. The bank's error did not cause the market to fall. If the applicant is a dealer in documents (some kind of importer for an industry) and would be unable to dispose of the documents if they are defective in any way, perhaps the applicant should be able to avoid reimbursing the issuer. *See* §5-111, cmt. 2.

b. If, on the other hand, the defect causes the applicant loss, as it does when the goods are destroyed on the dock while they are not covered by marine insurance, surely the applicant should be able to resist reimbursing the issuer.

293.   a. The bank should not pay. If it does, it would not be justified in charging its customer's account. The courts generally have been quite strict in applying the expiry date of a letter of credit.

b. The expiry applies to the presentation of the documents. If the beneficiary gets the documents to the counters of the payor bank, in this case, the issuer, prior to the expiry, the beneficiary has satisfied the credit. It does not matter that the issuer does not pay or does not determine that the documents are conforming until after the credit expires.

c. There may have been a time when and courts where this kind of argument would work, but that time and those courts are long gone. As you may know, in every courtroom there is a boom, and when a bank lawyer makes this kind of argument, the judge lowers it. These facts are a classic candidate for estoppel. The bank delayed, and the beneficiary did nothing because of the delay. The beneficiary relied to its detriment. Under classic estoppel, the bank will not be heard to say that the certificate is unsigned. The courts have uniformly so held. Note, moreover, that §5-108(b) requires an issuer to give notice of defects in the documents and precludes the issuer from claiming that a document is defective if the issuer fails to give timely notice and to describe the defect in the notice.

    d.   If there is no detrimental reliance, some courts will not estop the bank. However, under Article 14(d) of the Uniform Customs and Practice for Documentary Credits (UCP 500) (1993) and §5-108(b) & (c) the bank must give notice of defects without delay, not more than seven days after it receives the documents. If it fails to give that notice or if it fails in the notice to specify all of the defects, the bank is precluded under UCP Article 14(e) and under §5-108(c) from saying that the documents are nonconforming. These rules apply without regard to reliance and detriment.

294.   a.   The issuer must pay. *See* §5-108(a).

    b.   No. If the bank is relying on the goods, perhaps it should require an independent inspector's certificate to the effect that the goods conform. Then the bank would have some protection. Otherwise it must pay against conforming documents, the nonconformity of the goods in the underlying transaction notwithstanding, as the section indicates. Id.

    c.   It is possible that the information the bank obtained clashes with the certificate sufficiently that the certificate is fraudulent. In that case, §5-109(a)(2) permits the bank to dishonor. Note that §5-109(a)(2) also gives the bank the prerogative of honoring in these circumstances if it can do so in good faith. Article 5 does not require the bank to determine who is telling the truth: the person claiming defects or the independent inspector. Most letter-of-credit issuers, jealous of their reputation as issuers, will pay or will insist that their customer obtain an injunction stopping payment. *See* §5-109(b). Courts have been properly concerned, however, that the fraud exception not swallow the general rule that banks must pay against facially conforming documents. The courts and §5-109(b) have, therefore, crafted serious limits on the fraud exception, as the following problems explain.

Section 46. *The Exception for Fraud*

295.   a.   Yes. This is the type of case in which the courts are inclined to enter an injunction. This is a case of "material fraud," the kind of fraud §5-109(b) addresses. Nonconformity of the goods or the documents to the underlying transaction will not justify a refusal to honor the beneficiary's draft. The kind of fraud in this problem is not just a case of nonconformity, of green diodes instead of red ones, or of 3/4-inch diodes instead of 13/16-inch diodes. The courts distinguish between breach of warranty cases and outright fraud: shipment of rubbish instead of bristles, just to pick an example out of the air. (The example comes from Sztejn v. J. Henry Schroder Banking

Corp., 31 N.Y.S.2d 631 (Sup. Ct. 1941), which is the seminal case on the fraud exception.)

b. No, not unless the petitioner satisfies the equity prerequisites, most importantly by showing no adequate remedy at law and a probability of success on the merits. *See* §5-109(b)(2) through (4).

296. This is a common scenario in Middle Eastern transactions. The Saudi buyer, the beneficiary of the Saudi bank's guaranty, understands the American law of letters of credit and the problem of the fraud exception. The buyer, therefore, has structured the transaction in a way that insulates the buyer from the risk of an injunction against payment. It is difficult under these facts for the U.S. bank to show that its beneficiary, the Saudi bank, has practiced fraud. The fraud, if there is any, is being practiced by the beneficiary of the foreign bank's guaranty. All is not lost, however. First, if the applicant, the U.S. seller, can show that the beneficiary of the credit and the guaranty beneficiary are in cahoots, there may be grounds for an injunction, assuming always that the equity prerequisites are satisfied. Even if the applicant cannot obtain an injunction, he can sue for fraud or its equivalent in Saudi Arabia. Bear in mind that he entered into the arrangement knowing that payment under the credit could be effected by presentation of documents. Courts are generally unsympathetic to applicants that enter into agreements with foreign parties and then complain that they do not like to litigate in foreign courts. The Saudi Arabian system of law differs from the common-law system, but it is a civilized system followed in many countries. Sellers in the United States that want petrodollars will have to adjust their prices or investigate the buyers' creditworthiness and commercial honor. If the sellers do not want to accept the risk of having to litigate in Saudi courts, they may have to satisfy themselves with the domestic market. Of course, U.S. sellers and Saudi buyers often agree to arbitrate their disputes, sometimes before a panel in some place like Switzerland. Under this set of facts, the Saudi buyer will have the funds during that arbitration, because the issuer will pay.

297. a. Most courts will not issue an injunction here. This dispute is really one in the underlying contract over the landlord's and the tenant's performance of the lease promises and covenants. The landlord has structured the transaction so that he will have the funds during the litigation of that underlying dispute, and most courts will not disturb this allocation of risks that the parties agreed on before the fact (ex ante). As long as the dispute is contractual and the beneficiary is acting under some color of right, most courts will not enter the injunction. There are other courts, however, that will issue it, to the detriment of the letter of credit and in conflict with the parties' ex ante allocation of risk.

b. Same reasoning. The courts usually want to know whether the beneficiary is trying to take the applicant's money "without any shred of honest belief," as one commentator has put it, in its right to that money. These facts do not reflect that kind of egregiously fraudulent conduct or "material fraud," as §5-109(b) describes it.

298. a. If the large corporate beneficiary submits false documents, even if the corporation is practicing the most egregious fraud, the court should not enter the injunction unless the applicant can show that his remedy at law (a cause of action against the corporation for fraud) is not adequate. Normally, a cause of action for fraud against a solvent defendant is a sufficient remedy at law, and the court will put the applicant to his legal remedy and deny the injunction. *See* §5-109(b)(3).

b. Some courts appear to be moved by the applicant's charge that payment under the credit must be enjoined to avoid the applicant's bankruptcy. The notion that the embarrassment of the applicant should provide grounds for an injunction is a little bit silly, though at least one court has accepted it. Another court opined that the applicant should have been embarrassed to seek an injunction against payment.

c. If the bank pays over facially nonconforming documents, it has breached its obligation to the customer-applicant under the application agreement; and the applicant will have a cause of action against the bank to recover any damages that breach causes. Given that remedy at law against a solvent bank, the applicant has little cause to seek an injunction.

299. Lending Bank is probably a holder in due course of the note, so that Applicant has no defense to Lending Bank's claim under the note, the fraud of the general partner being cut off by §3-305(b). Thus, Applicant has not demonstrated that it has a good chance of success on the merits. Applicant should lose on the merits, and to enter an injunction against payment would only make it necessary for Lending Bank to sue in order to recover. Injunctions should not be used to that wasteful end.

Section 47. *Transferring Interests in Letters of Credit*

300.   a. No. Second is entitled to enforce the credit under its terms. The credit does not call for payment to a holder in due course. Typically, a negotiation credit contains a negotiation clause: "We hereby engage with drawers, indorsers, and bona fide holders of drafts drawn under and in compliance with the terms of this credit that we will honor your draft if presented on or before the expiry." That language calls for payment to the holder of the beneficiary's draft. Second is such a holder.

b.&c. If Second is a holder in due course, the injunction may not issue. *See* §5-109(a)(1)(i). [Note that this is not a §5-109(a)(1)(iii) case because Second did not take the draft *after* acceptance.] Normally, one would expect that Second would have the burden of showing that it is a holder in due course. *See* §3-308(b). Here, however, some authority holds that the petitioner seeking the injunction must allege facts showing that it is more likely than not that it will prevail on the merits. Because the petitioner will not prevail on the merits if Second is a holder in due course, those authorities put the burden on the applicant as petitioner to show that Second is not a holder in due course. One would guess that a petitioner that alleges that Second is not a holder in due course may have done enough, since no applicant will be in a position to disprove the holder-in-due-course status of Second, which will be in possession of the facts on which that issue turns. Thus the burden of going forward with the evidence should perhaps fall to Second.

d. If the credit is straight, Second's status as a holder in due course is irrelevant. Second does not, moreover, fit any of the other categories of parties protected in §5-109(a)(1) from injunctions. If the petitioner can satisfy the prerequisites for an injunction, the court should not make the holder-in-due-course inquiry. A bank that negotiates the beneficiary's draft under a straight credit does not act as a nominated party. The straight credit does not run to "indorsers and bona fide holders."

e. Most courts that have addressed the issue hold that once the issuer honors the time drafts and renders them acceptances, Article 3, not Article 5, governs. The cases arose under the old version of Article 3 and held further the issuer must pay the holder in due course and, perhaps, must pay any holder. Presumably, the result will be the same under new Article 3. *See* §§3-305(b), 5-109(a)(1)(iii). Certainly, the fraud defense to payment of the acceptances is cut off by the holder in due course rule. Such a holder must take after the acceptance, however.

301. If the resulting company expects to draw on the letter of credit, it may want to have the credit amended so that its drafts and certificates, rather than those of the pre-merger subsidiary, will be acceptable under the credit. Corporate counsel and bankers claim that the hard-and-fast rule against transfer of the right to draw creates problems. The only case in point permitted the parent to draw. Section 5-113 probably reaches the same result.

302. The courts have held almost uniformly that personal representatives— trustees, executors, and receivers—may draw under the credit. Some banks write into the application agreement a clause making it possible for the bank to honor the drafts of the beneficiary or its successors or personal representatives, including the trustee in bankruptcy. Section 5-113 probably permits these personal representatives to draw on the credit.

303. One case has permitted the FDIC to draw on a credit issued to a bank that later became insolvent. In the lower court, the judge ruled that when the FDIC acted as receiver, it could draw, but that when, as receiver, it transferred the credit to the FDIC as insurer, the transfer was voluntary and not by operation of law and therefore forbidden by letter-of-credit law. On appeal, the court held that Congress' intent to facilitate the resolution of bank insolvencies by the federal agency overrides state letter-of-credit law and that the FDIC could draw whether it acted in its capacity as receiver or as insurer. [So it goes.]

304.   a.   In order to secure his own bank, Exporter may assign to it the proceeds of the German credit. The credit is not transferable, but the proceeds of all credits may be assigned. In this particular case, since the assignment is for security, it involves the creation of an Article 9 security interest in the beneficiary's right to payment under the credit (which Article 9 defines as "letter of credit rights." §9-102(a)(51)). The Code fashions a complex of provisions to deal with this secured transaction. The manner of creating and perfecting the security interest is for the assignee/secured party to obtain control. Under the Code and in practice, banks use notification procedures to effect the assignment. A beneficiary must notify the paying bank (here, the New York bank that confirmed the German bank's credit) of the assignment and obtain that bank's consent to the assignment. That consent conveys control to the assignee/secured party for Article 9 purposes. *See* §9-107. Control, moreover, leads to attachment and perfection of the security interest. *See* §§9-203(b)(3)(D), 9-314(a). When the beneficiary draws on the credit, the confirming bank will pay the assignee/secured party, Exporter's bank, rather than the beneficiary.

b.   Exporter must draw the draft. The right to draw cannot be transferred unless the credit is transferable. This credit was not transferred; its proceeds, the letter-of-credit rights, were assigned. The beneficiary is still Exporter, and Exporter must draw the draft.

305.   a.   First has an automatically perfected security interest in the standby credits, which are supporting obligations under Article 9. *See* §9-308(d).

b.   GDC must sign the draft and the certificate. This feature of the credit makes it vulnerable security, for GDC can refuse to sign the documents. If it does, and unless First can obtain a court order requiring GDC to sign them, the standby credits will expire without a conforming draw.

Section 48.   Issuer Insolvency

306.   a.   The Supreme Court has held that despite confusing language in the Act, the beneficiary is not a depositor and not entitled to insurance under the deposit insurance scheme.

b.   To the extent that the FDIC prefers the beneficiary out of the assets of the failed bank, the allocation would be in violation of the Act. To the extent that the FDIC provides its own funds to the liquidation or the sale of the failed bank, it may prefer one class of creditors over another.

c.   Not at common law. Whether this rule conflicts with the National Bank Act or the Federal Deposit Insurance Act has not been resolved by the courts, but there is good reason to support the rule. The deposit is in the nature of a trust. Generally, trust deposits, unlike general deposits do not become assets of the bank and are not available to its general creditors.

4. WIRE TRANSFERS

Section 49. Wire Transfers

307.
    a. The San Francisco Fed charges the account of First Bank, which must maintain an account with the Fed.

    b. If the receiving bank does not know that the name and the routing number do not refer to the same bank, it may credit the account according to the number. §4A-208(a)(1). If it knows that the name and account differ, it cannot accept the order. §4A-208(b)(4).

    c. Acceptance occurs when the San Francisco Fed acts on the p/o, that is, when it sends the p/o to the Atlanta Fed. *See* §4A-209(a).

    d. Payment occurs when the Second Bank of Atlanta accepts it. It accepts the order in one of the ways specified in §4A-209(b).

    e. Under its contract with Insurance Co. or under wire transfer system rules, a bank may have to accept, but the Code does not require it to accept. *See* §4A-209, cmt. 5. Under Fedwire, the system used in the Problem, Second of Atlanta's account at the Atlanta Fed will be credited by the time Second receives the p/o. Under §4A-209(b)(2), such an arrangement constitutes automatic acceptance of the p/o. *See* §4A-209, cmt. 6.

308. It depends on the adoption by the bank of a security procedure. As §4A-202(b) suggests, no bank in its right mind will accept payment orders unless it has established such a procedure. If the bank does establish it and if it is commercially reasonable and the bank follows it in good faith, the employer will generally bear the loss. The customer can avoid the results of the general rule by proving that the unauthorized p/o was not the work of an employee entrusted with wire transfer duties or proves that the person responsible for the unauthorized p/o gained access to the system through the bank and not through the customer.

309. If the beneficiary's bank knows that the number and the name refer to different persons, it should not act on the order. The order cannot be accepted; it is an unacceptable payment order under §4A-207(a). However, if the bank does not know of the discrepancy, it will credit the account by number, or its computer technology will so credit it. That action by the beneficiary's bank is proper. *See* §4A-207(b)(1). In that case, the originator, if the originator is a bank, will have to pay the beneficiary's bank. §4A-207(c). If the originator is not a bank, the originator's bank will bear the loss unless it can show that it has notified the originator in writing of the fact that the originator will bear the loss incurred by virtue of such a discrepancy. Comment 2 (third paragraph) discusses the scam cases. The originator can recover from the person whose account was credited unless that person gave value in good faith, as it did in the scam cases. *See* §4A-207(d) & cmt. 3 (2d paragraph). The only other recourse for the originator that issued this discrepant order is against the fraudulent parties who have long since departed the scene.

310.   a.   An originator may cancel an order as long as beneficiary's bank receives the notice of cancellation in sufficient time to act on it before it accepts the order in one of the ways specified in §4A-209(b). Note, however, that under §4A-209(b)(3) and Fedwire rules, Third will have accepted the p/o when the Federal Reserve Board credits its account. *See* §4A-209(b)(2) & cmt. 6. Note further that the Code makes allowance for a different result if the beneficiary's bank consents. *See* §4A-211(b). It will consent if it can recover the funds from the beneficiary. It can recover funds from a bad-faith beneficiary if the funds are still in the beneficiary's account. *See* §4A-211, cmt. 4. Note also, that a receiving bank (not the beneficiary's bank) that has not executed the order by sending it on to the next bank must accept a cancellation. There is no reason it should not defer to the wishes of the sending bank, but the cancellation must arrive at the receiving bank in time for it to stop the order from its journey to the next bank.

b.   No. Under §4A-211(b), the notice is late if the bank has accepted the order. Under §4A-209(b)(1), the bank that notifies the beneficiary has accepted the order.

311.   Insured's bank has acted erroneously. It may recover $1 million from Insured and must try to recover the balance from Insurance Co. *See* §4A-303(a).

312.   No, unless the Insured's bank has otherwise agreed—and there is little chance of that. *See* §4A-305(a) and (c). Bear in mind that Article 4A governs wholesale wire transfers. Consumers are seldom involved. The originator of a wire transfer that wants to play like a boat river gambler is going to take his losses. Users of the wire transfer systems will have to know that they should wire their funds early or arrange for their own verification procedures to see that the funds arrive on time. The rule may strike some as harsh, but it is a quite sound rule.

Table of Statutory Sections

References are to sections and to problem and answer numbers.

UNIFORM COMMERCIAL CODE

Article 1 (New)

§1-103(a)	40, 135
§1-103(b)	7, 209, 213, 223, 232, 233, 241, 247
§1-201(b)(3)	24
§1-201(b)(9)	106, 127, 129
§1-201(b)(21)	211, 212, 224, 245
§1-201(b)(29)	§18, 95, 123, 150, 177
§1-201(b)(30)	§18, 26, 95
§1-201(b)(35)	2, 25, 27, 28, 99, 139, 168, 186, 187
§1-201(b)(37)	208
§1-203	25, 139, 168
§1-203(b)(2)	168
§1-203(c)	168
§1-203(d)	168
§1-203(e)	168
§1-204	9, 31, 226
§1-204(2)	26
§1-305(a)	233
§1-309	207

Article 1 (Old)

§1-102	40, 135
§1-103	7, 209, 213, 223, 232, 233, 241, 247
§1-106(1)	233
§1-201(3)	24
§1-201(9)	106, 127, 129

§1-201(20)	211, 212, 224, 245
§1-201(32)	§18, 95, 123, 150, 177
§1-201(33)	§18, 26, 95
§1-201(34)	95
§1-201(37)	2, 25, 27, 28, 99, 139, 168, 186, 187
§1-201(39)	208
§1-201(44)	9, 26, 31, 226
§1-208	207

Article 2

§2-319(4)	261
§2-320(4)	261
§2-325	283
§2-326	2
§2-401(1)	1, 2, 3, 26, 27, 28, 138
§2-401(2)	1
§2-402(2)	12, 172
§2-403	7, 154
§2-403(1)	4, 5, 6, 9, 10, 26, 181, 182, 183, 184
§2-403(2)	7, 8, 10
§2-403(3)	8
§2-501(1)	31, 174, 177
§2-505	187
§2-505(1)	187
§2-506	282
§2-507	178, 180, 185
§2-507(2)	178, 179, 181, 185
§2-511	178
§2-512	261
§2-513	261
§2-513(3)(a)	261

BANKRUPTCY CODE

MISCELLANEOUS STATUTES

Index

References are to problem numbers unless indicated otherwise.